THE BONAPARTES

Dynasties

General Editor: Nigel Saul

Published

Forthcoming

The Bonapartes

The History of a Dynasty

William H. C. Smith

Hambledon and London

London and New York

Hambledon and London
102 Gloucester Avenue, London NW1 8HX

175 Fifth Avenue
New York, NY 10010
USA

First published 2005

ISBN 1 85285 462 6

A description of this book is available from the
British Library and from the Library of Congress.

Typeset by Egan Reid Ltd, Auckland, New Zealand,
and printed in Great Britain by Cambridge University Press.

Distributed in the United States and Canada
exclusively by Palgrave Macmillan,
a division of St Martin's Press.

Contents

Illustrations

Plates

Between Pages 86 and 87

Family Trees

To My Friends

Introduction

The events and people dealt with in this book are set within the context of French history, but it is not intended to be a history of France; rather it is a study of the emergence of a family that was to become France's Fourth Dynasty. Members of the family were destined to rule the country during two separate periods (both ending in national defeat). They, nevertheless, left an indelible mark on the French nation.

When Napoleon Bonaparte came to the realise that he was destined to be much more than a successful general, he at first had no thought of becoming a ruling sovereign and the founder of a dynasty. Not an ideologue with a preconceived programme, he was a decisive pragmatist with a flair for grasping opportunities, whether political or military. As he himself said, 'On s'engage, et puis on voit', which could be translated by 'You make a start and see what happens next'; a simple precept that served him well both as a soldier and as the ruler of the French nation.

'By 1793 the Revolution had led to the execution of Louis XVI, and to a decree of the Convention declaring monarchy to be abolished forever in France, it is therefore surprising that in less than a decade the country had acquired an Emperor. To justify the establishment of this new monarchy to the French people, Napoleon stated, 'I am the Revolution', claiming to represent in his person a summation of revolutionary doctrine. By establishing a dynasty, he claimed he was providing the essential link with the entire revolutionary inheritance. In other words; the fact that the dynasty issued from the Revolution would be was its claim to *legitimacy* in the eyes of the French people. Legitimacy was the key word, for the Bourbons, although dethroned by the Revolution, still claimed the throne by right, regarding the new dynasty as a vulgar and illegitimate usurpation by an upstart general.

Lacking a dynastic inheritance, Napoleon created a new one, whose claim to an historic antecedent was that of classical Rome, with its consuls and emperors, and its continued stress on republican values. By linking the imperial system to the Revolution, however, Napoleon created contra-dictions and ambiguities within his regime. These difficulties were exacerbated by the fact that the problems facing the new dynasty had to be resolved not just within France but within the context of Europe.

As the self-proclaimed heir of the Revolution, Napoleon inherited the wars which it had unleashed, together with the expansionist drive with which they were associated. No one likes armed missionaries, avid to preach revolutionary doctrines (and enforce French annexationist aims), whether led by a Republican general or a newly-crowned Emperor, with the effron-tery to establish his dynasty on revolutionary principles. It was inevitable that the reactionary powers, who had consistently opposed the Revolution by force of arms, would be equally determined to oppose the new dynasty, a trial of strength that was only ended on the field of Waterloo.

The victors of 1815 were to find, however, that Napoleon's dynastic legiti-macy did not depend simply on the sword for its existence, for the evolution of Bonapartism as a political force ensured the future role of the dynasty in the development of France, even though Napoleon's only legitimate son, Napoleon II, died in exile in Vienna, never having had the chance to reign. The troubled period between 1815 and 1848 came about because of the inability of other dynasties to stabilise a country that in essence remained as Napoleon had left it. This situation was only resolved in 1848, when Louis Napoleon took up his imperial inheritance. The nephew of Napoleon I, he restored the Empire, taking as his title Napoleon III.

It was an ill-starred dynasty. Both rulers lost their only sons young, and with them the hope a dynastic continuity, tragedies which proved fatal to the imperial succession, though not to the ideas that the dynasty had represented to the French people. It could be argued that the dynasty had done its work so well that France could, and still does, benefit from its achievements. One of the arguments of the Bonapartists was that 'the Republic is in the Empire', the one containing the other, since both were descended from the Revolution. It is a claim has substance, given how much the constitution of the present Fifth Republic owes to the legacy of the Fourth Dynasty.

The Founder

At 9 o'clock on the morning of 2 December 1804 a procession of carriages left the Tuileries palace in Paris. In the leading carriage was the Pope, Pius VII, brought from Rome for this special occasion, followed immediately by the carriages containing cardinals and other ecclesiastics. The secular dignitaries, ministers, councillors of state, diplomats and other officials came in a further procession immediately behind the papal convoy. One hour later came the principal personages: the Emperor Napoleon and his consort Josephine. Their coach was a splendid affair of glass, gilt and painted wood surmounted on the roof by a crown held up by four eagles, for eagles, together with bees, were to become the identifying symbols of a new dynasty. They were the outward signs that France, seemingly recovered from its republicanism, was about to become a monarchy again.

But what was this new monarchy to be? It was unlikely to resemble that of the Bourbons, whose last representative, Louis XVI, had also been the last sovereign to live in the Tuileries. He had left it for imprisonment and execution, seeing his palace for the last time from the window of the carriage taking him to the guillotine on the morning of 21 January 1793. Some months previously, in September 1792, the revolutionary government had decreed that 'royalty is abolished in France'. Now, seemingly, it had been restored, but in an ambiguous manner, for the coinage of the new Empire displayed on one of its faces the words *République Française* and on the reverse *Napoléon Empereur*. In its way these inscriptions summarised not only the nature of the new dynasty but also the history of its appearance and triumph: if the origin lay in the Republic then it was clearly a Republic which had evolved into something rather different. But if the inscription appeared ambiguous, one thing was not, for the coin bore the effigy of the man who had brought all this about – Napoleon Bonaparte on his way that morning to be crowned Emperor of the French at the cathedral of Notre-Dame.

Born in Ajaccio on 15 August 1769, Napoleon was, and remains, the most famous Corsican of all time. At the moment of his birth, the island was French but remained very much its own self, so that while he would benefit from the French connection, Napoleon could not escape his Corsican inheritance. The island was dominated by familial loyalties, and disputes were made all the more bitter because, in a small population, everyone knew everyone else and there were multiple interrelationships. In a society that was poor, and where the possession of small areas of land was important, there was frequent litigation about boundaries and titles, generating further sources of grievance which often culminated in the dreaded vendettas. Napoleon was born into a turbulent society, harsh and unforgiving, something which undoubtedly left its mark on him as a future soldier and lawmaker.

Napoleon's father, Charles Buonaparte, had been born in 1746 and married off in 1764, at the age of eighteen, to the fourteen-year-old Letizia Ramolino, a marriage arranged by the bridegroom's uncle, Lucien Bonaparte, who was a priest. Neither party was rich but their modest holdings of land made them, by Corsican standards, comfortably off, though the family house in Ajaccio was far from luxurious. Unsurprisingly, Letizia was a careful housewife and more than frugal in her ways all her life. Within a month of the marriage, Charles left for Rome, ostensibly to study law, but a marked disinclination to work led to his return to Corsica, where he set up house with his wife at Corte and then resumed his legal studies. Perhaps it was his youth that made it hard for Charles to settle, for he was far from being uneducated. He spoke French and Italian, as well as his native Corsican, and had a working knowledge of both Latin and Greek.

There was a further impediment to the living of a settled life and that was the political situation in an island where feelings ran high and were expressed with violence. Technically part of the Genoese Republic, Corsica had, during the course of the eighteenth century, developed national aspirations and was seeking some form of independent status, and this movement had found a leader in Pasquale Paoli. He had served in the Neapolitan army and now commanded the Corsican forces opposing the Genoese, with the rank of general. The Genoese, seeking to end the problems caused by an island which seemed more bother than it was worth, sold it to France in 1768. Paoli tried to hold out against the new occupying power, but was defeated and forced to flee to England, leaving behind him a further source of civil conflict in which Napoleon's own family became embroiled. Charles Buonaparte, as a member of the minor Corsican nobility, had been for a time a supporter of General Paoli, indeed had been his secretary, before eventually identifying himself with the French administration. Paoli's position at the head of a quasi-autonomous Corsican Republic led to his becoming identified with true Corsican nationalism, something which by implication made the partisans of France appear as traitors to their country. From this situation sprang the enmity between the 'Buonapartists' and 'Paolistas' that was to dominate Napoleon's youth, having as its background the guerrilla war against the French forces stationed on the island and their Corsican supporters. It was as a result of having aligned himself with the French that, after a dangerous journey across the mountains from Corte, Charles Buonaparte and his wife Letizia had arrived as refugees in Ajaccio in May 1769.[1]

Already the mother of one son, Joseph, born in January 1768, Letizia was, at nineteen, heavily pregnant with her next child. On the morning of 15 August she went to hear mass in the cathedral of Ajaccio, because it was the feast of the Assumption of the Blessed Virgin, but labour pains forced her to leave the church and return home. She had barely time to reach her house before a boy was born. He was immediately, as was customary, given conditional baptism with the name Napoleon. The formal christening eventually took place in July 1771, performed by the baby's uncle, Archdeacon Lucien Bonaparte, who had arranged the parents' marriage.

Napoleon's birth was followed by that of six more siblings: Lucien, Maria-Anna (known as Elisa), Louis, Pauline, Caroline and Jerome, all of whom, together with their eldest brother, were destined to form part of the dynasty which Napoleon was to found. Joseph would become King of Naples and then King of Spain, so that his sister Caroline's husband, Joachim Murat, could be given the Neapolitan throne. Louis would become King of Holland and Jerome King of Westphalia. Of the males, only Lucien, because he quarrelled with his brother, did not acquire a kingdom. The girls were also beneficiaries, though in their own view they never acquired enough. Caroline married Murat and ultimately became Queen of Naples, while Pauline became Princess Borghese and Elisa Grand Duchess of Tuscany. As for the indispensable co-author of the family (who was to have thirteen pregnancies between marriage and the death of her husband), Letizia received the title of the Mother of the Emperor and was always known as *Madame Mère*. Napoleon's dynasty therefore resembled all dynasties in that it was a family affair; and, like all dynasties, it was riven by jealousies, disputes and assorted manifestations of ingratitude.

Madame Mère had as her unofficial motto 'Pourvu que ça dure' (provided it lasts), a healthily realistic appraisal of the situation, for all turned upon her second son, and if he should fall the whole edifice would crumble. It was Napoleon's astonishing career, a reflection of his genius, which made all of this possible, though even he would have been the first to admit that he was lucky in his time of birth. Napoleon believed in luck and it is therefore no denigration of his genius to see the belief as being part of his character. It was something which in later life led him to reject those whom he felt lacked the aura of having luck on their side. But if luck did lie in the fortuitous union of Corsica with France – which enabled him to benefit from the educational, and later military, opportunities which were open to him – his genius revealed itself in his knowing how to utilise and exploit these opportunities.

The childhood and youth of the future Emperor are, as is frequently the case with great men, the subject of legend, anecdote, disputed facts and, needless to say, historical debate. The most profitable approach therefore is to take what is known and easily verifiable, beginning with the child's entry (at the age of nine years and eight months) to the military academy at Brienne. As a noble, but insufficiently wealthy to provide for his son's education, Charles Buonaparte was eligible to apply for one of the six hundred places in the king's gift at the military academies. Thanks to the support of the application by the Count de Marboeuf, the principal French representative on the island (and some said susceptible to the charms of Letizia), Napoleon was awarded one of the coveted places. Thus began his relationship with metropolitan France. Contrary to legend, Napoleon was not a brilliant student at Brienne. Nurtured like all of his contemporaries almost everywhere in Europe on Plutarch's lives, and study of the classics, Napoleon was formed in a literary culture that recognised the cult of the hero. In his case, however, any ill-effects that such a cult were counterbalanced by his love of mathematics: 'geometry is a supreme abstraction, like great poetry', he said, and it was one subject in which he shone. His mathematics teacher considered him to be his most promising pupil, but this was the only bright spot in what seems to have been a difficult time, for the boy was not happy. Teased by his fellows because of his Italian accent and, unsurprisingly, not inclined to be particularly sociable, he felt himself to be isolated: 'By the time I reached puberty', he admitted to Las Cases at St Helena, 'I became morose and low spirited, taking refuge in reading', which became for him a real passion, almost an obsession.[2]

In 1781 Napoleon made his first Communion: later he was to say that he wanted to believe, indeed needed to believe, but reason shook his capacity for acceptance 'and that [happened] before I was thirteen'. There is nothing really very remarkable in all this, nothing that distinguished Napoleon from many young people at the same age or even older. For what it is worth, article one of the will he dictated at St Helena on 15 April, 1821 stated, 'I die in the Catholic, Apostolic, and Roman religion in whose bosom I was born over fifty years ago'. An act of policy? Or had something remained? He left no specific request for masses to be said after his death, nor was there any bequest to religious foundations, but he had asked that a priest be sent to St Helena, and he received extreme unction on his death-bed. Perhaps Napoleon lived with a not unusual mixture of agnosticism, superstition and belief. What is certain is that he believed in himself and the more he achieved the more sure he was of his capacities.

As for his youth, one of the major sources, the so-called *Mémoires* by Bourienne, is tainted and needs to be used with great care. Certainly they had known one another in youth and Napoleon had been mindful of this when he achieved power. Bourienne became one of the imperial secretaries, but a series of financial speculations and serious embezzlement led to his final dismissal in 1810. He then became an agent of the Bourbons and in 1829, old, ill and needing money, agreed to give his name to an account written by someone else, Charles de Villemarest. The author was hostile to Napoleon, invented episodes and anecdotes, and even forged documents. Bourienne seems to have been either unwilling or unable to control the work which appeared under his name, its reliability only being accepted because of the author's known association with Napoleon.[3] What does seem beyond doubt, for there are fortunately other sources, is that the period at Brienne was difficult for Napoleon: when taunted by his fellow students he tended to respond with blows and his generally antisocial attitude made him isolated and unhappy. It must have been a relief when, in September 1784 after an examination, he was accepted for entry into the Royal Military School at Paris where he arrived towards the middle of October. His first report described him as 'a slight dark young man, melancholy, inward-looking and austere in manner, yet liking discussion and a great talker'.

In 1785, having come forty-second in a class of fifty-eight, Napoleon was assigned to Valence to an artillery regiment, and for the next four years his life was that of an ordinary garrison officer. Its dullness, fortunately for Napoleon, was interrupted by various forays to his native Corsica to look after the family's affairs. The death of his father in 1785, coupled with the absence of Joseph, the eldest brother, meant that the second son became the virtual head of the family. It was a difficult inheritance: the financial affairs were in a mess thanks to some unwise agricultural experiments by Charles and his subsequent death. The situation was exacerbated by the fact that his widow had been left with four children all under ten years old. These problems kept Napoleon in Corsica from September 1786 until the same month one year later, with one interval in Paris to press the financial claims of his family against the government. But in December he rejoined his regiment, which was now quartered in the town of Auxonne. Here he helped to alleviate the monotony of garrison life by reading – and writing – but above all he found great satisfaction in being able to follow the lectures on artillery directed by the Baron du Teil, the author of a book *On the Use of Modern Artillery*. These clearly made a deep impression on the young lieutenant, for among his notebooks which have survived from this period no less than three are devoted to studies on the deployment and use of artillery.

It was not all study, for it appears that at this period of his life (he was eighteen, almost nineteen) living with his regiment made the young Buonaparte more sociable and outgoing. He entered fully into the life of the regiment and was so well integrated that his fellow subalterns asked him to draft a constitution for a society they were creating, designed to protect their rights and interests. This process of assimilation, perhaps best described as an acceptance of 'Frenchness' linked to a growing ease in the company of young men and women, led to a lightening of the tight personality which had been noted on his arrival at military academy. This sense of 'Frenchness' was soon to find another form of expression other than an ability to be at ease socially, for by the late 1780s a crisis had been reached in the government of the kingdom that had resulted in an ever-increasing demand for reforms. The *ancien régime* was breaking down and the pressures caused by a financial and administrative crisis led ultimately to the decision by Louis XVI to summon the States General – a body that had last met in 1614 – in an attempt to find a solution. Their meeting, in

The Early Bonapartes

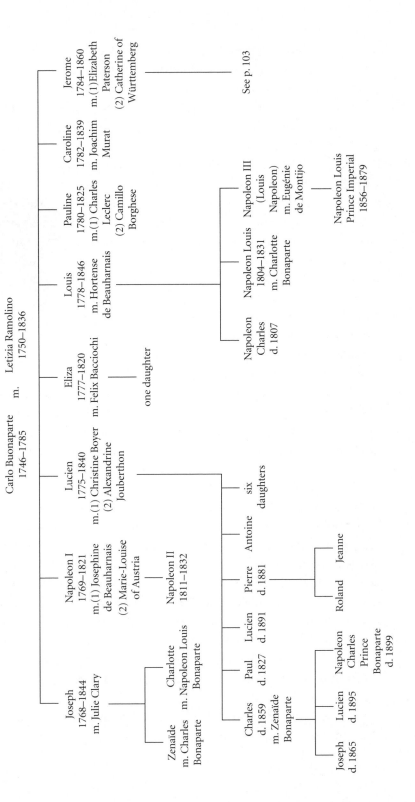

Carlo Buonaparte 1746–1785 m. Letizia Ramolino 1750–1836

Joseph 1768–1844 m. Julie Clary

Napoleon I 1769–1821 m.(1) Josephine de Beauharnais (2) Marie-Louise of Austria

Lucien 1775–1840 m.(1) Christine Boyer (2) Alexandrine Jouberthon

Eliza 1777–1820 m. Felix Bacciochi

Louis 1778–1846 m. Hortense de Beauharnais

Pauline 1780–1825 m.(1) Charles Leclerc (2) Camillo Borghese

Caroline 1782–1839 m. Joachim Murat

Jerome 1784–1860 m.(1)Elizabeth Paterson (2) Catherine of Württemberg

Napoleon II 1811–1832

one daughter

Napoleon Charles d. 1807

Napoleon Louis 1804–1831 m. Charlotte Bonaparte

Napoleon III (Louis Napoleon) m. Eugénie de Montijo

Napoleon Louis Prince Imperial 1856–1879

See p. 103

Zenaïde m. Charles Napoleon Bonaparte

Charlotte m. Napoleon Louis Bonaparte

Charles d. 1859 m. Zenaïde Bonaparte

Paul d. 1827

Lucien d. 1891

Pierre d. 1881

Antoine

six daughters

Roland   Jeanne

Joseph d. 1865

Lucien d. 1895

Napoleon Charles Prince Bonaparte d. 1899

May 1789 at Versailles, which was hailed as the first move in a process that would produce much needed reforms, in fact unleashed the Revolution.

The upheavals in France produced a large number of pamphlets and books dealing with the various problems facing the government, together with propositions for their solution. Napoleon was himself a contributor to the debate, but he was less a proposer of reform than of revolution. In October 1788 he began to write on the theme that 'Kings enjoy an usurped authority in the twelve kingdoms of Europe', a title which gives a clear guide to the content. It has been said of this pamphlet that it makes clear the author's position: 'Before the fall of the Bastille, before Robespierre and Danton, Bonaparte was already a Republican.'[4] Republican he may have been in sentiment, but the young officer did his duty when it came to suppressing a riot in the town of Auxonne – an early indication of an important facet of Napoleon's character: he never cared for disorder.

In order to deal with the financial complications arising from the confused state in which his father had left the family property, Napoleon spent virtually two years, from 1789 to 1791, in Corsica, and so those years which were critical in the development of the revolutionary process in France, affected him only through the events on the island. Because of this, and despite his increasing tendency to *Frenchness*, Napoleon's preoccupation as the *ancien régime* fell apart was therefore less with France than with his native island. He had never really lost touch with family obligations and now all his former hero-worship of Paoli resurfaced, since it seemed possible that the general would return from his English exile and could again become the liberator and regenerator of the Corsican nation. When Napolean returned to the island, in September 1789, he took the lead in bringing his fellow-citizens up to date with the changes brought about by events in France. A volunteer National Guard was organised – complete with tricolour cockades – and an address was presented by it to the National Assembly in Paris, which resulted in a decree making Corsica a part of France, a part of *La Nation* in the new meaning which the Revolution had given to the word. As a quid pro quo, all Corsicans were to enjoy the full rights and liberties of French citizens as defined by the revolutionary decrees. It was at this point that Paoli returned from his long exile in England.

What is important to note here is that, if Napoleon's 'Frenchness' did not run deep, Paoli's Anglicisation was fundamental to his attitude.

Convinced of the great virtues of the English parliamentary and monarchical system, Paoli became ever more disenchanted with France as the
Revolution gathered momentum. Two events crystallised his opposition.
The first in 1791 was the enactment by the National Assembly of the Civil
Constitution of the Clergy, designed to give retrospective validation of the
sequestration of all church property by the revolutionary government and
the creation of a state-supported clergy with elected bishops, having only
tenuous links to the papacy. Confronted by a refusal of a section of the
bishops and priests, the Assembly decided to enforce its decree by demanding that all ecclesiastics swear an oath of acceptance of the Constitution on
pain of being deprived of their livings. This was the key moment in what
became the great divisive struggle within France that was to endure until
Napoleon ended it in 1801. The King was antagonised, for Louis felt himself
to be perjured, since he was sworn to defend the church and its interests.
He was a devout Catholic for whom the situation became intolerable once
the Pope condemned the Civil Constitution.

The King's reaction led to an unexpected phenomenon in many parts of
France, since it produced an alliance of 'Throne and Altar'. This was to have
serious consequences because it involved the majority of people for whom,
until then, the revolutionary process had remained an affair of politics and
remote from their daily concerns. Although glad to be rid of feudal dues
and contributions to the church, the people as a whole did not support a
concerted attack on their religious customs and beliefs. When, suddenly, it
was *their* parish and *their* priest who were threatened, events ceased to be
remote and became immediate in an age when local loyalties were pre-
eminent. The immediate outcome was unrest, and in parts of France virtual
civil war, as the country divided on this issue.

In Corsica the results split the national movement, already alarmed by
the consequences of the King's abortive flight in June, leaving behind a
document in which he repudiated all the concessions he had made since
the beginning of the Revolution. Because of the obvious threat this posed
to the continuance of the monarchy, in which he was a firm believer, Paoli,
supported by Pozzo di Borgo, the Corsican deputy in the National Assembly
in Paris, took the side of the Royalists and clericals. The crisis came when
there was a riot in Ajaccio on Easter Sunday 1792, in the course of which a
battalion under Napoleon's command fired on the citizens.[5] Hostile
reaction to this event, plus the fact that overstayed leave had led to his being

struck off the army list, decided Napoleon to return to Paris to defend his conduct and clear himself. It was not the first time, nor would it be the last, that he would employ the tactics of justification in person (revealing a growing sense of self-confidence).

From May to September 1792 Napoleon was in Paris – the period which saw the fall of the monarchy, the September massacres and the victory by the revolutionary armies over the invading Prussian army at Valmy. He was an eyewitness to the attack on the Tuileries on 10 August and saw the King, the Queen and their children flee to the safety of the Assembly. This spectacle, together with the heaped up corpses of the Swiss Guards who died defending the royal family, confirmed Napoleon in his hatred of 'the dregs of the populace' and what it was capable of doing. At Auxonne and Ajaccio he had done his duty; to the end of his political career, he never weakened in his abhorrence of the 'populace', even when it would have served him and his cause to have enlisted its support.

The shortage of officers in the army, as a result of emigration by those hostile to the Revolution, meant that Napoleon was not only reinstated (with back pay), but promoted to captain. Perhaps more surprisingly, in view of an already long period of absence, he was again given permission to return to Corsica, escorting his sister Elisa, whose school, a royal foundation, had been closed by the revolutionary authorities. Napoleon arrived in Corsica in October 1792 to find the situation considerably altered. France was now at war with Prussia and Austria, exposing Corsica to a possible attack at a time when the island was torn by internal rivalries, now exacerbated by the increasing hostility between Paoli and his supporters and the Bonapartes. The more pronounced Paoli's hostility to France became, the more he found himself opposed by Napoleon's family. The execution of the King in January 1793, followed on 1 February by the French declaration of war against England, brought matters to a head. Alarmed by Paoli's hostile attitude, the Convention in Paris issued a decree for his arrest which, thanks to Napoleon's direct intervention, was withdrawn, but it was too late. An attempt to seize Ajaccio by Buonapartist partisans failed, and the family, its property having been seized, was forced to flee to France: Paoli handed over Corsica to the English, who promptly garrisoned the island. As a consequence a young Irishman serving as a captain in the British army, and also born in 1769, was quartered in the house of Madame Buonaparte. His name was Hudson Lowe. It was his first encounter with members of a family who would play a key part in his later life.

Forced by circumstances to break with Corsica, and destined never to return, Napoleon was about to find new opportunities on a wider stage. He was, after all, a professional soldier, and France was now seriously at war, and furthermore a war that was not going well. A majority of the French departments were in open revolt against the central government and the external enemies of the Republic were threatening invasion. A joint English and Spanish force had occupied the harbour of the great naval base of Toulon, and it was there that Napoleon was dispatched as artillery commander. His success in ending the siege forced the enemy to withdraw, led to his promotion to brigadier-general, and brought him to the notice of both the Ministry of War and the Committee of Public Safety. His career seemed to be well and truly launched, but in July 1794, Robespierre fell from power and Napoleon became politically suspect because of his closeness to Robespierre's brother Augustin. He survived an investigation into his links with the now disgraced Jacobins, and was able to underline his loyalty to the Convention by dispersing a Royalist riot in Paris in 1795. For this loyal service he was promoted to the rank of major-general and, to complete his promotion, named as commander of the army of the interior.

The collapse of the Convention in the Thermidorean reaction meant that in 1795 a new system of government was introduced. Known as the Directory, it was headed by an executive of five Directors assisted by two chambers for which 'controlled' elections were held. By the simple process of nominating two thirds of the outgoing deputies, the new assembly very much resembled the old and it was this which had provoked the riot suppressed by Napoleon in October 1795.[6]

If the constitutional process was flagrantly dishonest, in that little changed at the top, a new society was beginning to emerge which would have an effect on events, for, after six years of upheaval and the experience of the Great Terror, when the public prosecutor could boast 'heads are falling like slates', there was a desire for normality. 'Society' was re-emerging and Napoleon found himself in a position to enjoy its benefits, having helped to establish it by his victories in the field and on the streets of Paris. Among his new patrons was Barras. Born an aristocrat, he had moved from support of the Terror to becoming a key player in the overthrow of Robespierre. He was now one of the Directors, who not only helped with

Napoleon's promotion but provided the young general with a wife, by finding a home for his former mistress, Josephine de Beauharnais.

She was thirty-two, a widow (her husband had been guillotined in 1794) with two grown-up children. She was an aristocrat by birth (her family was Tascher de la Pagerie from the island of Martinique), by education and by marriage, for her first husband had been the Vicomte de Beauharnais. She was highly sophisticated and well able to move in Society, which meant in other words that her liaisons were normally well conducted and that the concept of a marriage implying fidelity was quite frankly beyond her. In any event, the problem did not immediately arise since Napoleon began by following where others had been before. He made her his mistress.

Why did he marry her? The short answer is he fell in love, a hopeless romantic and sexual love of a man of twenty-six who had had very little experience of women: 'My character rendered me naturally timid in their company. Madame de Beauharnais was the first woman who gave me a degree of confidence.' So, in spite of her fading looks, bad teeth, and frivolous and extravagant nature, not to mention the two children, Citizen General Buonaparte and the Citizeness Beauharnais were married on 9 March 1796 in a civil ceremony as prescribed by law. Both lied about their age: Josephine gave 1767 as her year of birth, not 1763, and Napoleon gave his as 1768. At St Helena the Emperor declared that he had not been deceived by his wife's action but felt he must try to reciprocate.[7]

The wedding gift from the Directory was an appointment to command the Army of Italy. This had become the crucial area for military campaigns since, as Prussia and Spain had abandoned the war, only Austria remained as an adversary on the Continent. The Italian campaign was the first real Napoleonic triumph, not just because of battles won, including Lodi, fought on 10 May 1796, but because of what he realised about himself. 'It was only on the evening after Lodi that I realised I was a superior being and conceived the ambition of performing great things.' It was from this moment on that he signed his name Bonaparte (the 'u' was suppressed), as if he was indicating that a new phase in his life had begun.

The campaign was not over, for the Austrians fought tenaciously, but they were hampered by war on two fronts, since there was also a French army on the Rhine to be dealt with, and by the spring of 1797 they were compelled to seek an armistice. Presumably anxious to begin performing 'great things', Napoleon went much further than the conclusion of a simple armistice. The agreement signed at Leoben was really a peace settlement, and was recognised as such by its confirmation six months later at Campo Formio. In plain language the general had conquered Italy, and the peace terms were his, though the government in Paris was, for form's sake, associated with them. Since it continued to lurch from one political crisis to another, the Directory was in no position to quarrel with the army on whose loyalty it relied to carry through the various *coups d'état* which permitted its survival, and which provided it with money from the loot acquired during its victorious wars. Nevertheless, the Directors were far from unaware of the danger posed by their reliance on their generals and were eager to keep them occupied, particularly as the wars tended to be profitable. Given Napoleon's status after his outstanding success in Italy, there was a particular desire to keep him occupied: in November 1797 he was appointed to command of the Army of England, since the British government gave no sign of coming to terms and remained at war.

It was, however, clear to Napoleon that there could be no serious campaign against England without maritime power, as the failure of the recently attempted landing in Ireland under the command of General Hoche had shown, for an army would have to be ferried across the Channel and the success of such an undertaking would depend on a degree of luck as well as good seamanship. It was unfortunate for France that its navy had been weakened by the defection of many officers as a result of the Revolution, something that seriously affected its capacity to wage war at sea. In view of what had happened to Hoche, it was not too difficult for the newly appointed commander to dissuade the Directors of the dangers of their proposed invasion of England.

In any event Napoleon had his own plans: he wanted to invade Egypt, to cut British trade with India, and to achieve complete control of the Mediterranean; this being the sort of grand design which appealed to him. Ironically, it was the self-same lack of naval power which had made him reject the idea of an attack on England that was to make a nonsense of this grand design by nullifying the military successes of the French army in Egypt, for Nelson's victory at the battle of the Nile invalidated the whole Egyptian campaign and the vast project initially associated with it.

For Napoleon, the check to his plans in Egypt was a decisive moment, and significantly his next moves were based upon political and not military considerations. The decision to leave his army blockaded in Egypt and to return to France was a bold one, for it risked being seen as treason, cowardice; or indifference to the fate of his troops. But the Turks had been decisively defeated at the battle of the Pyramids (July 1799) and the army was, for the moment, safe. Furthermore, the continuing political weakness of the Directory, coupled with defeats suffered by the French forces in Italy and on the Danube, seemed to threaten the unravelling of French domination in Europe. England's work in financing and creating the Second Coalition appeared to be on the edge of success: the collapse of France's finances (the budget deficit for 1799 was four hundred million francs) meant the army could not be paid and the paper money in circulation was now virtually valueless. It was clear that only drastic measures would suffice to deal with the crisis.

In this context it is well to remember that contemporaries knew what the result of internal weakness and an inability to provide strong leadership could be, for the kingdom of Poland had disappeared from the map as a consequence of these very failings, partitioned among its three neighbours, Prussia, Russia and Austria. It was also not forgotten that, when France had been in turmoil at the beginning of the Revolution, the same powers had been only too willing to profit from its situation. By 1799 the political classes in Paris had come to the view that, in order to bring an end to the present crisis that seemed to threaten the country with dissolution, a strong executive was needed with a sword in its hand. Napoleon's views coincided with the politicians with one vital difference: they thought to use the general, wildly popular now because of his victories, and then discard him; Napoleon was determined on the reverse.

The fact that Napoleon was well informed about the political situation at home, in part thanks to the newspapers thoughtfully provided by the English fleet cruising off the Egyptian coast, was a reminder that the same fleet stood between him and France. Some way must be found to run the blockade, avoiding the very real risk of capture, but there was no alternative. Napoleon entrusted the command of the army to General Kléber and, having ordered that two frigates and two smaller vessels be prepared for sea, all with the utmost secrecy, set sail for France on 24 August.[8] The little flotilla, skilfully navigated by Admiral Ganteaume, successfully evaded the roaming English ships, and on 13 October, six weeks after leaving Egypt, Napoleon landed at St-Raphael. All along the route to Paris he was received with acclamation in the towns through which he passed, so that by the time he reached the capital he could be in no doubt about the extent of his popularity. The only question was how it could be used. In fact the route was already mapped out. While it is clear that the success of the *coup d'état* of the 18 and 19 Brumaire (9–10 November) 1800 would have been impossible had Napoleon not been central to it, it is equally clear that a great deal of preparation had already gone into planning the *coup*.

Napoleon was able to join what was virtually a ready-made conspiracy by political groups in Paris determined to change the existing political structure. To this end it was proposed to devise a new constitution. This was in line with what was almost a traditional method of changing a regime during the revolutionary period, three having already been tried since 1789. Almost equally traditional was its proposed author. The man in question was Joseph Sieyès, among the more interesting of those who had been propounding political ideas since 1789. Sieyès was in fact a priest, having chosen holy orders as a means of escape from poverty, but his real belief was in the perfectibility of society, the product of an ideal state which could be created if the right method of government could be found and established by a constitution. His search had led to his participation in the making of the various constitutions which had been tried since 1789 – except the one which had established the Directory. As a consequence, he disliked it intensely and was determined on its revision, to which end he had got himself elected in 1799 as one of the Directors. It was at this point that Napoleon entered the picture in the role of the strong man, 'the sword' who would defend the new structure as set out in a draft proposed by Sieyès. The new constitutional organism would consist of three consuls, forming the executive, assisted in government by an elected legislative body and a Senate, with the tacit understanding that the man who had been responsible for the making of it all would be one of the consuls.

The main participants in the proposed changes in the structure of the government hoped that it might be achieved with a semblance of legality, avoiding unhappy precedents by which constitutional change was brought about by a *coup d'état*. Napoleon himself hoped that any suggestion of a *coup* in which he was the prime element could be avoided and for this he counted on the help of his family. The plan was that his brother Lucien, who was president of the existing lower house, should try to persuade its members to vote through the new scheme, thereby making it legal. It seemed to be possible, but the whole affair was bungled and, without

Lucien's decisive action at the critical moment, it might well have foundered. Napoleon, confronted by a violent opposition from the deputies
– who demanded that he be declared an outlaw and arrested – proved
unable to deal with the situation. Lucien, showing remarkable skill as
President of the assembly, managed to prevent a vote being taken on the
motion to declare his brother an outlaw, but in the end the desire to give
the whole business an appearance of legality failed, though at least there
was an avoidance of bloodshed. The troops, who had been awaiting the
outcome of debate, became convinced that 'their general' was in danger
and they invaded the Legislative Chamber. At the sight of the soldiers, the
deputies, feeling themselves threatened, fled, the Directory was at an end
and the new provisional government installed.[9]

The affair produced very little public reaction: after all, the Republic had
already known a number of illegal acts since its inception. In any event,
the Republic, as such, would continue, now with three Consuls at its
head instead of five Directors. There was even a hope of greater stability
because the army, represented by Napoleon, was in alliance with the
'constitutionalists', represented by Sieyès. The three Consuls were duly
nominated by the provisional government, Bonaparte, Sieyès and Ducos;
the two latter were political allies who were also linked by being regicides.
The first task was to produce the new Constitution which, in Napoleon's
view, should be 'short and obscure' and, in spite of Sieyès reputation as a
constitutional expert, the final document reflected the views of Napoleon.
'What is in the new constitution?', asked contemporaries, 'There is
Bonaparte' was the answer.

The Constitution of the Year VIII as it is known (the dating comes from
the Revolutionary calendar) was, in fact, quite short.[10] At the head of the
executive were the three Consuls, but only the First Consul held any real
power: to him belonged the initiative of the laws, the nomination of
ministers and the right to make war or peace. The legislative power was
split into four: the Council of State (its members nominated by the First
Consul) prepared the legislation, which was then discussed by the
Tribunate. The agreed text of the law was then sent to the Legislative Body,
where it was voted on, which meant either accepting or rejecting the text
presented with no possibility of amendment. The fourth body, the Senate,
had the task of deciding if the laws proposed were or were not in accordance
with the constitution and so it had the power to annul any which it

considered unconstitutional. This fragmentation of the 'parliamentary' power virtually paralysed the Legislative Body's ability to oppose the First Consul; at best its role would be advisory. Clearly, therefore, in this new 'short' constitution, there was nothing obscure about the position of Napoleon. This was the tacit understanding when, in accordance with Republican principles, the Constitution was submitted to the popular vote: this was not a referendum on a new system, it was a plebiscite favour of one man.

Once the constitution had come into force, the original two Consuls, Sieyès and Ducos retired, and two new men were named: Cambacérès and Lebrun, neither of whom were in any way inimical to Napoleon who, in 1802, became Consul for life – a change once again ratified by the people. The other two Consuls continued to exist, but they were now nominated by Napoleon himself and not by the Senate. The young general who, on the eve of the battle of Lodi, 'had conceived the ambition of performing great things' had made a spectacular beginning.

2

Towards a Dynasty

In the making of Brumaire, and in its ultimate success, the role played by members of Napoleon's family was of great importance. The activities of Joseph and Lucien, particularly the latter at the most critical moment, decided the issue when success of the *coup* hung in the balance. This family support is understandable because Napoleon had not at any time lost touch with his family, nor they with him, and it was this closeness which led the Count of Provence (the future Louis XVIII) always to refer to the Bonapartes as 'a tribe'. Since the tribe had prospered largely as a consequence of Napoleon's success, they all had a vested interest in furthering their brother's career.

Joseph, the eldest, who had established himself financially at an early stage by marrying Marie-Julie Clary, the daughter of a rich merchant in Marseille, had continued to consolidate his fortune as a result of his nomination as Commissioner for War of the Army of Italy. This was an extremely lucrative post, which came to him as a direct consequence of his brother's military career. Probably, for the same reason, he was elected to the lower house of the Directorial Assembly. As a result of his status as a deputy he was sent occasionally on diplomatic missions by the Directors, providing him with valuable experience in conducting negotiations, for which he revealed a talent. In between times, he had acquired at great expense one of the most desirable residences in France, the château of Mortefontaine, forty kilometres to the north of Paris. Here he affected the role of 'literary gentleman' and kept a good table, something which gave him useful connections in the artistic and literary world that he used to further the interests of his brother.

Lucien had long since abandoned his youthful destination, the priesthood, to become the most overtly political and republican of the family, as proof of which he had contracted a marriage with an innkeeper's daughter. He never got on well with Napoleon, even though he had saved the day for him at the critical moment during the *coup d'état* of Brumaire.

It seems that Lucien acted in the belief that he would work together with Napoleon to save the Republic and then re-establish it in a revivified form on a surer foundation than that of the Directory. Like others who had indulged in similar hopes, he was irked to find that he had worked *for* rather than *with* his brother, though he was rewarded by him for his help by being made Minister of the Interior in the ministry formed after Brumaire. He proved incapable of fulfilling the post to his brother's satisfaction, so, in a move calculated to estrange him still further, Napoleon sacked him. Lucien's answer was to publish, in 1800, a pamphlet entitled *Parallels between Caesar, Cromwell and Bonaparte*, a literary effort which, as its very title must have indicated, went down badly with the First Consul. To extricate himself from what had become a difficult situation, Lucien appealed to his mother, through whose intervention he obtained the post of ambassador in Madrid. There he distinguished himself by making a fortune based on taking enormous bribes from the Spanish and Portuguese governments on a promise of furthering their interest in Paris. He was never to be truly reconciled to Napoleon, calling him an 'ingrate' who owed his success entirely to his sibling, an attitude which did not, however, prevent him from being among those pushing for the establishment of the Empire in 1803–4. Tribal interest overcame rancour.

The two youngest brothers, Louis, who had been in Egypt with Napoleon as an aide-de-camp, and Jerome, who was fifteen in 1799, played no direct part in the events of Brumaire, though they seem to have accompanied Joseph when he set out to meet Napoleon as he travelled towards Paris from his landing at St-Raphael. Their aim had been to inform their brother of Josephine's misdeeds during his absence, of her infidelities and extravagances, in the hope that the evidence against her would bring about a divorce. That Josephine must be got rid of was the one point on which all the Bonapartes agreed – for they all hated her. What inspired such a tribal hatred? After all Josephine had, like them, not been born in metropolitan France but on an outlying island, though there was a world of difference between the culture of Corsica and that of Martinique. The narrow, poverty-stricken and faction riddled atmosphere that produced the Bonapartes had nothing in common with the lush, aristocratic plantation culture of the French West Indies. Josephine's family, the Tascher de la Pagerie, might well have employed members of the Bonaparte family – but would not have married them.

Perhaps to a family which, ostensibly, cultivated simple republican virtues, this aristocratic background, as exemplified by Josephine's frivolous and extravagant behaviour, was an affront; or possibly it was simple jealousy. Certainly the latter affected the behaviour of Napoleon's sisters.

From the Bonaparte family's point of view, the most dangerous aspect of the marriage was that Josephine had brought to it her two children by Alexandre de Beauharnais: Hortense, who in 1796 was thirteen, and her brother Eugène, who was fifteen. This was the more important as, at the time, there were no second-generation male Bonapartes. It was especially alarming in that Napoleon never made any secret of his affection for his two stepchildren, in particular his stepson Eugène de Beauharnais. Since it was the view of all Napoleon's siblings, not to mention his mother, that all good things should come to, and remain in, the family, it was imperative that Josephine and her children be excluded from any share in her husband's riches and fame.[1] Unfortunately for the family, two things impeded their plans. The first was Napoleon's passionate attachment to Josephine – though it cooled after the crisis of 1799; the second was her position in the crypto-aristocratic society of the Directory which made her useful, for she had had a role in the events leading up to Brumaire.[2]

Josephine's relations with Barras, whose mistress she had been, gave Napoleon a means of direct communication with one of the key Directors, already committed to constitutional change, and whose support was essential until the *coup* was over. Josephine was also linked to other important groups with funds at their disposal through Madame Tallien, who had been in prison with her during the Terror, and who had, like her, only escaped the guillotine because of Robespierre's fall. Thérèse Tallien was now the mistress of Ouvrard, a wealthy banker and speculator, who had links to Cambacérès, with whom Napoleon had close relations, and so to the plotters.

In any event, whatever her usefulness in the furtherance of her husband's political ambitions, Josephine's future was, in marital terms, secure. She survived not only the campaign of denigration mounted by her in-laws but, more importantly, survived the dramatic moment when Napoleon, on his return from Egypt, had threatened to divorce her. As proof of his acceptance of her, he paid her debts – amounting to some two million French francs – as soon as the new government was in place in 1800.

Napoleon had not achieved power, however, simply in order to pay his wife's debts. Having seen himself as 'the best type of Caesar: one who builds', he now began the reordering of France, a project which first and foremost required an end to war. On Christmas Day 1799, he wrote personally to both King George III and the Emperor Francis of Austria offering peace negotiations, which both sovereigns refused, as indeed Napoleon probably expected. The real point of the offer was to convince opinion in France that the war was not sought by the First Consul but by the enemies of France and the Revolution. If they would not have peace, then Napoleon would give them war. Since geographically Austria was the available enemy, another campaign was launched against her possessions in Italy, culminating in the French victory (a close run thing) at Marengo, a victory which soon became part of the Napoleonic legend – thanks to the carefully edited army bulletins prepared for public consumption. Although the Italian campaign had only been a qualified success, when its effects were added to the victories of General Moreau in Germany, the strain of war on two fronts forced Austria to make peace. As a consequence, the Second Coalition against France, brought about by English diplomacy and gold, was wrecked.

The immediate gain from Marengo was that it consolidated Napoleon's position at home and it gave him the breathing space he needed to deal with the internal situation. What was needed, above all, was a solid administration and the restoration of the normal authority of government. There must be an end to the arbitrary nature of 'revolutionary justice', as exemplified in the infamous *Law of the Suspect*, and respect for properly constituted law be enforced. As a first step towards the assertion of a central authority, a system of prefects was introduced, in February 1800, and with them came a reform of the entire system of local government. The effect of this reform is easy to summarise: government ceased to be local, since all was now to be directed from the centre, enabling Napoleon to say in March 1800: 'here everything goes from good to better. The prefects are going to their posts and I hope that in a month France will at last be an organised state.' Bonaparte had succeeded in stabilising the government in Paris, and now the prefects became his instruments in the more difficult task of bringing order to the rest of the country.[3] What facilitated the process was that the Revolution had cleared away all the old vested interests and legal barriers which had impeded royal authority: now, given the Napoleonic impetus, a new system could be built on the débris.

To make certain of the consistency of approach and continued direction from the centre, Napoleon made the Council of State, put in place by the constitution of the Year VIII, the dynamo of the new machinery. Here was a body of experts, chosen by the First Consul, composed of the most able men who could be found, irrespective of their political past – for Napoleon asserted that 'I am national'. His aim was to end, not perpetuate, the divisions caused by the events of the last decade. And so moderate Royalists, ex-Jacobins and others learned to work for the state: 'Bonaparte', it was said, 'assembled all the talents in every sphere and fused all the factions.'[4]

The creation of a functioning administration was a tremendous achievement, given the condition of France in 1800, but the essential complement to it was a coherent system of law that would be acceptable because of its rationality, and that would preserve the gains of the Revolution while ending its excesses. The result of the work of the legal committees, whose meetings Napoleon himself frequently attended, was the Code of Laws which bear his name and which appeared as the various specialist committees finished their deliberations. The most important for the whole of society was a Civil Code: clear, concise and well structured, it enshrined the revolutionary principles of equality before the law, freedom of conscience and the secular state; above all, it confirmed the right of individual property combined with the right to work. Although it can be argued that the Civil Code simply leant towards consolidating a middle class which had benefited from the Revolutionary upheaval, and although both a Criminal Code and a Commercial Code were yet to be added, it was the Civil Code which was to have most effect outside of France. Exported along with the armies of Napoleon, it was to affect the legislative structures of many other European states profoundly. The sweeping away of archaic, confused and confusing legal systems was one of the benefits which Napoleon conferred on Europe as a whole.

If by 1800 Napoleon had gained a breathing space in relation to France's external enemies, and had made considerable headway in the reordering of affairs at home, the internal situation was still far from satisfactory. Among the events which had precipitated the fall of the Directory had been its weakness in the face of the Royalist revolts in the west of France and in Normandy, two regions where the counter-revolutionary forces were being maintained in the field by the supply of arms and other necessities from England. It was clear to Napoleon that the civil war must be ended. Although the Directory had made half-hearted attempts to negotiate with the royalists, it was the consular regime that made serious and definitive moves. On 17 December 1799, Napoleon offered pardon, the re-establishment of religious practices and a return to normal life. He even met leaders of the Royalists, who, if they failed to persuade him to restore the Bourbons, at least achieved terms for a satisfactory pacification of the regions which had been in revolt for so long. Just in case there were hesitations over acceptance of the terms, this policy was accompanied by a military campaign whose success led to the virtual collapse of the Royalist cause in its armed manifestation. Henceforth Royalists would have to, and did, resort to plots and assassination attempts if they wished to overthrow the new regime.

To reinforce his determination to unite the nation behind him, Napoleon now began the work of healing the religious schism. Brought about by the enforcement of the Civil Constitution of the Clergy, this was one of the most catastrophic legacies of the Revolution, and one which had been at the root of much of the civil disturbance across the country. Napoleon had already shown his willingness to work towards an end to the religious problem by allowing the unofficial return of priests who had fled their parishes and lived in emigration. Their return did much to pacify local discontents, and served also to underline the change of policy under the new regime, but the key to any real reconciliation between the state and the church depended on the attitude of the papacy. Once again fortune favoured Napoleon. Pius VI ('Citizen Pope', as he was referred to during the Directory) died in Valence, where he had been kept prisoner since 1798, in order to remove his influence from Rome and to underline his subordinate position to the French government, actions which had antagonised most of Catholic Europe. Significantly, by a decree of December 1799, Napoleon ordered that Pius should receive a fitting burial and that a proper monument be erected on his tomb, gestures intended to be a visible manifestation of his goodwill towards the papacy. In March 1800, the conclave held in Venice elected as Pope Luigi Chiaramonte, a gentle Benedictine monk, the candidate of Spain (and France) against the hopes of Austria and the Bourbon Pretender. Taking the name of Pius VII, the new pontiff showed himself to be equally conciliatory in his attitude to Napoleon and, as a consequence, was able to begin his reign by returning to Rome without any hindrance from Paris.

In June 1800, on his way back from the battle of Marengo, Napoleon gave further indication of his intentions, when he met a senior cardinal and discussed with him the administrative reorganisation of the church in France. Significantly, no spiritual matters were raised, and it was on the basis of this proposed reorganisation that the Pope began negotiations. Napoleon, with his customary lack of patience, thought that the whole business could be wound up quickly – after all he was the one in a position of strength; but, like others before him, he underestimated the strength of unhurried papal diplomacy. Rome had centuries of experience and had seen many previous interlocutors come and go. Exasperated by the delays, Napoleon tried the threat of military action – he would occupy the Papal States – and even added a hint of spiritual blackmail by announcing he would turn Protestant: 'others will follow me'. The Pope remained unmoved, though, as a precaution, and remembering what had happened to his predecessor, he did sound out the King of Spain as to the availability of a refuge if Napoleon proved really threatening. Prudence was, after all, one of the cardinal virtues.

The negotiations between the papal emissaries and the French dragged on until, in a decisive session lasting twenty hours, a compromise agreement acceptable to both sides was produced. Success was due to the skill and patience of Joseph Bonaparte, who again showed great capacities as a negotiator in difficult circumstances – including having to put up with his brother's outbursts of temper.[5] In essence what was decided was that Rome would recognise the French Republic while the French state would recognise the Catholic faith as 'the religion of most Frenchmen'. The Pope regained authority over the church in France, but the terms of the Concordat had been negotiated between equals and could be revised if the state should find it necessary. Even more pertinent was the fact that the French clergy became state functionaries, in that they were paid by its authority, for there had been no question of restoring to the church the lands and properties confiscated and sold off by the revolutionary govern-ments. The acceptance of the irrevocability of the revolutionary land settlement by the church was certainly the one aspect of the agreement that made Napoleon's initiative palatable to those who had no desire to see religious practice restored in France.

The Concordat of 1801 was not perfect, nor did it always provide the best solutions, but in the immediate term it brought an end to one of the most virulent causes of civil discord and marked a new beginning. That was what Napoleon had intended. Just to make sure that the Pope had understood the situation and the relative positions of the parties involved, the Organic Articles, which were added *after* signature, underlined the subordination of the church to the state. All papal bulls needed a governmental imprimatur; the clergy were to wear French and not Roman ecclesiastical dress; and there was to be one catechism in use by all the French dioceses. The famous Gallican Articles of 1682, emphasising the jurisdictional independence of the church in France, had to be taught in all seminaries. Pius protested, accusing Napoleon of bad faith, but by way of reply the government put the Protestant clergy on exactly the same footing as the Catholic, that is equal in the eyes of the state. In a further move in 1806, Napoleon regulated relations between the Jewish community and the government by establishing the Sanhedrin as a central organisation with which the state could deal. Henceforth the Catholic faith would be the one 'professed by most Frenchmen', but as an institution the church would have to learn to live with other state recognised bodies.[6]

The church did, however, benefit from an unexpected recognition of its restored place in France. On Easter Sunday, 18 April 1802, the Concordat was to be officially proclaimed and to mark the occasion there was to be a celebration of a solemn Mass and Te Deum at the cathedral of Notre-Dame, now restored to Catholic worship. This type of ceremony was, given the circumstances, not out of the ordinary, but its complexion was totally changed by the fact that it was attended officially by the First Consul, together with his two colleagues. They drove from the consular palace of the Tuileries to the cathedral in a procession of carriages, followed by the foreign ambassadors and representatives of the various government institutions, accompanied by the cheers of the crowds, the pealing of church bells (virtually silent for a decade) and salvoes of artillery. Not everyone appreciated what one commentator described as a 'religious farce'. In particular, the generals and higher-ranking army officer behaved so badly in Notre-Dame that it required a sign of displeasure on the part of Napoleon to bring them to order. The Mass was splendid and, to emphasise the new spirit of reconciliation, the sermon was preached by the Archbishop of Tours, who had preached at the funeral of Louis XV and at the Coronation of Louis XVI, and who now received the oaths of the newly consecrated bishops.

Having very publicly taken the sting out of the religious quarrel, Napoleon was reaping the benefits. One of the strengths of the Royalists had been their ability to count on the support of the church. This was now to a great extent withdrawn, thereby depriving royalist agents in France of a network of communication, based on the parish clergy, one which had been particularly strong in staunchly Catholic areas. Furthermore, the swearing in of the new bishops at Notre-Dame was in accordance with an important clause of the Concordat, namely Napoleon's insistence that the Pope remove from their titular sees those bishops who had emigrated – principally to England – thereby further weakening not only the links with royalism but also with France's enemies. To counterbalance this, he had seen to it that the so-called 'constitutional bishops', that is those who had accepted the Civil Constitution of the Clergy of 1791, were also removed. France was, in fact, to have a new episcopate – there was even an alteration in the distribution of the dioceses, and so the First Consul could be hopeful of both support and obedience.

With the church once again integrated into the structure of the nation there now remained the problem of the *émigrés*, those who had fled the Revolution and who in some instances had actually borne arms against France. In 1800, as a result of the end of the civil war in the Vendée, Napoleon decreed an amnesty which actually benefited not just those in that region, but also permitted many *émigrés*, who had returned clandestinely, to regularise their situation. A further decree of 26 April 1802 authorised the return of all those nobles in emigration except those who had borne arms against France.

This was an important move, since it sorted out the diehard Royalists from those prepared to accept an accommodation with the Revolution – which in many instances had stripped them of their estates and driven them into exile. Napoleon's aim was clear: the returned nobles who could be persuaded to serve the new dispensation would, by rallying to him, weaken the position of the Pretender, who served as a focal point for all those in emigration who pinned their hopes on a restoration of the former dynasty. Their 'King' was Louis XVIII, brother of the executed Louis XVI, who since 1791 had moved about those European courts which were prepared to give him refuge. In 1800 Louis tried a direct approach, by writing to Napoleon, hoping to find in him a General Monck who would restore his King to the throne as had happened to Charles II of England in 1660. The answer was definitive and discouraging for, on 7 September 1800, Bonaparte wrote: 'your return to France is not a thing to be wished for; it could only be accomplished over the corpses of one hundred thousand men'[7]. Realising that he could be spending a considerable time abroad, Louis settled in England as a pensioner of the English government, which, taking the long view, considered him a useful card to have in hand, to be played if an occasion presented itself and France should need a king.

Deprived of any real chance of either military success or mounting a successful counter-revolutionary *coup* the Royalists turned to assassination as a means of doing away with the 'usurper'. On 28 December 1800 an attempt was made with explosives on the life of Napoleon and Josephine on their way to attend the opera. The street where the explosion of the 'infernal machine' took place, the Rue Saint-Nicaise, gave its name to the attempt which provoked retaliation not only on those who were responsible but on the Jacobins, who were blamed for the outrage in spite of clear evidence pointing to the Royalist group. Once again the Napoleonic balancing act was responsible: having clipped the wings of the Royalists, he now turned is attention to the Jacobins, those who were unrepentant in their republicanism, and were growing more and more disaffected as Napoleon's policies began to take clear form. For them, the immediate consequence of the attempt was the deportation without trial to France's overseas possessions of 130 men who were suspected of being a threat to the established order. Most were to end their days in exile, for Napoleon never relented against those whom he considered to be an 'internal disease', more deadly than any external threat since it led to civil war.

By 1801 the restructuring of France had begun in earnest and the new regime had made clear the broad outlines of its future policies. What was needed now was an end to the war and the signing of a peace treaty that would be more than a truce. Marengo had been an important victory, especially in helping to consolidate Napoleon's position inside France, but, as already noted, it had not ended hostilities. Austria, although defeated in Italy, was not vanquished in Germany. It needed the defeat of its armies by General Moreau at the battle of Hohenlinden in December 1800 to force the Emperor Francis to ask for an armistice. This led ultimately to the holding of a peace conference at Lunéville in Lorraine in 1801. England was invited to send representatives but refused to participate, thwarting Napoleon's hopes of bringing about a general settlement. Lunéville, how-ever, at which the chief negotiator was Joseph Bonaparte, provides a clear indication of Napoleon's aims once it is seen as part of the series of treaties concluded in the period 1800 to 1802. The treaty of San Ildefonso with Spain, which brought about the return of Louisiana to France, led to a second treaty at Aranjuez by which Spain promised to attack Britain's ally Portugal. There was also the treaty of Mortefontaine with the United States, based on a joint refusal to accept England's right to stop, search and seize at sea any ship suspected of trading with her enemies. The thrust of all these treaties was to make England amenable to negotiation through isolation, a strategy which gained an unexpected bonus as a result of the actions of the Tsar Paul I of Russia, whose admiration for Napoleon led him to leave the English camp. Under his aegis the Armed Neutrality of the North (linking Russia, Denmark, Sweden and Prussia) was established, aimed at ending England's Baltic trade, of great importance to it for naval supplies. The English response to this menace was an immediate and two-pronged attack designed to break the threat to her position in northern Europe. In St Petersburg a conspiracy was hatched to assassinate Paul and to replace him with his son Alexander. The plotters were a mixture of court nobles and military officers who feared for their own positions and who resented the pro-French policy of their ruler. The extent to which the English embassy in St Petersburg was involved in all this remains a subject for debate: what is undeniable is that the ambassador had complete knowledge of what was intended. The conspiracy was a success and Paul was murdered in March 1801.[8] As a result, any immediate threat of a Russo-French entente was averted. The second thrust of the English offensive was the attack by Nelson on Copenhagen in April which destroyed the Danish fleet and removed the immediate threat of hostile control of the Baltic Sea. As a result of these events the Armed Neutrality collapsed, but England's position remained precarious due to financial strains, the alarm caused by a serious insurrection in Ireland in 1798, and by discontent at home exacerbated by the very bad harvest of 1799.

In the event, the way to opening negotiations leading to a cessation of hostilities came about in an odd manner unconnected with the war – for Pitt's resignation in 1801 was occasioned by the King's refusal to accept his plan for the granting of Catholic Emancipation. Pitt had conceived this idea of granting religious and political toleration as a means of making the Act of Union between Britain and Ireland more palatable to the Irish Catholic majority. The Union had been decided on as a result of the threat of armed French intervention in Ireland, as had been made manifest in

1798, since it was felt in London that only complete control by Britain could avoid a recurrence of such a danger to its military position. Pitt's promise of Catholic Emancipation was to be the reward for acceptance of the new political dispensation, but George III refused to consider it on the grounds that it would violate his coronation oath to uphold the Protestant religion.

The negotiations with France were begun by Pitt's successor Addington, whose credentials for office were that he was a liberal Whig, an anti-Catholic and against a continuation of the war. He was therefore able to fill the role of peacemaker that Pitt would never have been able (or willing) to do. Anglo-French dscussions continued from February 1801 until March 1802 when a treaty was signed at Amiens in northern France. The terms of the treaty were, at first reading, quite straightforward: England returned to France all the colonies taken from her in the war, keeping only Ceylon, taken from the Dutch, and Trinidad, taken from Spain. These seemingly modest gains were of great strategic importance for Britain's maritime power. The same reason lay behind the attempt to keep control of Malta, which Napoleon wished to neutralise by giving it back to the knights of St John of Jerusalem. In an attempt to hinder the implementation of this clause, the English negotiators obtained a three-month delay in the withdrawal of their troops from the date of the ratification of the treaty. The importance, from Napoleon's point of view, was that France gave away virtually nothing while England appeared to have recognised the treaty of Lunéville, which virtually confirmed French control of the Continent.

By 1802 Napoleon had secured an advantageous position for France abroad, had established firm government at home and had ended the threat of civil war. He could claim to have redeemed the promise made at Brumaire: 'Citizens, the Revolution is now settled in the principles in which it started: it is completed.' In England a war-weary populace greeted the news of the signing of the peace with an outburst of public rejoicing to mark the end of a decade of war. But was it really over? Lord Malmesbury, a hardened and sceptical diplomat, commented: 'peace in a week, war in a month'. In the event he was somewhat out in his calculations, but his instincts were sound, for the war was to be resumed. When it was, the situation in France had altered considerably because of changes in the governmental structure.

As a result of the successes at home and abroad (the Concordat and the Peace of Amiens) there was such a degree of support for Napoleon that it was felt essential to express in some way 'the gratitude of the nation', an idea which was assiduously cultivated by Joseph and Lucien Bonaparte. They were supported by other dignitaries, including Talleyrand and Cambacérès, though there was considerable opposition among member of the Senate and among the generals. The plan was to change the constitution so that Napoleon would become First Consul for life, thus ensuring the continuity and stability of the regime. In order to effect a change of such importance, it was decided that a proposal should be submitted to the nation, which would vote on it in a plebiscite. A ratification by popular vote would prevent accusations of imposition from above and would maintain the revolutionary principle of the people's right to participation. On 11 May, a few weeks after the splendid ceremony at Notre-Dame, the voters were asked to give their answer to the question: 'Should Napoleon Bonaparte be named Consul for Life?' By August the results were known: 3,568,885 'yes', 8374 'no', in a vote of more than 40 per cent of the electorate. There seems little doubt that the vote reflected a genuine expression of popular support, though there were naturally accusations of trickery and fudged arithmetic, in large measure inspired by disgruntled Royalists who feared what a Life Consulate might lead to.

Napoleon's new status meant a considerable increase in his powers: among others the right to nominate his two colleagues, the right to nominate his successor, and the right to grant pardons, on appeal, to those convicted by legal process. It was this last which underlined the extent to which the Republic had become monarchical in its outward form, though still animated by the spirit of the Revolution, and it was precisely this which made it so formidable. It seemed to the world that France had acquired an uncrowned King, one who disposed of more power than had Louis XVI when he became King in 1774. For the France of Napoleon, the most populous country in Europe, had freed itself from all the archaic constraints which had hampered the old monarchy, thwarting necessary reforms, and was now motivated by the triumph of its revolutionary ideals. When considering the reasons for the breakdown of the Peace of Amiens it is well to remember Napoleon's own comment: 'between older monarchies and a young republic the spirit of hostility must always exist'.

Rather than asking, therefore, what went wrong with the Peace of Amiens, it might be more profitable to ask if there had ever been a possibility that it would actually work. The failure of the English to evacuate

Malta was the official reason put forward for the breakdown of the peace, once the English government proved unwilling to give up what it considered the key to the control of the Mediterranean, but in fact there were deeper reasons. The increase in Napoleon's power and the evident strengthening of the consular regime seemed to indicate that the reorganisation of areas of the Continent, in accordance with the treaty of Lunéville, heralded the establishment of French political and economic hegemony. This was a situation which England could never accept, for control of the major ports would enable France to expand its maritime empire, and thus threaten England's vital commercial interests while at the same time depriving her of continental European markets.

These factors would, in themselves, have been sufficient to alarm the English government, but there was a further dimension, one which was to help in keeping the war going for another decade, for the struggle between the two countries had become one of rival ideologies. From the moment when the French revolutionaries began not simply to make war, but showed their determination to export their ideals, the threat of war, allied to the spirit of the Revolution, had never ceased to be perceived by the English governing classes as a menace to the whole political structure of the kingdom. It was therefore essential that any continental power which showed a tendency to accept France's right to exist, as a symbol not just of conquest but of enlightened reform, had to be brought to heel and enlisted in the cause of counter-revolution. It was fortunate for England that the vagaries of Napoleon's policies, and his seemingly limitless ambition, enabled his greatest enemy to pose as a beacon of liberty rather than the protagonist of reaction. At the same time, the image of Napoleon as a cruel and blood-thirsty tyrant was assiduously cultivated to make certain that hostility to France and its leader did not falter.

Unfortunately for his opponents, an unforeseen consequence of English demonisation of Napoleon was that, rightly or wrongly, he became identi-fied with reform, with the ideals of the Revolution and with an attempt to form a European Confederation which would bring peace and stability to the Continent by putting an end to English interference in its affairs. There was just enough truth in all this to make it believable to contemporaries and, above all, to give it considerable force in the future.

Napoleon may have intended the treaty of Amiens to be a serious commitment to peace, or he may have seen it as providing a breathing space, allowing him to consolidate his authority further. In the event, neither the peace nor the breathing space were achieved, for England, aware that an agreement that allowed France to dominate the Continent could never be tolerated, would not be bound by Amiens. Already incontestably in breach of the treaty over Malta, England now compounded the offence by seizing one thousand French and Dutch ships in English ports without the formality of a declaration of war. In retaliation, Napoleon ordered the arrest of all British subjects in France and the confiscation of all ships and merchandise belonging to England. As an almost symbolic gesture, proof that things were back to normal, Pitt returned as Prime Minister. The war that was now resumed would last for twelve years, but its effects would last for nearly a century.

In England the war was seen as an affair of defending the status quo: internally it was in defence of the oligarchic and aristocratic society that governed the kingdom, while abroad it was fought for the traditional purpose of preventing any one power from dominating the European Continent. For France, the problem was of a different order: internally there were conflicting elements which had to be reconciled, though Napoleon had certainly reduced their capacity to make mischief, and the authority of the state and the action of regular government had to be established and maintained. None of this would be helped by the conditions prevailing in time of war, and all had also to be maintained against a background of perpetuating the gains of the Revolution and recognising the new social order it had produced. Since becoming First Consul, Napoleon had gone a long way to finding a solution to these serious problems, but he was still faced with the inevitability of the dislocation that war would bring and the consequences arising from it. Above all, how could the threat of counter-revolution be finally removed if England, its principal protagonist and banker, was not beaten decisively?

As proof of the reality of this threat, Napoleon found himself the victim of a further assassination attempt early in 1804 – an attempt made all the more alarming because it included among the conspirators two generals, Moreau and Pichegru. The plot was clearly linked to Royalist agents financed by the English government, as police investigations soon revealed, and by March 1804 all the leaders had been arrested and imprisoned.[9] The affair then took a dramatic turn, for interrogation of the suspects revealed that they anticipated the arrival of a Bourbon Prince to assume leadership of the plot. Napoleon became convinced that the Prince in question was the Duke of Enghien, the son of the Prince of Condé, who lived in Baden, a few kilometres from the French frontier. It was decided that this young man should be seized and brought to trial in France, a gross violation of all extant laws of protection, for the Prince lived in Baden by permission of its Duke. The seizure, and execution, of the Duke of Enghien was an action which has traditionally always damaged Napoleon's reputation, though he himself never denied responsibility for what had been done. In fact, in his will, dictated in 1821 on St Helena, he explicitly justified the affair: 'I had the Duke of Enghien arrested and tried because it was necessary for the security, the interest and the honour of the French people ... And in similar circumstances I would act in the same way.'[10]

Given the use made of the event by Napoleon's enemies, both then and now, it is perhaps worthwhile examining the reasons behind this affair, described by the cynical Talleyrand as 'worse than a crime, it is a blunder'. Given that Talleyrand himself was a party to the whole affair, he should perhaps have considered another of his bons mots about missing a good opportunity to say nothing.

To begin with, it was clear from an examination of the papers seized at Enghien's residence that he was indeed engaged in an active correspondence with émigré groups both within France and abroad. Since, in the case of those newly re-established in France, it was Napoleon who had permitted their return, it was clear to him that they must not be allowed to act as a 'fifth column' engaging in plots in the hope of a Royalist restoration. Such activities could now be seen as a double treason, not merely to the First Consul but also to the country itself, since France was at war with England, whose government supported the Bourbons by giving them refuge and by subsidising their plots against Napoleon.[11]

The ramifications of this plot of 1804 revealed just how widespread and how dangerous for the regime was the work of English agents operating in France. Such people and their backers needed to be shown that, as Napoleon said, 'this is not a children's game'. In any event the majority in France was convinced that the government of the Consul for Life would give them what they wanted: consolidation of the gains of the Revolution together with a stable society. It was unlikely that there would be much agitation about the death of a Bourbon Duke who was virtually unknown, when some ten years previously the guillotine had dispatched the King, the Queen and assorted

Princes of the Blood. Since the Bourbons were now associated with England, their paymaster and the enemy of France, they were repudiated even more firmly.

So much then for the negative aspects of the affair – but did Napoleon have something further in mind other than the administration of a sharp lesson to those hankering after the past? There was indeed for him a more positive aspect, which concerned the future of the consular regime and its transformation into something which would be more secure and more durable. At the very moment when the idea of establishing the empire was being seriously discussed, and was, indeed, waiting to make its entry into history, Napoleon very brutally underlined his revolutionary convictions and his determination to prevent a Bourbon restoration. Furthermore, those who had returned from exile had, by openly attaching themselves to him, broken definitively with the former dynasty. It is this which makes the execution of the Duke of Enghien a watershed, for it can be argued that Napoleon, by his action, joined the regicides. If the country felt the need for a monarchy then a new dynasty was already available to answer its needs – a dynasty which would represent the Revolution and not the counter-revolution.

There can be no doubt that the effects of the affair of the Duke of Enghien speeded up what had become virtually an inevitable development: even those who had opposed the proclamation of the Consulship for Life were now agreed that the times had changed and that all must change with them. The question was quite simply how, and by what constitutional mechanism, an Empire should be proclaimed. As before, the machinery was set in motion by the Senate which, together with the Legislative Body, approached Napoleon asking him to accept the national will and to proclaim himself Emperor. As well as this institutional approach, a campaign was organised so that the nation could express its will as it had done over the question of the Consulship for Life. This resulted in addresses being sent to the Senate from various parts of the country asking that Napoleon Bonaparte, the First Consul, should be declared Emperor and in this form should remain at the head of the government of the French Republic.

One important question remained to be settled within the family. Napoleon and Josephine had no children, so it was necessary that the new Emperor should adopt an heir to provide for the succession. As a result of a discussion within the family, Napoleon adopted the son of his brother

Louis, born in 1802 of his marriage to Hortense de Beauharnais and called
Napoleon Charles; a shrewd move, for it cleverly married together the
family of the Bonapartes with that of Josephine, since Louis Bonaparte was
the father and Hortense was Josephine's daughter.

On 13 April at the palace of St-Cloud, where the Consulate had been
inaugurated in 1799, the question of the Empire was discussed frankly, for
it was quite clear that the principle had already been accepted, though it
now emerged that some of the senators were less enthusiastic for the project
than they had been at the beginning. It was too late for a change of heart,
however, for the matter had gone too far and the Senate, fearing that it
would be bypassed, tried to save face by setting up a commission to consider
the question. There could really only be one result of its deliberations, but
it did enable the constitutional forms to be observed. So, on 18 May 1804
(28 Floréal Year XII of the revolutionary calendar), a *senatus consultum* was
issued which stipulated by its first article that 'the government of the
Republic is entrusted to an Emperor, who takes the title of Emperor of the
French'[12]. The thing was done and France had acquired by way of its
Revolution a fourth ruling dynasty. It was hardly what had been intended
in 1789.

All that remained now was to consult the nation and to hold the plebiscite envisaged by the *senatus consultum* by which the people were asked to
vote, *not* on the establishment of the Empire as such but on the conferment
of heredity on Napoleon Bonaparte. 'The people wishes the imperial dignity
to be hereditary by direct descent, natural, legitimate and adoptive of
Napoleon Bonaparte, and in the descendance direct, natural and legitimate
of Joseph Bonaparte and of Louis Bonaparte.' The new regime was to be
identified with the family, whose dynastic claim rested on the will of
the people.

The results of the plebiscite were officially proclaimed on the
30 November 1804: 3,572,329 had voted 'yes', against only 2569 'no', in a
turn out of over 40 per cent.[13] In one sense the figures are totally unimpor-
tant, it is the fact that the event took place which matters – as contemporaries
were well aware. In Vienna one of the ministers of the Emperor Francis II
told his master: 'It is the Revolution which has been consecrated, thus
allowing the transmission of its calamitous precepts'. It now remained to be
seen how other European states would react to the emergence of the new
Emperor who owed his throne to revolution and a popular vote.

3

The Revolution Crowned

The transition from Consulate to Empire was less dramatic than might have been expected since, from 1802, everything except to the words 'Consul' and 'Republic' had already become monarchical. There had even been the reintroduction of a system of orders and decorations, banished as a symbol of monarchy by the revolutionary government, with the creation of the Legion of Honour. As a sop to egalitarian principles, it was made clear to those who denounced this as a retrograde step, and an affront to revolutionary principles, that it was designed to reward all those who had deserved well of the nation without distinction of class or profession. In the creation of a new orientation in society, however, the establishment of the Legion was only a small item. Much more remained to be done to produce an imperial court worthy of the new Emperor and Empress. It was not just a question of things, but also one of people, for, as Talleyrand waspishly remarked, 'there were many who did not know how to walk on polished floors'.

It was in this sphere that Josephine's influence was important, for she represented the link between the old aristocracy, with its manners learnt at Versailles, and the new class of would-be courtier which, for the most part, had little experience of courtly life or manners. In a wider context, however, it must be remembered that the *ancien régime* was not something lost in the mists of time but a system which, at one level of society or another, all the leading figures in the Empire had known. There was an added advantage since, thanks to the policy of reconciliation inaugurated in 1801, many were of the old nobility. Napoleon, as it happened, could claim descent from a noble family that could trace its origins back to the sixteenth century, but he rarely bothered to make much of it since his own career made recourse to ancestral deeds unnecessary.

What was now essential was to present the European powers with the fact of the new Emperor and the new Empire. To achieve this two things were necessary, if normal diplomatic protocol was to be observed. First, the

European sovereigns must be informed of the newcomer to their ranks; and, secondly, there must be a coronation which would establish a form of 'divine sanction' of the new dynasty.

The proclamation of the Empire was made known to those foreign courts that were at peace with France by means of a letter addressed to their respective sovereigns The language and style which was used in conveying the news of the proclamation of the Empire to Charles IV of Spain will serve as an example of the communications sent to all the other European monarchies so favoured:

> Most eminent, most excellent and well beloved good Brother, Ally and Confederate, the good relations which exists between our two states and the veritable interest which Your Majesty has always shown to the happiness and prosperity of France oblige me to tell you that it has pleased Providence to call me to the government of this Empire, and that in virtue of its laws and its constitutions the title and dignity of Emperor of the French have been conferred on me to remain in a hereditary manner in my family.[1]

With the exceptions of England and Sweden (an action which provoked the breaking off of diplomatic relations between France and those two countries), all the other European states which were officially informed recognised the Empire. Given France's domination of the Continent, as a result of its military strength and its alliances, such recognition was prudent. Apart from which, it was only a public demonstration: privately the other sovereigns mocked this latest bizarre caprice of Napoleon, though one country found it useful, since Francis II declared himself hereditary Emperor of Austria (a title that he kept when, in 1806, the Holy Roman Empire ceased to exist). A more serious reaction to the event soon manifested itself, however, for the major powers began the construction of a new coalition against France, as always under the aegis of England, with Alexander I of Russia as the prime mover on the Continent.

While these diplomatic transactions were taking place, Napoleon fulfilled the second obligation imposed by his new status. He had himself crowned. For him, it was indispensable as a means of giving dignity to his self-proclaimed rank, since it would put him on an equal footing with the other monarchs; even more importantly, it would help to consolidate the dynasty and the succession. To underline the importance which he attached to the ceremony he determined that the Pope himself would be present, thus spanning the millennium which separated him from the Emperor

Charlemagne, crowned Emperor by the Pope in Rome on Christmas Day 800. This time the Pope would come to Paris at the behest of the Emperor, so there would be no dispute as to who was pre-eminent in this new imperial dispensation. The identification with Charlemagne, which could easily be derided as some sort of medieval fantasy, was a deliberate act, for it put Napoleon in a European context. He would be more than Emperor of the French and his dynasty would not be identified only with its country of origin but would be presented as a pan-European monarchy.

Pius VII arrived in Paris in November 1804 and straightaway found himself involved in a delicate problem occasioned by the lack of any religious ceremony between Josephine and Napoleon when they had married. Fearful of a divorce, for she had failed to produce an heir to ensure the continuity of the dynasty, Josephine persuaded the Pope to make a religious celebration of her marriage a condition of his participation at the coronation. At first sight this may have appeared to be a shrewd move, in that the church was now a guarantor of the marriage, for Napoleon, after much complaining, was forced to accede to her request or face an embarrassing dispute with Pius. In a private ceremony, performed by Cardinal Consalvi on 1 December 1804, the two were duly married according to the rites of the church. Had Josephine forgotten that where marriage was possible, so also was divorce? At least for the moment, however, she appeared to have consolidated her position and had gained a point in her never-ending struggle with the Bonaparte family.

The next day, the coronation ceremony took place in Notre-Dame. In one striking innovation, contrary to normal practice in which the presiding ecclesiastic performed the act of crowning, Napoleon did not receive the crown from the hands of the Pope but crowned himself. That done, he then crowned Josephine as his Empress, with the result that, at the climax of the ceremony, the Pope found himself reduced to the role of a spectator at what indeed appears to have been a splendid piece of theatre.[2]

The setting was certainly one of great magnificence, with all the principal actors, and spectators, dressed as if for an evening at the opera: the women resplendent with jewels and the men, mostly in uniform, with their medals shining in the myriad candles which lit the cathedral. This impression of a stage performance was enhanced by a setting of the mass by Paisiello, who was an accomplished composer of opera but had little experience of church music on a grand scale. The actual ritual turned out to be an eclectic mix of a traditional coronation with all the usual trappings of monarchy, that is crown, sceptre, sword and the hand of justice, part of the traditional regalia of the kings of France, to which (an innovation) war added the orb. While the crown was new, the sceptre was reputed to have belonged to King Charles V (1338–80) and the sword to Philip III (1245–85), all designed to point up a continuity with the defunct monarchy. Although Napoleon agreed to the rite of the anointing with holy oil, he did not receive the sacrament at the communion, so that, apart from the blessings which took place during the mass, there was no point in the ceremony at which the Pope appeared as the most important participant. The papal action was limited to reciting the coronation prayers and, proclaiming the Emperor according to the traditional formula: 'Vivat imperatorem in aeternum!' (May the Emperor live forever), followed by the intoning of the Te Deum. Some further prayers were then recited, which ended the mass and the religious ceremony.

At this point, as the result of a previous agreement, the Pope retired to the sacristy of the cathedral while the second part of the ceremony took place. In this section there was, significantly, no reference to ancient traditions, for although Napoleon swore his constitutional oath on the Gospels, the content of the oath was a summary of the last decade of France's history. The text was presented to him by the President of the Senate, the President of the Legislative Body and the most senior President of the Council of State. Napoleon swore to maintain the integrity of the territory of the Republic, to maintain equality before the law, and the right of civil political and religious liberty. He swore that no taxes would be levied without legal consent, and that the sale of all property confiscated during the Revolution was irrevocable. Since this included all church property seized in 1791, it seemed that the Pope, by his presence at the coronation, had accepted this act of spoliation. This last part of the coronation ceremony was the key to the whole performance: there might be nobles and there might be the church, but the dynasty had sworn to maintain the principles of the Revolution from which it derived its real legitimacy. This was the guarantee that there would be no return to the *ancien régime*.

It was at this stage, after the swearing of the oath, that the newly appointed herald of arms turned to the congregation saying in a loud voice: 'The most glorious and august Emperor Napoleon, Emperor of the French, is crowned and enthroned. Long live the Emperor!' The cry was taken up by the people present and, in the middle of these acclamations, Napoleon left Notre-Dame, surrounded by the imperial dignitaries, while the choir sang the invocation 'Domine salvum fac imperatorem nostrum Napoleonem'. It was some little while afterwards that Pius VII, having waited in the sacristy until the departure of the imperial party, left the cathedral. His day was probably made more cheerful and agreeable by the fact that along the route of his carriage people knelt in the streets invoking his blessing and calling out in greeting. Apart from which Napoleon had given him one concession: he had agreed that in 1806 the revolutionary calendar would be abolished and the Gregorian calendar restored. This meant that Sunday became once again a recognised 'day' and so became an outward symbol of the return of religious practice. It was perhaps small return for all that the Pope had given, but the papacy was nothing if not patient and small concessions might lead to bigger ones in time.

What is clear is that, beneath an appearance of a calm acceptance of the events of this December 1804, there was a great deal of discontent among contemporaries. The Republicans were angered, and the anticlericals in particular were outraged, by the religious pomp which the coronation had occasioned. Few were deceived by Napoleon's ruse in presenting the Pope as simply a temporal sovereign, just visiting for the coronation at which he was then asked to assist, rather than head of the church. This tawdry nonsense (which fooled no one) especially angered the Catholics, who saw that it had been used as a means of subjecting the Pope to a series of calculated humiliations. Aware of the mixed reactions, Napoleon was far from satisfied with what he had done, but had no choice but to live with the consequences, hoping that time would diminish the acrimony it had caused.

As it happened, his most vexatious moments came about, not because of mixed public reactions, but from the anger and hostility manifested within his family. The problems which Napoleon confronted in his relations with his family predated the coronation and the proclamation of the Empire, and in some instances were not directly connected with these events. Of his brothers, Lucien, although a supporter of the idea of the Empire, had quarrelled yet again with Napoleon; yet again, because of his marriage. His first wife having died in 1800, Napoleon envisaged finding Lucien a royal bride, in accord with the family's new status, but once again Lucien defied him and married Alexandrine de Jouberthon, a rich, but not royal, widow.

The youngest brother, Jerome, who was seventeen in 1802, displayed an aptitude for frivolous dissipation and spending money, while leaving his brother to pay his debts. Hoping to remove him from the temptations of Paris, and life at the consular court, Napoleon had arranged for him to join the navy as an officer. Life at sea, however, did nothing to improve Jerome's character and his inherent tendency to irresponsibility found an outlet in choosing a bride in the United States of America. In spite of Napoleon's having specifically warned him that he should not contract any marriage without his brother's express permission, in December 1803 he married Miss Elizabeth Patterson of Baltimore. She was of good Irish stock and came of a wealthy family, and was well regarded in her native city, but she was quite useless in furthering the new dynastic system now envisaged by her imperial brother-in law. In this case Napoleon would be able to have the marriage declared null and void, because the groom was a minor and had married without parental consent, but in the meantime Jerome was sailing towards France convinced that the beauty of his new bride would bring his brother to acceptance of the marriage. Napoleon, on being informed of this, simply declared that he had no interest in Jerome's 'mistress', and that if he wanted to come to France he must leave her behind. To show his resolve in the matter, an order was issued for the arrest and deportation of Miss Patterson if she attempted to join her husband. Faced with the choice of obeying his brother or remaining with his now pregnant wife, Jerome hesitated over his course of action – but not for long. In May 1805 he renounced his marriage, was reconciled to his brother, and received an annual allowance of 150,000 francs. Madame Jerome left for England, where she was well received by a sympathetic populace as a victim of the monster 'Boney', and where she gave birth to a son in July 1805. The boy was baptised Jerome Napoleon Bonaparte and shortly after was taken by his mother to the United States of America to become the founder of the Bonaparte Patterson branch of the family.

As a consequence of their apparent determination to flout his will, Napoleon decreed that both Lucien and Jerome were to be excluded from the succession to the throne, with the result that, when the imperial establishment was promulgated at the moment of the proclamation of the Empire, they were not given the title of French Princes (*Princes Français*) as a public mark of their brother's displeasure. To underline their feelings of anger, neither Lucien nor Jerome attended the coronation, a move which had the support of *Madame Mère*, who remained with them in Rome.

Napoleon insisted that David include her in his famous painting of the event nevertheless.

The two brothers chosen for preferment were Joseph and Louis: Joseph was the eldest brother, while Louis had always been Napoleon's favourite, since he had been responsible for him while he was young. As far as their capacity for being of service to their brother was concerned, Joseph had already shown, by the negotiations over the treaty of Lunéville and in his success in producing acceptable terms for the Concordat, that he was a highly skilled diplomat. Louis had much less experience of public activity, but he was only twenty-one in 1799 and his contribution to date had been to act as an aide-de-camp to Napoleon in Egypt. He had been sent back to France in March 1799 with letters from his brother to the Directors; and, although he was in Paris at the moment of the *coup d'état*, his part in it seems to have been minor. His great service to Napoleon, and the family, was his marriage to Josephine's daughter Hortense de Beauharnais, providing a fusion between the two families and ultimately consolidating the new dynasty by producing sons. Until the birth of Napoleon's son, the King of Rome, in 1811 these children represented the succession.

In the context of family marriages, which caused Napoleon so much irritation, it is interesting to note that he never called into question Joseph's marriage to Julie Clary, the daughter of a rich merchant in Marseille: was it because he, as a young man had been in love with her sister? Or was it that he knew Joseph would not accept any interference in this matter? Whatever the reason, Joseph remained married to his original wife – but unfortunately they only produced daughters, ending any possibility of that particular line playing a part in the succession.

The existence of the Salic Law, reinforced by the terms of the Constitution of the Year XII, which prohibited any of Napoleon's sisters from having any part of the succession to the throne, did not prevent them from looking for titles and a recognised place in the imperial dynasty. Pauline was already a Princess in her own right, by her marriage to Prince Borghese, but Elisa and Caroline – particularly the latter – became hysterical at the thought that the hated Josephine would now be 'Her Imperial Majesty', while Hortense would also be recognised as an Imperial Highness. They demanded that Napoleon give them titles, and, after a fearful row, in which Caroline fainted with anger, their brother conferred on them the titles of 'Imperial Highnesses'. This resulted in an absurd situation when Caroline, by virtue of her rank, was admitted to the throne room, while her husband, Joachim Murat, was turned back at the door. Such were the unexpected traps which etiquette sprang on the new imperial family and the court, proof that when it came to playing at royalty there was more to be learned than an ability to walk on polished floors. What made all of these unseemly scenes and squabbles so damaging to Napoleon's family was the contrast they made with the dignified, gentle and aristocratic behaviour of Josephine and her two children.

For Napoleon, the coronation was not an end but a beginning: 'The French Empire will become the mother country of the other sovereigns of Europe.' It seemed to him that one of the best way to achieve this would be by making members of his own family kings. He began by offering the crown of an Italian kingdom to Joseph, who refused, on the grounds that to accept would exclude him from succession to the French throne, an argument which would seem to indicate a wider ambition. Napoleon then tried to win over Lucien by offering him the throne on condition that he abandoned his second wife, Alexandrine, an offer which Lucien refused outright. Since Louis had also indicated his unwillingness to be involved, Napoleon had no choice but to accept the crown himself, and so, on 26 May 1805, he was crowned King of Italy in Milan Cathedral. The ceremony was, in most of its forms, a mirror image of the coronation at Notre-Dame, but this time the oath that he swore to maintain the constitution had an additional phrase: 'to govern solely in the interest, the happiness and the glory of the Italian people'.[3]

Napoleon's brothers had done him a considerable disservice by refusing to accept the Italian kingdom, for it seems clear that Austria would not accept the fact of Napoleon as both Emperor and King, while a separate entity under one of the brothers *might* have been tolerated. It may well have been Napoleon's irritation with his brothers' lack of cooperation that led to his naming his stepson Eugène de Beauharnais as Viceroy of the Italian Kingdom, knowing the resentment this would provoke within the family. Resentment, however, was not confined to the family. Whether the reasons were personal or political, Austria was angered by Napoleon's action in establishing the new kingdom and joined the new coalition being created by Russia and England to attack France yet again.

The outcome of this new war altered dramatically the entire state system of the Continent, for the total defeat of the combined Austro-Russian forces at Austerlitz on 2 December 1805 was followed by the collapse of the coalition and a treaty with Austria which redrew the map of Germany. As a sign that the Holy Roman Empire was finished, two new kingdoms, Bavaria and Württemberg, emerged, while the duchy of Baden was elevated to the status of a grand duchy. Napoleon, who knew that Prussia had been inclined to join the coalition, took advantage of the situation to negotiate with King Frederick William, offering him the kingdom of Hanover as a reward if he would break definitively with England. By accepting the offer, Prussia sealed the fate of the coalition without any thought for the future; for what Napoleon had given he could also take away.

In Italy, Austria was obliged to recognise the Napoleonic reorganisation. This now included the kingdom of Naples, from which the Bourbon King Ferdinand was removed, to be replaced by Joseph Bonaparte. The first of the brothers to reach this dignity, this time the new King made no difficulties about acceptance. Joseph proclaimed his intention of 'working for the happiness of his people', with whom he wished to be identified, but in very short order it was made clear to him by Napoleon that he was there to govern in the interests of France, and that the interests of the Italians must take second place. The form which the *Grand Empire* would assume thus emerged early on, as Joseph himself discovered when he pointed out to the Emperor that his budget showed a substantial deficit and indicated that he expected a subsidy from France. Napoleon replied refusing any grant of money and instructing him to raise thirty million francs by taxing his Italian subjects: 'you are too soft-hearted', became a constant refrain of the Emperor's letters to his brother.

In spite of this lack of support, or perhaps because of it, Joseph showed himself to be a capable and energetic ruler. The feudal structure of the Bourbon kingdom of Naples was abolished, there was a redistribution of land, and the law code was reformed on the French model. Since it was clear that a programme of public works, roads, viaducts and improved public facilities of all kinds was very necessary in this impoverished and backward state, Joseph made a serious attempt to produce it, proof of his determination to rule his kingdom wisely.

Unfortunately for Joseph, he not only had his brother's demands to cope with, he also had to deal with revolts and military forays organised by the English, who remained in occupation of Sicily. Officially there to protect the Bourbon King Ferdinand, who had fled to the island with his Queen and court, English command of the sea meant that an invasion of the mainland was always possible, while a distribution of money by Ferdinand's supporters on the mainland encouraged the peasantry to be ready to support armed intervention. The benefits of French reorganisation of the legal system, coupled with more efficient tax collection, was not always received by the people with the enthusiasm the authorities expected. Apart from which, the church showed a sustained hostility towards the godless invaders.

By 1807 Joseph recognised the precariousness of the situation – the English had actually taken the island of Capri and entrenched themselves there – and became convinced that only a general peace could save not only his kingdom but the whole Napoleonic Empire. In March 1807 he wrote to his brother: 'Your Majesty must make peace at all costs … you should not hazard the unbelievable glory you have accumulated in the past ten years of your life.' The letter was ignored because Napoleon felt himself to be in a position of strength, and moderation was not on his agenda, particularly as, looked at from the Emperor's point of view, there was every reason to feel secure. The effects of the victory of Austerlitz continued to be felt throughout central Europe and enabled Napoleon to establish a Confederation of the Rhine, composed of the south German and Rhenish states, of which he became the protector. The result was to extend French influence into the heart of Germany. With a view to completing France's domination of the Rhine, Louis was made King of Holland in the summer of 1806.

Louis had married Hortense simply because his brother (and Josephine) had wanted it. The positive result of this union was that, until 1811, when the King of Rome was born, he remained the only member of the family to have sons who could ensure the succession. Unfortunately, by then the marriage itself had turned into a disaster: Louis became morose, cold and introspective, and morbidly suspicious of his wife, whom he accused of infidelity and of betraying him. These views were encouraged by the mischief-making of Lucien and Caroline, the former going so far as to accuse Napoleon of incest with Hortense, and the latter spreading rumours about her sister-in-law's behaviour in general. For his part, Napoleon seems to have hoped that by establishing the couple as King and Queen of Holland the dynastic links would be extended and the marriage would prosper again. It would be reassuring for the Dutch to see the establishment of their new rulers as a family, so the new sovereigns set off for The Hague accompanied by their two sons, Napoleon Charles and Napoleon Louis. The Emperor's advice to them was: 'Go, and reign and make your people happy', an injunction which produced a somewhat equivocal reply from Louis: 'My happiness has been in my living near to you … but since these people wish it, and Your Majesty commands it, I shall go and rule.'

Louis, who in spite of his moodiness and difficult temperament was both shrewd and capable in managing affairs of state, began his reign, like his brother Joseph, by identifying himself with the interest of his new subjects. Napoleon had already warned him that his duties as Constable of the Empire meant that he must always put the interest of France above others, but Louis was less malleable than Joseph and a clash of wills was inevitable. The decisive confrontation was postponed because of Napoleon's campaign against Prussia in the autumn of 1806, which led him to demand that Louis bring a contingent of his Dutch army and collect a year's taxes in advance to defray the costs. The swiftness of Napoleon's campaign in which he destroyed Prussian military might at the battles of Jena and Auerstadt, given Louis' share in the campaign and in the reflected glory of these victories, postponed any open rupture with the Emperor.

The return of Louis to The Hague brought no comfort to Hortense. In fact his behaviour was so difficult that there was a virtual separation – in spite of Napoleon's chiding his brother for his behaviour: 'Your quarrels with the Queen are known to the public. Show in your private life the paternal and soft side of your character and in your administration the rigour you display at home.' The sting in the last phrase was a reference to the treatment by Louis of his Dutch subjects, which, Napoleon considered, was marked by too lenient an approach and an habitual failure to subordinate Dutch to imperial interests. Unsurprisingly, the final breach with Louis came about because of his refusal to impose on his Dutch subjects the trading restrictions which were part of Napoleon's wider plans for a French-dominated Europe and which pressed particularly hard on Holland.

Meanwhile, in 1807, a domestic tragedy brought the estranged couple together: their eldest son, Napoleon Charles, died at the age of five and both parents were genuinely grief-stricken. As their grief drew them together, they resumed normal marital relations, which resulted in the birth of another son in April 1808. For a time it seemed as if the marriage might be saved, but unfortunately by the time the boy was born the parents had already parted again. Virtually from the moment of his birth, encouraged as always by the family gossips, it was hinted that Louis was not the father of this new child, who was christened Charles Louis Napoleon.

In spite of the subsequent collapse of the Third Coalition, Tsar Alexander was determined that the defeat at Austerlitz should not end Russia's chances of curbing Napoleon. He prevailed on the King of Prussia, who found France's position on the Rhine unacceptable, to join him in a joint attack on Napoleon. This renewal of the war ended in the defeat of the Prussian and Russian armies, first at the bloody battle of Eylau and then at the extremely hard fought battle of Friedland. Faced with the inevitable, Alexander I signed the treaty of Tilsit in July 1807. By so doing, he acquired room to manoeuvre in south-eastern Europe, while Napoleon could embark upon a further reconstruction of central Europe, a reconstruction which enabled him to bring about a new dynastic venture. As a punishment for its foolhardiness in renewing the war, France took all Prussian territory west of the Elbe. This became the kingdom of Westphalia and was given to Jerome to rule. The new kingdom was to be a link to the Confederation of the Rhine and, further to reinforce his position in Germany, Jerome, now freed from his American wife, was married to Catherine, daughter of the King of Württemburg.[4]

As a further punishment, Prussia was stripped of the lands she had taken at the Partitions of Poland, which were now formed into the Grand Duchy of Warsaw and attached to the Confederation of the Rhine. The possible geographical difficulties this involved were partly offset by the fact that the Tsar was now an ally of Napoleon and unlikely needlessly to upset the new arrangement – at least for the time being.

Napoleon's position on the Continent seemed to be secure: Russia, Prussia and Austria had been dealt with, and a new continental structure had been erected with key areas entrusted to the members of his own family. Only one major problem remained: how to force England to accept this situation and how the great land power could effectively reduce the great sea power. It is said that the victory of Austerlitz, and its implications for the future course of the war, hastened the death of William Pitt, but, in October 1805, Nelson's victory at Trafalgar had exposed the perennial French problem of how to get at England. It was this stalemate which led Napoleon to devise the Continental System, based on the reasoning that, if England's commerce was destroyed, thus crippling her financial system, the country would be brought to an economic standstill and forced to sue for peace. Given his mastery of the Continent, Napoleon would declare a blockade in reverse by excluding all English commerce with other European states: 'anyone engaging in trade in English goods is the accomplice of England' and, by implication, an enemy of France.

By a decree issued in Berlin in 1806, reinforced by a second one issued in Milan in 1807, Napoleon hoped to make it impossible for England to carry on any form of trade with the Continent, for even any neutral ship suspected of carrying English goods was declared open to seizure. England, for its part, retaliated by seizing any neutrals suspected of trying to trade with France, so neutrality became an almost impossible option for any would-be non-belligerent. Normal commerce became indistinguishable from high-risk smuggling.

For the continental blockade to be effective, it was essential that *all* European states with coastlines took part and enforced Napoleon's decrees; but not all states were prepared to accept a diktat which threatened their own economies. It was almost certain that somewhere there would be a refusal to conform. The crisis came about in 1807 when Portugal, England's traditional ally, refused to accept the blockade and declared the ports of Lisbon and Oporto open to English trade. Napoleon's answer was to intervene militarily in the Iberian peninsula, in order to assert his authority and close the breach in the Continental System. As a result of the French invasion, the Portuguese monarchy fled to Brazil, transported by English ships, while the Spanish monarchy was ended by Napoleon's action in forcing the King's abdication. In order to strengthen the French presence, and extend his own dynastic structure, the Spanish were provided with a new sovereign. Joseph Bonaparte was transferred from Naples to Madrid, where he was proclaimed King of Spain, while his brother-in-law, Joachim Murat, was made King of Naples, thus allowing Caroline to achieve her ambition to be a Queen. To Napoleon, all this may have looked to be a satisfactory solution to the problem of shutting out English commerce, but it must have been clear to him that continued success would turn upon his ability to control militarily all the areas involved. Only by rigorously applying a stranglehold to English trade would the blockade work, and indeed it did produce the grave economic difficulties Napoleon had envisaged, but every year brought even greater difficulties for the French, beginning with the Spanish revolt of 1808.[5]

The Spanish revolt, which was a popular uprising inspired by hatred of the French invaders, was soon seized on by the English, who were quick to see the opportunities offered to them to use their command of the sea. It was decided to assist the rebels by sending an expeditionary force, under Sir Arthur Wellesley, which landed near Lisbon. Even before the English landing the Spanish rebel forces had achieved an extraordinary victory when, at Baylen in southern Spain, they forced an entire French division to capitulate. This was an event that had immense repercussions throughout Europe, for here at last was proof that French armies were not invincible. Later in the year, further proof was furnished when General Junot was forced to capitulate to Wellesley at Sintra in Portugal.

By 1809 Napoleon's military plans for the Peninsula had begun to unravel, making Joseph's throne precarious. Known to the Spanish as 'Don Pepe Botella' (King Joe the Drunk), which was an unwarranted slander, for he was in fact an abstemious man, Joseph, during the three years of his reign, tried to reform the archaic laws and customs of Spain. To this end he attempted to draw to himself those enlightened members of Spanish society, hostile to the former Bourbon monarchy, a policy which had a degree of success.[6] Joseph knew, however, that, as in Naples, the only hope of establishing his dynasty in Spain would be to make peace with England, get rid of the French army, annexe Portugal and pacify the insurgents. Napoleon reacted to this analysis by ignoring his brother's advice, although it was obvious that Joseph could only rule in Spain, however he did it, on the back of French military power. There was little support for the French outside those small enlightened groups whom their enemies contemptuously called the *afrancesados* (the 'Frenchified'), whom they loathed. Ranged against these groups, and the French army, were the supporters of the Bourbon monarchy, the bulk of the clergy and the great mass of the peasantry, who provided the backbone of the anti-French guerilla forces.

It is difficult to avoid the conclusion that the years 1808–10 marked a crisis point in the affairs of the Empire. Napoleon found himself at odds with Tsar Alexander over the interpretation of the Tilsit agreement which not even a meeting between the two rulers, held at Erfurt, could really resolve. The meeting was held against the background of the Spanish and Portuguese disasters, and Alexander knew that, if the war continued, Napoleon would have to commit his *Grande Armeé* to the Peninsula, thus weakening the French hold on central Europe.[7]

The shaking of the military monolith by the events in Spain, together with an apparent worsening in Franco-Russian relations, led to a fresh attempt by Austria to assert its status as a European power. It proved to be an ill-advised move, and ended in defeat at the battle of Wagram. Since the Tsar refused to break with France, it obliged the Emperor Francis to sign the treaty of Schönbrunn in October 1809. The treaty provided for further annexations of Austrian territory, but, as well as this, Napoleon introduced a more personal note in the negotiations by sounding out the Austrian court as to whether there might be a possibility of his marrying one of the Emperor's daughters. The reason for these discreet enquiries was very simple: there was as yet no child of his marriage to Josephine and it was almost certain at this stage that there never would be. The time had come for a new marriage and, given the reputation of the Habsburg archduchesses for fertility, the Austrian Imperial House seemed an excellent choice for both diplomatic and dynastic reasons.

Josephine had known for some time that her position was becoming precarious because of her inability to produce a child and so assure the continuance of the dynasty. She knew that Napoleon had a son by his one-time mistress Eléonore Denuelle, and it was now also known that his liaison with the Polish Countess Marie Walewska had resulted in a pregnancy. Since clearly her husband was not infertile, there was only one conclusion to be drawn: Josephine herself was now barren. Divorce was inevitable and it came in December 1809, suggesting that the idea had been well established in Napoleon's mind before the recent triumph in Austria. Only the Bonapartes were pleased that at long last their cherished wish had been granted. Josephine was distraught and Napoleon himself was far from unmoved by the end of their fifteen-year relationship, which in spite of everything had meant much to him. As a sign of his deep feelings for Josephine he assigned to her Malmaison, the place where they had spent so much time together, and granted her the title of Empress in her own right. He also insisted that Hortense and Eugène remain with him, in spite of their offer to retire from court life now that their mother was no longer there.[8] Having finally disposed of Josephine, the Bonapartes felt they must act in order to organise the family future – and how better than by a marriage within it? *Madame Mère* devised a plan which would not only produce a potential bride but would also end the feud between Napoleon and his brother Lucien.

Lucien had a daughter, Charlotte, who was only fourteen but who was seen by Letizia as a perfectly suitable match for her uncle the Emperor. She informed Lucien that he must send his daughter to Paris, to her grand-mother, and at the same time he must of course show willing by agreeing to divorce his wife Alexandrine, and so please the Emperor by doing his will. Then, at long last, the family could present a united front.

Charlotte came to Paris and was presented to her uncle, who seems to have found her agreeable enough in that she looked like a Bonaparte, but his interest in her would certainly have ended there had she not foolishly compromised herself by writing letters to her father in which she gossiped and made fun of the family who surrounded her in Paris. Naively, she sent these letters by the ordinary postal service, apparently unaware that this was routinely intercepted by the police, with the important items being given by the Minister of Police to Napoleon for his information. The Emperor did not find his niece's comments amusing, and the family were outraged, so that the incident, together with Lucien's reiterated and cate-gorical refusal to end his marriage, torpedoed the hopes of *Madame Mère*. It would seem that in some way she had not really grasped what had happened to the family: their stage was now Europe, not Corsica, and marriage for the Emperor had ceased to be a 'familial' duty and had become a dynastic affair. He had already made up his mind on this, and a bride had been chosen: she was Marie-Louise, the daughter of the Emperor Francis of Austria and a great niece of Marie-Antoinette. The House of Bonaparte was now entering a new phase in its evolution. By allying itself with one of Europe's oldest ruling Houses, France's fourth dynasty would be in a strong position to refute the charge of its being inferior to other monarchies. In Vienna the idea of the marriage appears to have been accepted in the hope that, by strengthening the newly established dynasty, it would also end the cycle of war that had begun almost twenty years before. A strong Austro-French alliance seemed to offer a guarantee of stability in Europe and would enable Napoleon to use diplomacy, rather than war, to protect France's interests and the security of the dynasty. For his part, the Emperor Francis hoped that the alliance would strengthen Austria's position against any possible threat from Russia.[9]

Unfortunately, just at the very moment when it seemed as if the Bonapartes were entering respectable monarchical society, a series of events occurred that revealed how family problems could mar dynastic aspirations.

Once again the cause of the upset was the behaviour of Lucien. He had not seen his brother between 1804 and 1807 as a result of a violent quarrel which took place at their meeting at St-Cloud, angry scenes which had resulted in his refusal to attend the coronation. Relations had continued to deteriorate to the point where Lucien had left France and installed himself in Rome, where he was welcomed by the Pope and assigned a residence. If Lucien envisaged an ultimate reunion with his brother, he did nothing to facilitate a reconciliation, since he openly attacked the Emperor as 'the Caesar who killed the Republic'. Napoleon did make a serious attempt to heal the quarrel by arranging a meeting at Mantua in December 1807, but that once again ended in a blazing row because Lucien would not divorce and make a dynastic marriage, this time to a Spanish Princess. Having thwarted another of his brother's grand designs, for the Spanish marriage formed part of the Emperor's plans for the reorganisation of Spain, Lucien returned to Rome. He found that in his absence it had been occupied by French troops and the papal territory annexed to the *Grand Empire*. Deprived of papal protection, since the Pope's authority had been suppressed, Lucien now came within the jurisdiction of the imperial administration. He was confined by imperial order to the city of Rome, and, in ever-increasing financial difficulties, with a wife and seven children to support – including the unfortunate Charlotte who had been sent home – Lucien decided to leave Europe for America.

Because of English control of the sea Lucien got in touch with the English naval authorities, requesting passports and a safe conduct for himself and his family, something which he considered only prudent. It turned out to be rather *imprudent* the French authorities in Rome threatened to arrest him on the grounds of 'communication with the enemy' and he was forced to look for a vessel flying the American flag in order to be able to find a passage to the United States. In August 1810, with the threat of arrest hanging over him, he embarked with his family and a considerable retinue, apparently never intending to return from the New World. Unfortunately he never reached it, for the ship was seized by an English frigate, cruising off the coast of Sardinia. Lucien declared himself a prisoner of war and in December 1810 the family disembarked in England.[10]

With the British public's unerring capacity for getting it wrong, Lucien on his arrival was hailed as a hero, whose lifelong opposition to his brother virtually made him an honorary Englishman. Cheering crowds turned out to greet him and the press portrayed him as a victim of tyranny come to find refuge in the true land of freedom. He repaid this extravagant welcome by buying a country estate at Thorngrove, in Worcestershire, and setting himself up to live the life of an English country gentleman. He spent his time cultivating his estate, supervising the education of his children, and indeed adding to their number, for a son was born to him at Thorngrove. In the event, just as he had by choice absented himself from his brother's coronation, so now he managed to be absent from his second marriage – an event which provoked satirical comment throughout Europe. Whatever anyone else thought about Lucien's odyssey, his situation made Napoleon furious, for his brother's English captivity was a constant source of embarrassment to him. What made it worse was the knowledge that *his* embarassment may very well have made Lucien's predicament all the more agreeable to him. It turned out not to matter in the end: when the brothers met again both their situations had greatly changed, for the Empire had run its course and family ties were rediscovered.

4

An Heir without a Throne

The marriage with Marie-Louise did not come about because Napoleon claimed one of the Emperor of Austria's daughters as a species of war booty after defeating her father at the battle of Wagram in 1809. It was a marriage of convenience which offered something to both sides. For his part, Napoleon was resolved on a prestigious union which would help to reaffirm his own dynasty, a desire which had already led to negotiations with Tsar Alexander, who had eligible sisters. By 1809 it was clear that the Russian monarch would never agree to a dynastic union with the Bonapartes, just at the moment when the Vienna government had become convinced that only a period of peace could provide an exhausted Austria with a chance to recover. Marriage might do the trick: Napoleon would be linked to Austria, whose Foreign Minister, Prince Metternich, was convinced that there must be no more hostilities or the Austrian Empire would founder. In turn, Napoleon could hope that his close union with the Habsburgs would undermine support for them in Germany and Italy, thus strengthening France's military position. Apart from such practical considerations, this would be a prestigious union with one of the proudest and oldest dynasties of Europe, setting the seal of approval on the House of Bonaparte as Napoleon desired.

Fortunately for Napoleon, Emperor Francis and Metternich accepted that, in spite of personal antipathy to the prospective bridegroom, reasons of state, in this case the very survival of the Empire, meant that the marriage must be accepted. After some preliminary soundings, negotiations were begun in great confidence, at one point Metternich using his wife as an intermediary. Terms were agreed. These included the church's acceptance of the divorce from Josephine, something upon which Austria, as a Catholic state, had insisted. Finally, in February 1810, the official announcement was made that the Emperor of Austria had given the hand of his daughter in marriage to the Emperor Napoleon.

The main characteristic of Marie-Louise, Napoleon's prospective bride, seems to have been a docile acceptance of doing what someone else told her to do, though she did express fear on being told that she was to marry Napoleon. The Emperor Francis simply reminded her of her duty, saying, 'as soon as you're alone with the Emperor, you must do absolutely everything he tells you. You must agree to everything he asks you'. No doubt reassured by this profoundly sensitive paternal advice, Marie-Louise left for France at the end of March 1810. Since the last Habsburg bride had been Marie-Antoinette, the great-aunt of Marie-Louise, the eighteen year old was entitled to a degree of anxiety about her future, but in the imme-diate term it was to be imperial splendour all the way.[1]

By 1810 the court in France was well established. It may have lacked in the extreme formality and tradition of the court of Vienna, reputedly the most hidebound in Europe, but it did have a well-ordered structure, and it was above all noted for its brilliance and extravagance. The Emperor's household, responsible for court activities, spent ten to fifteen million francs per year out of the civil list of thirty-five million. In its form the court was an amalgam of ideas carried over from the *ancien régime* but adapted to the new circumstance. All the apparatus of court life, whether at the Tuileries, Compiègne or Fontainebleau, was maintained, including the ceremonial gatherings in which ostentation was the keynote, as if spectacle would compensate for the lack of aura conferred by a long-established and hereditary monarchy. But the Napoleonic court was not just splendid, it was very much *the* centre of France, simply because the Emperor was the mainspring of the whole machine. The court was also, literally, the centre of the *Grand Empire*, since many of the court officials were 'European' in accordance with Napoleon's wish to underline the nature of his Empire. An imperial nobility had evolved slowly from its inception in 1804 with the creation of the Legion of Honour, and had been subsequently enlarged by the endowment of the senators with land and money to enable them to fulfil the administrative duties implied by their rank. But neither of these rewards were hereditary, nor did they confer any privileges on the holders. They were simply a means of binding the recipients to the imperial regime and were not intended in any way to imitate the nobility of the *ancien régime*.[2]

A decisive step in the evolution of a 'nobility' came about almost inevitably after 1804 with the creation of the Empire, though it was not until 1808 that a decree was issued re-establishing the old noble titles of prince, duke, count and baron. But once again these titles carried no privileges, no exemption from taxes, and, if they were linked to any territorial area, it was to land situated outside the frontiers of France. In fact, the first ennoblement in 1807, a sort of trial run, created Marshal Lefebvre 'Duke of Danzig', a city which he had just captured, as a reward for his services. Lefebvre was to be the first of the new nobles, many of whom were Marshals of the Empire, but non-military grand dignitaries, high civil servants and ecclesiastics were all eligible for this new system of honours. So also were members of the old nobility who rallied to the imperial regime, something which created considerable friction when the new men saw the old nobility installed at court or in the administration, even though the latter were now equally unprivileged. As far as an external show was concerned, the Empire could therefore put on a splendid parade and, what is more, it could display itself in some of the finest palaces in Europe, which were part of its inheritance.[3]

All this meant that, when it came to receiving his new bride, the Emperor was resolved that the splendour of such receptions that had been a feature of the previous monarchy should be surpassed by the new dynasty. The fulfilment of his desire for this union with one of the traditional royal houses of Europe made it certain that Napoleon would seize the opportunity to organise a grand public demonstration of his new status. Contemporaries could also note that by his marriage he had revived the Austro-French alliance, so linking his regime directly with the foreign policy of pre-revolutionary France. The reception for Marie-Louise would be at Compiègne, in the château where Louis XVI, as Dauphin, had waited for Marie-Antoinette. Now raised to the status of *palais impérial*, large areas of the building had been redecorated, and splendid apartments prepared for the new Empress, who would, on arrival, be presented to the entire Bonaparte family, now themselves kings, queens and princes, with only Joseph and Lucien absent. As for the former Empress Josephine, she had tactfully removed herself to her château of Navarre in Normandy.

It is an interesting and revealing fact that, in a sense, much of this elaborate preparation was wasted, for Napoleon, impatient for his bride, rushed to meet her and was so taken with his prize that he insisted that the carriages press on to Compiègne that night, avoiding a halt that had been planned at Soissons to allow the travellers time to rest. They arrived at ten o'clock at night, when a poor, travel-worn Marie-Louise had to face not only the Bonapartes but also the entire court, which had, in accordance with protocol, assembled to greet her. Fortunately for her, perhaps, Napoleon, eager to take advantage of the proxy marriage that had already been held in Vienna, rushed his bride off to their private apartments – an action which summed up the contradictions between court etiquette and the more down-to-earth manners of the new era. Some of those present felt they had been spectators at an event which bore more resemblance to a rape than a marital consummation.

The raising of the female members of the family of the Emperor to royal status had not improved their manners, as the marriage ceremony on 2 April proved. Once again there was a dispute about carrying the new Empress's train, and this time the slight was felt to be even greater than in 1804, for now the wives of Joseph, Louis and Jerome were Queens in their own right, as was Caroline, thanks to her husband's Neapolitan throne. Their elevation to their new rank had also not been accompanied by an increase in gracious behaviour, and they made little effort to be agreeable to their new sister-in-law. Only Elisa, who came especially for the marriage, showed friendliness to her new sister-in-law and happily carried her train at the wedding ceremony.

In the end, of course, the marriage was not about etiquette or surly ill-mannered behaviour by in-laws, it was about procreation, and here the success was total. In March 1811 a son was born to Napoleon and Marie-Louise and given the title of the King of Rome. His father said of him, 'to take hold of the world, he will only have to stretch out his hands', but there were already indications that it might not be quite as easy as that.

The wedding of Marie-Louise and Napoleon had taken place in the Tuileries, solemnised by the Emperor's uncle, Cardinal Fesch. Even had he been minded to, there was no possibility of Pius VII attending, since, by Napoleon's instructions, he had been removed from Rome and was interned at Savona, near Genoa, where he remained a prisoner until June 1811. The Pope was yet another victim of the Continental System, since he had refused to close the port of Civitavecchia in the Papal States to what was now 'illegal' trade. This breach in Napoleon's blockade became an important point of entry for contraband goods, and in 1809 Napoleon declared the papal territories annexed to France, though the revenues and properties were guaranteed to the Pope. Pius replied to this with a bull of excommunication condemning 'all those responsible for this act of sacrilege', but not actually mentioning Napoleon by name, so that the Emperor was able to prevail on a majority of the College of Cardinals to come to Paris to be present at his marriage.

In support of the papal attitude, however, thirteen cardinals refused to attend, and it was clear that the problem of the papacy was not going to be conjured away easily. Initially, Napoleon drew comfort from the fact that the Catholic majority throughout the imperial domains, including the newly annexed Roman departments, did not appear to be unduly worried by the latest quarrel, but there was no guarantee that this would not change.The clergy throughout the Empire were bound to draw attention to the Pope's situation and it would not be too difficult to stir up anti-Napoleonic sentiments.

As for Napoleon, when the Pope had protested about his behaviour, he had replied: 'Your holiness is the sovereign of Rome, but I am its Emperor'. Faced with continued papal intransigence, he remarked: 'God has given me the will and the force to overcome all obstacles.' But perhaps he had forgotten the French adage 'qui mange du pape en meurt' (who eats the Pope dies of him), for Pius was to prove a most formidable if non-military adversary. Perhaps, considering the nature of his office, God had also given *him* certain special qualities. One of these turned out to be an ability to thwart Napoleon's desire for an obedient and smooth-running Department of Religious Affairs in France and throughout the Empire. This was particularly important in the case of France itself, where the Pope refused to grant investiture to bishops who were nominated by the Emperor, thus leaving many dioceses without a bishop. When the Pope persisted in this course of action he was moved from Savona to the palace of Fontainebleau, where Napoleon could confront him personally. It was, however, just at this point that a sharp turn in Napoleon's military fortunes forced him to consider a new approach to Pius VII.[4]

The breach between Napoleon and Alexander of Russia was, once again, a product of the continental blockade. This was a particular bone of contention, because a large part of Russia's exports, timbers, rope and other materials used in ships, went to England, the best customer for such products because of its fleet. There were, however, other factors at work, making a confrontation almost inevitable. Alexander found little support from Napoleon for his plans to acquire Constantinople and the Straits, in spite of what may have been understood at the Tilsit meeting. Napoleon viewed this opening up of the Mediterranean to Russian commerce as a threat. 'She [Russia] could be at the gates of Toulon, Naples and Corfu.'

The Tsar became aware of what he could expect in the shape of French cooperation in Russia's schemes. It was this realisation, of what Alexander considered to be Napoleon's bad faith, that angered the Tsar. At a personal level, Alexander had administered a snub to Napoleon, when the latter had made serious overtures for the hand of the Tsar's sister, the Grand Duchess Catherine, during the period when he was seeking a dynastic marriage. To prevent any hope of negotiations, Alexander rapidly married Catherine to the heir to the Duke of Oldenburg, thereby making it clear that he did not wish for a union with the Bonapartes. Napoleon, well able to interpret Alexander's action, retaliated by giving his backing to the choice of Marshal Bernadotte as heir to the King of Sweden against Russian wishes, and then by annexing Oldenburg, whose future ruler was Alexander's brother-in-law.

Underneath this seemingly rather childish game of tit-for-tat between sovereigns the really serious issues soon emerged, for in 1810 Alexander declared Russian ports open to neutral shipping, blowing a gaping hole in the continental blockade. More ominously for the future of Franco-Russian relations were the negotiations begun by Alexander in 1811 in an attempt to rally Polish support for a move to launch an attack on France's troops beyond the River Elbe. The Poles would, however, never abandon France for Russia, and Napoleon, informed of these manoeuvres, knew this. He also knew that Alexander had sounded out Austria, Prussia and Sweden with a view to renewing the war with Napoleon, but none of them were willing to risk it. The cumulative effect of all this was to make up Napoleon's mind to attack Russia. A sound defeat in battle would bring Alexander to his senses and show Europe who was master. Alexander, aware of the possibility of a French attack, issued a warning, which he delivered to Caulaincourt, the French Ambassador: 'Carry it to Napoleon, this honest and final notice, that once the war has begun one of us, either Napoleon or I, Alexander, must lose his crown.' Napoleon may have missed the implication of the message, which was that once hostilities began the Tsar would never negotiate, for he would be deposed and killed by his own nobles if he did so. The anti-French sentiments which had motivated the murder of his father were again being openly expressed in St Petersburg.[5]

One of the consequences of Paul's murder had been the strengthening of the French *émigré* presence. Many were officers in the Tsar's armies – his military councillor was the Count of Allonville – and there were also others

of importance in the civil administration. The most influential of these
was Pozzo di Borgo, a Corsican and a one-time companion of Napoleon.
He had opted for the Paolistas and had conceived such a deep personal
hatred for his former friend that it had become a vendetta. Since he was a
personal favourite of Alexander, and completely in his confidence, his
activities in St Petersburg were of great importance in stoking up hostility
to France and, above all, to Napoleon.

Aware that a diplomatic offensive was an essential prelude to the new
campaign, on 17 May 1812 Napoleon held a summit meeting at Dresden
attended by the Emperor of Austria, the Kings of Prussia and Saxony,
together with an assortment of other rulers. The whole affair was marked
by lavish ceremonies and military reviews. It was during the course of these
meetings that Napoleon revealed how he now saw himself by affirming that,
if his late uncle had been firmer, history would have been different. The
late uncle in question was, ironically, Louis XVI, now related to the Emperor
by his recent marriage. The other sovereigns present may well have been
surprised – if not amused – by Napoleon's new-found relationship.

The army eventually assembled by the Emperor for the invasion of Russia
was a European force: 675,000 men made up of French, Swiss, Flemings,
Poles, Dutch, Germans and Austrians. In all twenty nations and at least
twelve languages. It crossed the River Niemen on 24 June 1812 to begin a
campaign whose course and consequence can be summed up in a sentence:
675,000 men crossed the River Niemen in June, in December less than
100,000 returned to Lithuania. The rest had disappeared, and most of them
were dead.[6]

From the beginning, the campaign had been difficult. The Russian
decision to avoid a pitched battle, drawing the French deeper into the
country, did not suit Napoleon's strategic style. When he finally found the
Russian army at Borodino, protecting Moscow, the battle was bloody but,
contrary to his expectations, far from being decisive. The invaders also
experienced the extremes of the Russian climate, as the torrid heat of
summer was followed by torrential autumnal rains. Choking dust was
replaced by thick mud. Nevertheless, Napoleon occupied Moscow but its
inhabitants deserted it and burnt much of the city.

Faced by his inability to impose terms, and deciding against wintering
in Moscow, Napoleon decided to retreat. Short of supplies and harassed by
the Russian armies, this led to catastrophe. Frozen, famished and exhausted,

the 'wounded beast', as the Russian General Kutuzov called it, struggled to reach Poland and Lithuania, its wretched state made worse by constant attacks from Cossacks and bands of peasantry. Only the bravery and constancy of Ney, who commanded the rear-guard, provided some protection. But he was powerless against cold, hunger and disease. Not for the first time, nor for the last, the geography and climate of Russia, combined with the tenacity of its soldiers, had destroyed an army and mortally wounded an empire. The first signs of this came when in December, Napoleon abandoned the broken army and returned to Paris, alarmed by the implications of a political crisis that had erupted in October when a republican general, Malet, succeeded in convincing some of the leading political figures in Paris that the Emperor was dead in Russia. Initially the rumour spread by Malet and his handful of supporters created panic among the senior government officials, but the conspiracy was suppressed by those who kept their heads and who saw to it that Malet was arrested, tried and executed. Nevertheless, if the conspiracy had been successfully crushed, it revealed a very alarming breakdown in the imperial structure; for, if the Emperor *was* dead, why had no one thought of proclaiming Napoleon II with the Empress as Regent? Among all those left by Napoleon to carry on the government there was no evidence of dynastic thinking beyond the person of Napoleon himself.[7]

On his return to Paris Napoleon began to try and reassemble an army, at the same time dissembling, in order to avoid the truth about the Russian catastrophe becoming known. Furthermore, well aware of what had *not* been done, and to avoid a repetition of what had happened during the Malet conspiracy, when the succession had been ignored, he amended the constitution of the Empire. A decree of 18 February 1813 established a Regency under Marie-Louise, who would be assisted by a council composed of the Princes of the Blood (the Bonapartes) and the leading dignitaries of the Empire. To obviate any hiatus, the decree envisaged a coronation of the Empress Mother and even a coronation of the Prince Imperial, the King of Rome, during the Emperor's lifetime. Both these clauses were clearly destined to reinforce and underline a dynastic continuity, but equally clearly they were intended to strengthen the dynastic links with Austria, bringing the Emperor Francis closer to his daughter, son-in-law and grandson, and so ensuring Austrian support should Napoleon be threatened with loss of power.[8]

The question of the succession was not as yet pressing; what was impera-tive was a strengthening of France's military situation, for the magnitude of the Russian débâcle could not be concealed for ever, certainly not from France's enemies. The immediate consequences had been an alliance between Russia and Prussia, with the result that French forces had to be withdrawn from East Prussia and Silesia and redeployed to central Germany, bringing the enemy nearer to France. Increased Prussian military mobilisation forced Prince Eugène to abandon Berlin, which was not only a strategic blow but also a blow to Napoleon's prestige.

Napoleon responded to this threat by a raising an army of 500,000 men, but the effectives were largely on paper, for desertion, evasion of conscrip-tion and the inevitable delays in gathering a large number of men together reduced the real fighting men to half that number. There were two addi-tional weaknesses, one caused by the shortage of horses (80,000 had perished in Russia), so reducing the cavalry; the second, perhaps even more serious, was the virtual destruction of the Imperial Guard, the core of the army. After 1813 it had to be rebuilt from the remnant that had survived the Russian disaster, but although it was to conduct itself magnificently, the 'Young Guard' had not the time to develop the experience and superb fighting qualities of the 'Old Guard'.

In the diplomatic sphere, the attitude of Napoleon's father-in-law, the Emperor Francis, became the pivot on which future developments would turn, and already there were ominous signs. The leading Austrian general, Schwarzenberg, had withdrawn the Austrian contingent from the *Grande Armée* in December 1812, but as yet Francis was undecided as to what to do. He had burnt his fingers too often in recent wars with Napoleon, and he was not certain that the new alliance of Prussia and Russia would win if another campaign were begun. From Paris, Marie-Louise wrote to her father, presumably at her husband's instigation, saying, 'the Emperor is well satisfied [with his troops] and flatters himself that he will soon force his enemies to a lasting peace'. But Francis, better informed than his daughter, knew that Europe was in fact coming together for a final assault on the Napoleonic Empire.

Given the situation, Napoleon felt compelled to end the long-running quarrel with the Pope over the question of jurisdiction that had, in the end, antagonised Catholic opinion throughout Europe and now served as a rallying-point for anti-French movements. Napoleon's demand that bishops be invested in the name of the Emperor and not the Pope had guaranteed a refusal by Pius to consider negotiations. He persisted in his attitude, in spite of being alternately bullied and cajoled once he had been forcibly removed from Italy and installed at Fontainebleau. By 18 January 1813 the pressure of external events forced a compromise, and a document was drawn up which was simply a preliminary agreement intended to serve as a basis for a final settlement. Napoleon had failed to achieve the cesaropapism he sought but the Pope had made sufficient concessions for this document to be considered the foundation of a new Concordat. It was published as such by Napoleon, who also announced that the Pope would live in Avignon, demonstrating the close relationship between the pontiff and France. In order that the world might know that he had made peace with the papacy, Napoleon ordered that the conclusion of this agreement should be marked by the ringing of church bells and by the singing of the Te Deum in churches throughout France.

Clearly Napoleon hoped to assuage the anger of a large number of French Catholics, for this was no time to be faced with internal discontent. Troops had to be conscripted and taxes gathered in preparation for a military effort that threatened to be extremely demanding. But the benefits that Napoleon hoped for as a result of his agreement with the Pope were of short duration, for in March 1814 Pius refused to sign the new Concordat unless he could negotiate from Rome. Faced with threat of a disintegrating military situation, Napoleon ordered the return of Pius to Italy, but this was an empty gesture, for he had no longer control of the situation, and it was in May 1814, after the Emperor's abdication, that the Pope entered Rome of his own accord.[9]

The career of the two protagonists had run together, for the election of Napoleon as Consul in 1799 had been followed by the election of Pius VII to the papal throne in 1800, but it was inevitable that their relationship could never be easy, too much being at stake on both sides. What *was* interesting was that their quarrel really turned on the struggle about investiture, just as it had between the medieval papacy and the Holy Roman Emperor. In that context, at least, Napoleon was heir to a great tradition, for he inherited the age old question as to which should prevail, the spiritual or the temporal.

Between the two men in person there was some degree of mutual respect and understanding. At St Helena the Emperor said: 'Pius VII was truly a lamb, a totally good man, a worthy man whom I esteemed, of whom I was very fond and who I am sure for his part returned my feelings.' He was not wholly wrong, for in 1816 Pius wrote a letter to the Prince Regent indicating his forgiveness of all that Napoleon had done to him, pleading for the prisoner of St Helena, and asking if some easing of the conditions of his imprisonment might be possible.[10] Needless to say it had no effect whatsoever.

In April 1813 the Emperor Francis, recognising that some sort of end was now inevitable, wrote to Napoleon urging him to make peace, warning him that the continuance of the war was leading to social and political unrest within states, and threatening the thrones of the European sovereigns. Francis was clearly thinking primarily of events in Germany, where there was talk of a 'rejuvenated' country 'taking its place among the nations of Europe'. Since Austria considered itself to be a natural arbiter in German affairs, such a threat was alarming, particularly as it was inspired by Alexander I and the King of Prussia. As if to underline the ambiguity of his attitude, and to demonstrate that Austria was capable of military action, an anti-French rising in the Tyrol was suppressed. Its suppression was also an indication that Francis would not condone or support any popular movement (he obviously had Italy and Germany in mind), because, to him, such movements represented a 'Jacobin ferment'.

There seems no doubt that Austria would have preferred a peace that would have perpetuated the Bonaparte–Habsburg dynasty. This would not only prevent revolutionary upheavals in France, it would also maintain the balance of power in central Europe in Austria's favour. Francis and his advisers were alarmed by the possibility of increasing Russian influence in Germany, which had always looked to Vienna and which needed to be discouraged from looking to St Petersburg. But this plan proved impossible because of Napoleon's refusal to agree to any peace terms that would lead to the dissolution of his Empire. For him the issue was simple, and he spelt it out to the Austrian Chancellor, Metternich, in June 1813: 'Your sovereigns born on the throne can let themselves be beaten twenty times and return to their capitals. I cannot do this because I am an upstart soldier. My domination will not survive the day when I cease to be strong and therefore feared.' In a further interview some days later, Napoleon indicated to the Austrian Chancellor that he could not give up his conquests and sign a treaty which would deliver myself like an idiot to my enemies and rely for a doubtful future on the generosity of those whom today I am conquering. It is my father-in-law who entertains such a project! In what position does he want to put me vis-à-vis the French people? He deceives himself if he thinks that in France a mutilated throne can shelter his daughter and grandson.[11]

So there was nothing for it but war to the end and by now the end could not really be long delayed, though Napoleon's military genius was to give his enemies some bad moments. But even when the French were successful, as at the battle of Dresden in August 1813, Napoleon was incapable of turning victory into a rout. His troops, and he himself, were worn out – and he lacked cavalry. At Leipzig in October came the famous Battle of the Nations in which 320,000 enemy troops faced 160,000 French. Not only were the latter outnumbered but, in the middle of the battle, they were faced by the treason of the Saxon and Württemberg contingents, who went over to the enemy. By November the whole Germanic edifice had collapsed, Jerome had been forced to abandon his kingdom of Westphalia and Napoleon was pushed back on to the French bank of the Rhine. Elsewhere the picture was the same, as if a dam had broken and pent-up water was bringing down all in its path. Holland and north Germany, in particular the city of Hamburg, declared independence, while in Italy Eugène was unable to prevent a military collapse now that Austria had openly turned against France. Perhaps the worst of all, and the most wounding, was the defection of Murat, who in a bid to save his Neapolitan kingdom negotiated directly with the Austrians. Of this action Napoleon said: 'The conduct of the King of Naples is infamous, and that of the Queen unspeakable. I hope to live long enough to avenge myself and France for such an outrage and such horrible ingratitude.'[12] Elsewhere there was another betrayal, though Bernadotte, now heir to the throne of Sweden, had long since turned against the Emperor. In 1813, perhaps encouraged by his friendship with the Tsar Alexander, who had hinted that Bernadotte might be a successor to Napoleon, Bernadotte brought Sweden into the anti-French camp; but in his case the Emperor had long expected this defection.

Spain and Portugal were definitely lost by the summer of 1813, after Joseph had been defeated by Wellington at the battle of Vittoria in June, followed by the retreat of the army to France. By October, the last French stronghold had surrendered and Wellington had crossed the River Bidassoa and entered France, making it impossible any longer for Napoleon to pretend he had any control of events in the Peninsula. By the end of the year Ferdinand VII had been released by the French and restored by the Cortes – ostensibly to prevent the English design 'to foment anarchy, Jacobinism, the annihilation of the monarchy and nobility, and to set up a republic!' The Cabinet in London would have been startled to learn that this had been their object in driving the French from Spain.

The Empire was now virtually defined by France's own frontiers, but the Allies hesitated before moving in for the kill, partly because of a residual wariness over Napoleon's military skill, and also because they were not sure how the political settlement would evolve if Napoleon were removed. On the first count, the cautious approach was well founded, for the campaign of 1814, which Napoleon fought under the worst possible conditions, saw his military genius at its finest, giving him a series of brilliant victories in which he defeated the Austrians, the Russians and the Prussians. It was magnificent, but also pointless: in the end, the odds were overwhelmingly against the French and were not likely to improve. Apart from this, Napoleon was well aware that his own forces were beginning to disintegrate. In March he wrote sadly, 'the Young Guard melt away like snow'.

The political decisions could now no longer be postponed and the pace was forced because of the direct intervention of the oldest and most implacable enemy, now present on the Continent in the shape of Castlereagh, the English Foreign Secretary. By promising an immediate subsidy of five million pounds the minister was able to persuade Austria, Prussia and Russia to sign the treaty of Chaumont (binding also on England), stipulating that there would be no separate peace negotiations and that the allies would adhere to the alliance for twenty years. What was noteworthy was that England, uncharacteristically, thereby signed up to a continental presence for the whole of this period, though, in accordance with English traditions, it was stipulated that, in the case of renewed hostilities, its military forces could be mercenaries.

When it came to discussions about the political future, Castlereagh appeared vague, but this was simply diplomatic manoeuvring. The Cabinet in London was absolutely convinced that Napoleon must be removed and had virtually made up its mind to replace him by a restoration of the Bourbon monarchy, but the problem was that the Tsar was distinctly cool when a Bourbon restoration was proposed. He had already had sharp exchanges with Castlereagh on the subject, so an open dispute had to be avoided if the coalition was not to be threatened with dissension. Alexander was convinced that the bulk of the French population remained Bonapartist in sentiment, which was probably true, but the Royalists, having lived in the shadows for twenty years, now came out into the sunshine that shone on them again by courtesy of the coalition armies. France's extremity was their opportunity, and secret Royalist organisations, formerly working under cover, now began openly to take over in those areas where the Allied armies were in evidence. Sure of Wellington's advance in the south, the mayor of the city of Bordeaux hoisted the white flag of the Bourbons and proclaimed Louis XVIII as King. Meanwhile the Count of Artois, the brother of Louis XVIII, was at Nancy, attempting to rally eastern France for the monarchy.

As always in moments of crisis in the history of France, Paris was the key to the situation, as both Napoleon and those now working for his overthrow well knew. The Allies were also well aware of the role played by the city and it was this knowledge which led them to the decision to march directly on Paris, bypassing Napoleon and cutting him off from his capital. In fact this was a move which had much more than symbolic value, for Napoleon *had* intended that Paris should remain the focus of the government and administration, and that it should be defended in case of attack. To that end, and in accordance with the procedures established in 1813, the Emperor, before leaving for the army, had appointed Marie-Louise as Regent and named his brother Joseph as Lieutenant-General of the Empire. Other members of the family also came to Paris. Since their own kingdoms had been swallowed up by the advancing Allied armies, there was nothing left now but to rally to the head of the dynasty. Of the two younger brothers, Louis had been welcomed by Napoleon and kept in Paris as a member of the Regency Council, but Jerome was kept at Compiègne as a sign that his conduct and unreliability made him unwelcome. These were the family members, together with Queen Hortense, who were there to confront the advancing Allies.

Late on the night of 28 March, with the enemy within sight of Paris, a meeting of the Regency Council took place at the Tuileries. The key question to be considered was whether the Empress and the King of Rome should stay in Paris, a decision which implied that the capital would be defended, or should leave for somewhere safe but near the capital. The council members instinctively, and then by a vote, felt that Marie-Louise and her son should stay, in spite of an impassioned appeal by Clarke, the

Minister for War, that they should leave. The final decision came about because of Joseph's intervention, using, as the ultimate argument, a letter from Napoleon dated in February, saying that if the Regent and the heir to the throne were in danger of being captured by the enemy they must leave Paris. The letter was, in fact, ambiguous in its meaning, but it suited the majority of the council members to interpret this as an *order* from Napoleon, absolving them from any decision. Marie-Louise herself indeed chose to interpret the letter as an order from her husband because it led her to change her mind and agree to leave Paris. Joseph sent her, together with the three-year-old King of Rome, to Rambouillet outside of Paris.[13]

This was a fatal move for two reasons: first, the departure of the Empress and the heir unleashed a wave of panic in the city; and, secondly, all those who were now working for the overthrow of Napoleon had a clear field of action since the Regent was no longer there. Their hand was immeasurably strengthened by the departure of Joseph himself, leaving the defence of Paris in the hands of two marshals, Mortier and Marmont. They had, under their command, a considerable force of regular troops, plus the National Guard, to which could be added to the willingness of sections of the populace to fight, provided they were armed. But the Allies had manoeuvred correctly: without Napoleon's presence all his projects foundered, for at the top there was a loss of nerve, and there was no will to defend the city. Whatever chance there might have been of mounting even a token resistance was lost completely when Marmont capitulated.

The government, having already liquidated itself by breaking up the Regency, now fell into the hands of Talleyrand, who had manoeuvred himself into a position of assumed authority, having carefully prepared for a moment that he had been expecting for some time. Talleyrand, who had survived the Revolution from its earliest days, including all the regimes through which it had passed, always tried to be ahead of coming changes, and had for some time been in touch with the Bourbons. To make certain that he would not suffer personally from the change of regime, he had already received an assurance of pardon for past offences from Louis XVIII. Deploying all his skill for intrigue and double dealing, Talleyrand succeeded in forming a provisional government on 1 April 1814. Two days later he persuaded a ragbag of senators to use their constitutional right to depose Napoleon. The grounds put before the Senate to justify this action were that the Emperor had himself broken his oath to the constitution.[14]

The Emperor was at Fontainebleau where, on 1 April, he was informed that the Allies were in Paris, at which point General Caulaincourt, Minister of Foreign Affairs, urged him to abdicate in favour of the King of Rome. This, he argued, would cut across all the intrigues which were now coming to light in the city: if he abdicated in favour of his son the Allies would be faced with the legal continuity of the dynasty. In fact, it was too late for this, since the Senate had already pronounced the deposition of Napoleon, so the dynastic continuity as such was already non-existent. The departure from Paris of the Empress Regent, together with the heir, and the fact that Napoleon's brothers had also gone, meant that there was no one to argue the case for the dynasty. By its absence it seemed as if the family had abandoned the capital to its fate, and with it had sealed the fate of the Bonapartes.

In a desperate attempt to reverse the situation, Napoleon, who could still count on the loyalty of part of the army, tried to bargain his abdication against the proclamation of Napoleon II. He refused to believe that Francis I would not act to save his daughter and grandson and protect their dynastic rights. He was soon disabused on both counts: the rank and file of the army were loyal, but the marshals refused to consider any military offensive and insisted on abdication, while Francis showed no inclination to launch a diplomatic and dynastic counter-offensive in favour of his grandson. In a letter to Marie-Louise, he pointedly informed her that 'he had obligations towards his allies', the inference being that he would not risk his own throne by quarrelling with the coalition for the sake of some nebulous future for his grandson.

In the end, reflecting the reality of the situation, the Allies disposed of the problems as they wished. By the treaty of Fontainebleau, Napoleon was given the sovereignty of the island of Elba but with no right of inheritance for his son. The Emperor could keep his title and would be paid a pension of two million French francs a year from the French funds. As for Marie-Louise and the King of Rome, they were now separated from Napoleon, though it appears that for a time both husband and wife thought that they would soon be reunited. In the meantime, Marie-Louise was given by the terms of the treaty the duchy of Parma, with the right of reversion to her son.

As for the hopes of both husband and wife that they would be reunited, they soon proved illusory. The Austrian court undertook the task of dealing with Marie-Louise, who was easily prevailed on by her father to return to her family in Vienna, while, for their part, the Allied commissioners set out with Napoleon for Elba. To make it less humiliating for the fallen monarch, he was escorted by detachments of his own guard commanded by General Drouot and Marshal Bertrand. As for the Empress, once Francis had safely ensconced his daughter, with her son, in Vienna there was little hope of her being able to join Napoleon. Marie-Louise had never displayed courage and strength of character but had always been inclined to do what she was told by others. Interestingly enough, within her own family, she was advised to join her husband by her grandmother, Marie-Caroline of Naples, a sister of Marie-Antoinette and no friend of Napoleon. Angered by the treatment of her grand-daughter, and sympathising with the plight of Napoleon, she urged Marie-Louise to defy her father and Metternich. 'If they are adamant you must tie the sheets of your bed to your window and escape disguised. That is what I would do.' Unfortunately, Marie-Louise was not made of such stern stuff and, in any case, she was now exposed to something much worse, namely the fact that her father connived at her seduction by Count Neipperg, who was deliberately chosen as her aide-de-camp because he had a reputation as a skilled seducer. By September 1814 he and Marie-Louise were lovers, while, at the same time, her son was inexorably drawn into the Habsburg family and allowed as little contact as possible with the French personnel who had followed him into exile.

Napoleon remained on Elba for ten months. As its sovereign he was able to organise it in his usual efficient way, beginning with the administration, at whose head he appointed men who had accompanied him from France. Working through them he reformed the system of customs dues, rebuilt the fortifications to protect the harbour at Porto Ferraio, reformed the medical services, built roads and planted new vineyards. For any ordinary mortal this would have represented a prodigious achievement; for Napoleon it was, of course, merely a temporary pastime.

He himself was installed in the Murini palace, where he was joined by his mother and by his sister Pauline, who unlike Caroline and Elisa, never wavered in her attachment and affection for her brother. As an object of curiosity, he was besieged by visitors, many of them English, whom he received affably and often invited to dine at his table. On one occasion, Countess Marie Walewska came with the son he had fathered in 1810, a child who so resembled the King of Rome that many on Elba thought that it *was* Marie-Louise and her son come to join the Emperor.

To outside observers it seemed that Napoleon had settled to his new life and surroundings, but in fact nothing could have been more illusory. Any idea that Napoleon could turn around his life and personality because he found himself in 'reduced circumstances' should not have been entertained by any except those wanting to believe it. Well aware of what was happening in France, through reliable information supplied by a network of under-cover agents, who provided a means of smuggling correspondence between Elba and sympathisers in France, Napoleon watched closely the evolution of events. The ineptitude of the restored Bourbon monarchy and its admin-istration meant that within six months of its return most sections of society in France, from nobility to peasantry, had become alienated. It was not difficult, therefore, to stimulate anti-Bourbon sentiment, particularly if it is borne in mind that the Bourbons had not been restored by the will of the nation, which was at best indifferent or at worst openly hostile.[15]

Louis XVIII might style himself 'King of France by the grace of God', and date 1814 as 'the nineteenth year of his reign', but one claim was unprovable and the other was untrue. As far as the population was concerned, he was there because it suited the Allies and helped to avoid an outbreak of civil disturbance. Above all, the Bourbons were accepted because they brought peace to a country that was war weary, but France needed careful handling to bring it to a real acceptance of the price to be paid for this. It seemed that the sheer impossibility of any further hostilities would be sufficient to guarantee a consensus, but this was an imposed consensus, the product of exhaustion rather than agreement. Underneath the torpor produced by weariness lay the reality of two Frances, one the France of the tricolour, the other the France of the Bourbon lilies, which for many, particularly the army, represented the flag that had flown alongside that of France's enemies since 1792.

The revival of overt and ostentatious religious practice, including public processions and ceremonies of penance, revived the anticlerical feelings which Napoleon had managed to assuage. To this was added the insolence of the nobles who returned from exile, and who, it was thought, would soon demand return of the lands taken at the Revolution, and then attempt to restore the full system of the *ancien régime*. By the spring of 1815 opinion in France had reached a high point of discontent, but it lacked direction and focus until, on 1 March, Napoleon landed at Antibes and the lightning found its conductor.[16]

The situation in France was certainly the prime factor that finally decided Napoleon to launch himself on the extraordinary adventure known to history as the Hundred Days, but there were other elements. He was angered that, in spite of promises, Marie-Louise and the King of Rome had not been allowed to join him; also, well informed as he was, he may have heard of her liaison with Neipperg. Furthermore, the Bourbon government had defaulted on the pension promised to him by the treaty of Fontainebleau, in spite of protests to the government in Paris by Alexander I and the Emperor Francis. It was strongly rumoured that the same government was prepared to countenance, if not actually organise, an assassination of the Emperor, and it seems clear that there were moves on foot to deal more harshly with Napoleon. In December 1814 English newspapers talked of deporting him to an island far from Europe, with St Helena already being mentioned.

Thanks to the wide reach of his system of informants, Napoleon knew that the Allied powers attempting to thrash out a peace at the Congress at Vienna were bogged down in a series of disagreements about the future structure of Europe. Mutual hostility had reached such a degree that at one point France, Austria and Britain had signed a secret treaty directed against Russia and Prussia. Like most secret treaties its contents were suspected, though the Tsar Alexander had no certain knowledge of its terms until the moment of Napoleon's return to the Tuileries. While going through the King's secret correspondence, it was discovered that Louis XVIII had left behind his copy of the treaty. Napoleon immediately sent it to Alexander. With gentlemanly disdain, the Tsar feigned to ignore it.

Napoleon's gamble paid off, perhaps even more spectacularly than even he could have envisaged. Landing on 1 March with a handful of supporters, he entered the Tuileries at nine o'clock on the evening of 20 March, literally carried by the crowd who surrounded him crying *Vive l'Empereur*! Already the tricolour flag had been hoisted and floated over the palace, while Louis XVIII was well on the road to Belgium, off once more into exile. What made this occasion quite different was that he set out accompanied by some of Napoleon's best marshals.

Once installed again in Paris, Napoleon was able to evaluate more precisely the reasons why he was there and to assess them. What worried him was the nature of the support which he had unleashed: 'nothing astonished me more or than this violent hatred of priests and nobles which I found to be widespread as at the beginning of the Revolution. The

Bourbons have succeeded in reviving all its spent force'. The young lieutenant who had put down rioting mobs in Auxonne and Ajaccio, and who had not hesitated to provide 'a whiff of grapeshot' to the same end in Paris, had not suddenly become converted to the virtues of revolutionary violence. It disgusted him, as it always had done, and it must be controlled. It was this sentiment that led to his lack of enthusiasm for the proffered support of the twelve thousand Parisian workers and old soldiers who paraded before him in May 1815, though he badly needed men.

The problem, however, was that, if popular support was rejected, could the more settled sections of society be counted on to show the same enthusiasm for his return? The liberal bourgeoisie, those who had benefited from the Revolution and had consolidated their gains during the Empire, would need to be convinced of the value of a Napoleonic restoration. They also had a profit and loss account to deal with, and the lack of enthusiasm displayed by this group for the Bonapartist cause in 1814 led to an attempt by Napoleon to show that in 1815 he was a changed man. As a pledge for the future, he announced 'no more war, no more conquests'; and, in a further attempt to show positive proof of change, he produced the famous Additional Act to the Constitutions of the Empire. By its clauses it seemed that the revived regime would be more parliamentary and less the rule of one man, since greater consultation with the elected chambers was promised. Restrictions on the press and on freedom of speech would be modified, taxes were only to be raised by consent of the Legislative Body, and in general there was to be a loosening of the imperial regime. This was all well and good, but the question exercising the minds of critics and supporters alike was how deep these changes went. They were not a fundamental reform of the imperial structure, they were simply to be tacked on to that which already existed. This produced an ambiguity that was a source of worry to many who doubted the sincerity of Napoleon's conversion and thereby weakened his position.[17]

In accordance with Bonapartist tradition, a plebiscite was held for the people to give its verdict on the changes outlined in the Additional Act, but this time, whatever the government's hopes may have been, the plebiscite was a failure. Out of a possible five million electors only just over one and a half million voted, and of that number the 'yes' vote only reached a little over one million. Those abstaining won by a massive majority, proof that the country was discontented, uninterested or simply exhausted. Certainly it was alarming proof that those eligible to vote were lacking in enthusiasm, and they were the very ones Napoleon needed to rally to him. An added worry was that the analysis of the returns showed that the regime appeared to have lost the support of the towns, whose votes were mostly hostile. What must be remembered, however, about this plebiscite is that it was conducted under extremely unfavourable conditions. All the previous consultations had been organised by local officials favourable to the regime, whereas in 1815 there had been insufficient time to appoint new men and the local officials were those appointed by the royal government. This undoubtedly affected the results in areas under their jurisdiction.

Nevertheless, Napoleon did not in any way show himself perturbed by this ambiguous popular reaction and the results were proclaimed with great pomp at the famous ceremony on 1 June 1815, held on the great open space of the Champ de Mars in Paris, the scene of so many of the set-pieces of the Revolution and the Empire. The idea was that the Emperor, together with the electors, representing the people, should swear an oath of loyalty to the new constitution and pledge themselves to the national monarchy in a demonstration of unity around the dynasty.

Since the Empress and his heir were absent, the ceremony was crippled from the start, because it underlined the fact of their absence and struck at the whole idea of dynastic continuity. Napoleon had therefore to make the ceremony focus on himself. Together with his brothers, Joseph and Lucien, he presented himself to the army and to the people wearing an extravagant version of his imperial robes. Unfortunately, many observers felt that the whole affair was not really suited to the gravity of the situation and seemed more like some sort of operatic performance, just at a moment when everything was extremely serious. It was a measure of the recognition of this seriousness that led to the army being given a prominent position in the whole affair, for no one could now delude themselves about the inevitability of war. This reliance on the military was given prominence by Napoleon's decision to use the occasion to present them with new eagles for the regimental standards.

It was to be the last great imperial pageant, for reality lay in waiting as the forces gathered by the Allied coalition prepared for an assault on France. On 13 March they had decreed 'Buonaparte' to be an outlaw whose breaking of the treaty of Fontainebleau placed him 'beyond the pale of civil and social relations'. He could be 'hunted down' in the words of Louis

XVIII's proclamation to the French people. It was the equivalent of a demand for unconditional surrender, because it meant that there would be no discussions and no treating with him; he must either win, or lose all hope of re-establishing himself.

Napoleon knew this, because he had already tried for peace, sending emissaries to the Tsar and to Francis I, agreeing to accept the terms of the treaty of Paris which had been laid down by the Allies; but there was no reply to his overtures. There was no alternative but to prepare for the inevitable battle on which, clearly, his future and the future of France would depend. It came at Waterloo, near Brussels, on 18 June 1815, and if there are such things as decisive battles, then this was certainly one. Napoleon's key strategy of preventing a fusion between the Prussian and English forces failed, and by the evening the French army was broken, leaving the Old Guard with one final great moment as it protected the fleeing army on its road to France. In spite of the advice of Joseph and Caulaincourt that he stay with the army and rally it around him, Napoleon decided to play a political game by returning to Paris. This time he was outmanoeuvred by those who were determined to make an end of the imperial adventurer and on 21 June, with no seeming alternative, the Emperor abdicated.

It must also be remembered that, political intrigue apart, there was an added dimension to the defeat at Waterloo. Napoleon had been vanquished by his two most implacable enemies, Prussia and England, with some assistance from a small Dutch contingent. For purely military reasons, the result of troop dispositions, neither Austrian nor Russian forces were present on the battlefield, a circumstance which would affect the course of subsequent events when there was a hiatus after the departure of Napoleon. In Paris the Legislative Bodies decided to appoint commissioners to find out what terms the Allies envisaged as the price of an armistice, only to find that, with or without Napoleon, the Allies were in no mood to talk. Wellington swiftly cut through any discussions about future developments and what role the chambers might play in them. 'What they had best to do is immediately proclaim the King. Their King is nearby, let them send him their submission.'

Suddenly, all the intrigues which had surrounded the second abdication of Napoleon, and from which the competing political groups in Paris hoped to profit, were shown to have been futile. Those people who had, in their various ways, imagined that, once Napoleon had gone, they could begin to negotiate and produce a new political settlement for France drawn up in their favour which they would present to the returning sovereign were out-foxed. They had tried to control the situation by declaring 'the throne vacant until the nation expressed its will', but they were swiftly made aware of their lack of authority by Wellington's diktat.

In extremis, in an attempt to manifest some semblance of authority, and under pressure from a minority faithful to the fallen Emperor and led by Lucien Bonaparte, they proclaimed Napoleon II as the legitimate heir of his father, 'according to the constitutions of the Empire'. Since there was no question of setting up a regency in the form prescribed by the constitution, as amended in 1813, this proclamation had no real import beyond its immediate promulgation. It served, however, to maintain the Empire as a phantom, without substance, but whose existence even in this form might prevent any popular uprising in favour of the fallen dynasty. The proclamation of the young Emperor was issued in such a way as to explain the situation:

> Napoleon Bonaparte has abdicated. The Prince Imperial, his son, has been recognised unanimously by the chambers as his successor to the Empire, under the name of Napoleon II. While awaiting his return, a government commission will direct affairs. Commissioners had been named by the chambers and they will approach the foreign powers in order to organise peace which will come to France and to the world.[18]

All of this actually meant nothing, except as an example of political humbug, because, even as they went through the motions of perpetuating the dynasty, the legislators knew that it was now their turn to disappear. On 8 July the chambers ceased to exist as a result of the return of Louis XVIII, and their dissolution automatically ended the reign of Napoleon II, which dated from 22 June. Given the extraordinary way in which the reign had begun and ended, the future of the Bonaparte dynasty was very far from clear. It was evident that there was an heir, though he was only four years old and lived in Vienna, while in Paris the throne of France was already occupied. In 1815 it needed great optimism and loyalty to envisage the bringing of the two together.

5

No Justice for Bonapartes in France

On 25 June, the day that Napoleon left the Elysée Palace, on his way to Malmaison, the first step in his final departure from France, the future political programme of the restored monarchy was defined in a proclamation by Louis XVIII. He had crossed back into northern France in the wake of the Allied armies, and his proclamation, known as the proclamation of Cateau-Cambrésis, the town where it was issued, stated that there was to be 'no pardon for the instigators and the authors of this horrible plot. They shall be given over to the vengeance of the laws, proposed by the chambers I intend to summon immediately.' The important word was 'vengeance', for this time the Royalists were determined to be implacable, attributing the success of the Hundred Days to the lenient policy of the First Restoration. Although a second proclamation, issued at the town of Cambrai, slightly modified the first, the general import was unchanged.

Not everyone had waited for the appearance of the royal proclamation to begin a policy of vengeance. In Provence, no sooner was news of Waterloo known than a 'White Terror' broke out resulting in the murders of Protestants, Republicans and Bonapartists in all the major cities, including Nîmes, Avignon, Toulouse and Marseille, where Royalist mobs assuaged old, and new, hatreds. One of the unfortunate side-effects of Napoleon's return had been that many had dared openly to rally to his cause, thereby exposing themselves to their enemies when the cause was lost.

What of the former Emperor? At the Elysée, on the night of 25 June, he held a family council with Joseph, Lucien and Jerome, where it was agreed that all of them should make arrangements to go to America. Lucien suggested that he should go to London to ask for a safe-conduct for the brothers, something which Joseph denounced as an act of madness. He proved to be correct, for Lucien, on reaching Boulogne, thought twice about going to London, and left for Italy, where he was immediately arrested at Turin. It seems certain that exactly the same thing, or worse, would have happened had he set foot in England.

Jerome decided to put himself under the protection of his father-in-law, the King of Württemberg, so that in the event the only one to follow in Napoleon's footsteps was Joseph. Intending to embark for the United States, he made for the port of Rochefort and it was here that the Emperor caught up with him on 3 July. On the same night that Joseph left the Elysée, heading for the coast, Napoleon himself left for Malmaison, intending to make it a staging post on his journey, but once there he lingered, apparently without purpose, seemingly caught in a web of memories, about which he spoke endlessly to Hortense. Josephine was no longer there to greet him, for she had died in May 1814, within a few weeks of his own arrival on Elba. Her death had come about as a consequence of her desire to provide for her two children and ultimately because of her rather touching vanity. She had become friendly with Tsar Alexander on his visit to Paris, whom she cultivated in order to protect Hortense and Eugène, fearing the vindictiveness of the restored Bourbons. As a result, she managed to secure for Hortense the title of Duchess of St-Leu and also a guarantee of Alexander's protection for her son. All of this Josephine achieved by using her natural charms and the elegance of her manners, combined with a judicious round of entertainment provided for Alexander. Ironically it was her talent for this which killed her, for after a dinner party at Malmaison she walked with Alexander in her famous rose garden, wearing only one of the gauzy lightweight dresses in which she delighted. Already suffering from a cold, she caught a severe chill and in three days was dead at the age of only fifty-one. The ex-Empress left the house to her son, Eugène, but, having learned of Napoleon's intention to stay there, Hortense had installed herself in order to receive him. The stay there must have proved an emotional strain on Napoleon, not least because circumstances made of it a place of farewells. Marie Walewska came, bringing their son Alexander, as did Eléonore Denuelle bringing 'little Léon', the son Napoleon had fathered in 1806. Above all, it was the memories that the place held of Josephine and of happier times which had to be exorcised.

Napoleon's continued presence on French soil alarmed the 'Provisional Government' in Paris, which wished only for his speedy departure. In June, Wellington had helped to focus minds on what would come next, and had expedited the return of the King. It was now the turn of Marshal Blücher, the Prussian co-victor of Waterloo, to move affairs along. Implacable in their desire to seize Napoleon, detachments of the Prussian army roved

round Paris, one having been charged with the specific mission of appre-
hending the Emperor and shooting him.

Made aware of this, Napoleon finally gave the order to move. Within a
week, travelling south west, he reached the port of Rochefort on the Atlantic
coast, where on 8 July he found his brother Joseph. It immediately became
clear that there was a problem, since the entire coastline was closely
patrolled by English ships. If it was Napoleon's intention to try and escape
by sea in order to go to America, it would be a dangerous undertaking. At
one stage it was suggested that the fugitive should board a smaller ship, fast
enough to run the blockade, and that, should the English stop and search
it, the Emperor should conceal himself in a barrel! Napoleon rejected this
as being unworthy of him and degrading to his status. Joseph at this point
offered to impersonate him, so that his brother could escape, but Napoleon
refused.

From Rochefort Napoleon and his small group of followers moved to
the Ile d'Aix, and it was there that Napoleon took the decision to surrender
to the English. In spite of the vigorous protestations of his entourage, negotiations were opened with Captain Maitland of the *Bellerophon*, who already
knew what he had to do. Determined not to be caught unprepared, and
possibly forewarned by their agents in France, the Admiralty had had given
him precise instructions: if Napoleon was intercepted, he was to be held
and brought as soon as possible to the nearest English port.

Joseph waited in the area until he knew that Napoleon had finally
embarked on the English ship. Only then, on the night of 24/25 July,
together with his small suite, all with visas for the United States, did Joseph
depart. He would arrive in America under the name of 'Monsieur
Bouchard'.

Did Napoleon realise what he was doing by giving himself up in this
way? Did he have some extraordinary notion that the British government
would allow him to live quietly, as Lucien had done, in a country house in
the shires? He had apparently said to Marshal Bertrand, 'There is always a
danger in entrusting oneself to one's enemies, but it is better to risk relying
on their sense of honour than to be in their hands as a prisoner of war'.
This explains his famous letter to the Prince Regent, in which he put himself
under the protection of the laws of England, a protection 'which I ask from
Your Royal Highness as the most powerful, the most constant, and the most
generous of my enemies'. He came, he said 'like Themistocles to sit at the

hearth of the British nation', but the England of Lords Liverpool and Castlereagh was not fifth-century Persia. The English oligarchy had been badly frightened by the Revolution and Napoleon – that was why it had spent twenty-five years as the driving force of the counter-revolution – and it would show itself to be ruthless and determined in its revenge.[1]

The moment he set foot in the ship's boat that was to ferry him to the *Bellerophon* Napoleon was lost. The same day that he surrendered, the Cabinet in London had met to decide on the place of his exile, Lord Liverpool indicating that the Cape of Good Hope or St Helena would be the most appropriate. Further consideration led to the final choice of St Helena and on 30 July Napoleon was informed of the government's decision. Although he protested that he had boarded an English vessel of his own free will, and could not therefore be seen as a prisoner, he had either forgotten, or had refused to remember, that at Vienna he had been publicly put 'beyond the pale of Civil and Social Relations'. The legal meaning of this was hard to define, but it implied outlaw status. In any event, whatever it might or might not mean, the English government had no intention of allowing lawyers to debate the matter. Indeed Lord Liverpool regretted that Louis XVIII had not seized Napoleon and had him executed for treason. The extraordinary scenes occasioned by the *Bellerophon*'s arrival at Torbay and then at Plymouth, when sightseers surrounded the vessel, waving at any person on board they assumed to be Napoleon, only increased the government's resolve to send the man as far away as possible. They also feared a threat to use Habeas Corpus to force the appearance of Napoleon before an English court. The *Bellerophon* was ordered to put to sea and it was at sea that Napoleon was transferred to the *Northumberland*, the vessel designated to carry him to St Helena.

Whatever Napoleon thought or expected, and whether his last weeks in Europe were full of wrong decisions, hesitations and finally a great mistake, or whether it was all carefully orchestrated, leading to a very public exit from a theatre which he had dominated for so long, is a source of debate. What emerged clearly was that 'General Bonaparte', as he was now to be styled, had no intention of going quietly. He could be physically removed from centre stage, but he could not be silenced and he would prove to be a very voluble martyr, ensuring that his island prison would become known as something more than a way station on the voyage to England for the ships of the East India Company.

So ended the episode known to history as the Hundred Days. Recognition of its importance has meant that it is now taken as a measure of political success or failure, and 'the first hundred days' has become a threadbare political cliché by which administrations and governments are judged on the basis of what they have achieved in their first days in office. In fact, the real importance of the episode lay in Napoleon's having sown confusion in the minds of contemporaries by his political actions in 1815. The Additional Act, and the seemingly liberal regime which it ushered in, led many to believe the Emperor's claim to have been obliged to pursue harsh and illiberal policies in order to defend the gains of the Revolution against the hostile counter-revolutionary powers. Given peace and stability in Europe, the whole structure of the Empire would have been different. This example of what one might call 'confusion marketing', assiduously cultivated by the later writings emanating from St Helena, was to have an enormous impact on nineteenth-century France, and indeed on Europe as whole.

The vindictive behaviour of the restored monarchy did much to help foster a feeling of sympathy for the fallen dynasty, for on 16 January 1816 the royal government agreed to the confiscation of all property belonging to the Bonapartes and banished the family from France. Any member of the family, either by direct descent or by marriage, if found on French soil, was liable to the death penalty. When the Duke of Richelieu tried to intervene on behalf of Queen Catherine, the wife of Jerome, Louis XVIII made his famous comment: 'There is no justice for Bonapartes in France.'

Exiled from France, the family were scattered, reduced to the status of high-class refugees, put under surveillance in any territory which gave them asylum, and allowed to move residence only by authorisation from the powers of the Waterloo coalition which had drawn up the treaties at Vienna. Dynastically all seemed lost, for Napoleon II was a virtually unknown infant whose memory could only be cherished by die-hard Bonapartists. Sadly, history remembers him as the Duke of Reichstadt, the title conferred on him by his grandfather in Vienna, when even the child's baptismal name was changed in a concerted effort made to make him forget his father.

Of the remaining possible successors, in the line laid down by the constitution of 1804, Joseph had managed to reach the United States. On arrival he first rented a house in the centre of Philadelphia, together with a second property in Fairmount Park, to the west of the city. But Joseph, who after all had twice been a King, and whose taste had always run to the luxurious, was disquieted to find himself a simple tenant, so he looked for a property to buy commensurate with his former status. The estate which he purchased was known as Point Breeze, situated on the Delaware river; and on 22 January 1817, having established himself, 'Mr Bouchard' became the Comte de Survilliers, the title Joseph used from now on, and was granted citizenship of the state of New Jersey.

Joseph had paid $17,500 for his estate but, as he had done at Mortefontaine and at others of his properties, there was to be alteration and enlargement of the house and land to the tune of $30,000. It was fortunate that Joseph was a wealthy man and able to set himself up in such grand style.[2] His wealth also allowed him to provide for many French and Spanish refugees, those who had served him when he was King of Spain. It seems clear that, in addition to these payments, sums of money were sent to St Helena, presumably out of funds which Napoleon had entrusted to Joseph, for we know that he had received very substantial amounts in the last two weeks before the fall of the dynasty. These sums were used by Napoleon to pay off his creditors and to pay his followers and the servants who were with him at Longwood. To protect his personal fortune, Joseph had put his properties in Europe in the hands of his bankers, or, in the case of Mortefontaine, in the hands of a relative of his wife Julie. This prevented them from being confiscated under the law passed by Louis XVIII.

Julie, whose relations with her husband had always remained amicable in spite of his constant infidelities, refused to join him in the United States, but she, like all other members of the family, was compelled to find a refuge somewhere, since she was forbidden to reside in France. She first found shelter in Frankfurt, but then in 1820 established a home in Brussels. She was never to join Joseph in America but remained in Europe with their two daughters, Zenaïde, born in 1801, and Charlotte, born in 1802, playing *her* dynastic role by finding suitable husbands for the girls.

The constitution of May 1804, which established the Empire, also provided for the succession, and since the terms had remained unaltered at the moment of the final collapse in 1815, its provisions were deemed by the family to remain in force. The relevant articles laid down that the Emperor would be succeeded by his son, either natural or adopted, as indeed had been the case in 1815. But, if there was a hiatus, as in 1815, and there had been no proper establishment in legal forms of a Regency, as set out in

1814, then the order of succession went from Joseph to Louis, both Lucien and Jerome being excluded.

The problem was that in 1815 Napoleon was on St Helena, and had in any case abdicated, and Joseph was in the United States. Only Louis remained in Europe. Since there was no vacant throne, it did not really seem to matter a great deal *what* the line of succession actually was. For those who thought it *did* matter the legal Emperor was now Napoleon II, who had been proclaimed in 1815 by the Legislative Bodies in Paris, though none of the young Emperor's uncles evinced any desire to put forward their nephew's dynastic claims – even in writing. Since the boy was in Vienna, 'not a prisoner but in a very special position', as one of his tutors expressed it, it could not be expected that any of them would mount an armed crusade to rescue *l'Aiglon*. What supporters he had were closely watched by the secret police of the various countries where they had found refuge; even had they been inclined to desperate measures, there was little hope of any such a project prospering.

Nevertheless, from time to time rumours of attempts to rescue Napoleon from St Helena, or to carry off Napoleon II from Vienna, circulated in the various European capitals, though cynically one supposes that secret police-men were often tempted to foment such rumours in order to ensure their own continued employment. There was no need for alarm: the Waterloo coalition had made certain that the Bonaparte family would give no trouble – a situation that, for the most part, its members found to be acceptable.

Louis, ex-King of Holland, had abdicated in 1810 in favour of his son, a pointless exercise since Napoleon had simply annexed the territory and suppressed the kingdom. Louis then went into exile in Austria, a move calcu-lated to irritate his brother, but this was an exile which came to an end in 1813 when Austria joined the coalition against France. Louis then moved to Switzerland and made an attempt at reconciliation with Napoleon, but it foundered on his demand to be recognised as King of Holland. The Emperor refused, on the grounds that the kingdom of Holland no longer existed, but, at the same time, informed Louis that he could return to Paris as a French Prince. The argument was still going on when the collapse of Napoleon's position forced Louis to agree to return to Paris in 1814, where he was accepted by his brother, but he was to play no significant role in the last months of the Empire. When Napoleon abdicated in 1814, Louis left for Rome.

During the Hundred Days, Napoleon, in an attempt to pull the family together, offered Louis a seat in the Chamber of Peers, but he had refused, preferring to remain in Rome in order to pursue his bitter dispute with Hortense over the custody of their children. In 1814 he had publicly protested about her acceptance of the duchy of St-Leu from the hands of Louis XVIII, not because he considered it an insult to the imperial family but because it gave Hortense an independent status. Presumably he feared that this would prejudice his case for custody of the two sons.

It is interesting to note how the legal system continued to function almost normally, even though the episode of the Hundred Days interrupted Louis' court case, for in July the Paris court gave a judgment in his favour. As a result, the eleven-year-old Napoleon Louis was sent to join his father in Italy. Having obtained charge of the elder boy, Louis wrote to Hortense in 1819 that 'in a certain time Louis must also come to me', something Hortense was resolutely determined to prevent.

In the meantime Louis had managed to keep his feud with Napoleon alive by publishing, in 1820, a book on the governance of Holland that painted a very unflattering portrait of the former Emperor's policy. The book merited a mention in Napoleon's will: 'I forgive Louis the libel he published in 1820, full of false assertions and forged evidence', but this forgiveness did not extend to any bequest and so could hardly be construed as a final reconciliation between the brothers. As far as maintaining the rights of the dynasty was concerned, or helping to produce a defence of the legitimacy of the Empire, Louis was a resolute non-starter, deploring any attempts to draw attention to members of the imperial family.

The most wayward of Napoleon's brothers was Lucien, whose conduct and behaviour over the decade 1804 to 1814 seems to have been designed to provoke the Emperor in ways which even Louis could never achieve. Napoleon's dictum, 'I recognise no relatives but those who serve me', had meant that, for a part of the time at least, Louis had been of service and Napoleon had reacted accordingly. Napoleon's attempts to shore up the rocky marriage with Hortense were certainly sincere and may well have sprung from a strong affection for a brother whom he had virtually brought up. That it all failed is unsurprising, given the circumstances, but at least there was reasonable contact between the two men up until 1810. In the case of Lucien, all contact had virtually ceased after 1804, though, in view of the fact that Lucien was constrained to live in England for nearly four years, from 1810, this is less surprising.

1. The Bonaparte family. Top row, left to right: Lucien, Letizia (*Madame Mère*), Joseph; second row: Jerome, Hortense de Beauharnais, Caroline, Elisa, Pauline, Louis; third row: Josephine, Napoleon, Marie-Louise. Lithograph by Becquet.

2. Napoleon I (1769–1821) and his brothers. Left to right: Joseph, King of Spain; Louis, King of Holland; Lucien, Prince of Camino; Jerome, King of Westphalia.

3. Napoleon Bonaparte as First Consul.

4. Napoleon I in coronation robes.

5. Napoleon's abdication at Fontainebleau, 1814.

6. The battle of Waterloo, 18 June 1815.

7. Napoleon II, the Duke of Reichstadt (1811–1832).

8. The Empress Eugénie (1826–1920).

9. Napoleon III (1808–1873).

10. The death of the Prince Imperial in the Zulu War, 1879.

On the fall of Napoleon in 1814, Lucien was able to leave England and return to Rome, where he was once again welcomed by Pius VII and given the title of hereditary Prince of Canino. It was in Rome that he learned of the landing of Napoleon in France in March 1815. He tried, but failed, to dissuade his impetuous brother-in-law Murat from avoiding open action in favour of Napoleon by invading the Papal States as a first step to rallying Italy to his cause.[3] Lucien's own contribution to his brother's cause was to leave Rome for Paris, to offer his services to the 'Republican Emperor'.

This rallying to Napoleon may have seemed like an act of quixotic and spontaneous generosity, and a desire to heal old wounds, having about it a certain nobility, particularly given the hazardous nature of Napoleon's enterprise. But Lucien's motives were always complex. He saw himself as the 'Great Citizen', the uncrowned brother who had eschewed all the titles and splendours of the Empire. Who in the family was better fitted to underline the dynasty's revolutionary principles which the Emperor was now reassuming?

Yet this radical had no objection to princely living, such as he had enjoyed in Rome, and in Paris he installed himself in the Palais-Royal, while at the same time accepting the title of French Prince (Prince Français) which Napoleon now conferred on him, though he did not revoke his exclusion from the dynastic succession. At the same time Lucien adjured Napoleon to embrace 'the enormous party of the Revolution against the infinitesimal party of the *ancien régime*'. In other words the Consulate should be revived and the constitutional reforms of the Additional Act enlarged.

After Waterloo, Lucien, supported by the staunchly Republican Carnot, tried to persuade Napoleon to revert to the revolutionary principles of 1793 and declare 'La Patrie en danger' with the establishment of a Committee of Public Safety. Napoleon's refusal to do so led to Lucien's alternative suggestion of an immediate abdication that would, when Napoleon II was proclaimed, safeguard the dynasty. It was undoubtedly thanks in large part to Lucien's bitter struggle with the Legislative Bodies that Napoleon II *was* eventually proclaimed. Lucien argued that 'every interruption in dynastic continuity means anarchy', but it is far from clear what he hoped to salvage from the wreckage of the Empire by the proclamation of his nephew. Whatever his immediate intention, the action ultimately turned out be of great importance for the future of the dynasty.

With the return of Louis XVIII, and the resumption of royal power,

Lucien was, like all the family, proscribed. He again made his way to Rome, putting himself once more under papal protection. The Allies demanded his banishment, hoping to force him out of Europe, but the Pope resisted all the pressures put on him and the exile remained in Rome until 1819. He then moved to the town of Viterbo, still inside the Papal States, where he lived in his usual extravagant fashion while doing his best to maintain the twelve children he had fathered by his two marriages.

In the *Mémorial*, Napoleon spoke highly of Lucien, in spite of all the difficulties that there had been between them, and his esteem for his brother was justified, for Lucien remained loyal to the cause of Bonapartism. Having been informed that during the crisis of July 1830 there had been cries of 'Long Live Napoleon II!', Lucien produced a written project for a revised constitution of the Empire. This document was finalised in 1833 in collaboration with Joseph, who came to London for a family conference. It represented, in essence, a revised 'consular constitution' putting forward the elective principle as the key to the re-establishment of the Empire. The acceptance of the elective principle represented a serious break with the concept of hereditary succession as established in 1804, and it was put forward, as we shall see, for a specific reason.

Both Joseph and Lucien, with the support of Louis, were alarmed by the fact that Louis Napoleon (Louis' younger son) clearly considered himself to be in the line of succession, and they all feared the consequences of this young hothead as the imperial heir. Lucien seemed to have forgotten the argument he put forward in 1815 that a break in dynastic continuity meant anarchy, but it soon became apparent that his nephew had not. To be fair, whatever criticisms can be made of the conduct of Joseph, Lucien and Louis, it must be recognised that they were serious men whose convictions and ideas had often led them into conflict with their brother and made his life difficult. But they were convinced that they had a responsibility to prevent Louis Napoleon from having a place in the succession. Their motives were mixed and partly selfish – they wanted a quiet life – and also because they considered their nephew to be too hot-headed. His actions risked putting the family in danger. When it came to the youngest, Jerome, the problems were largely of a different kind. Apart from his matrimonial blunder in marrying Miss Patterson, which had exasperated Napoleon and led to his direct interference, Jerome appeared to have one great advantage in his relations with Napoleon, in that he was really not interested in affairs of state. He asked only that his imperial brother should treat him well, and generously, which Napoleon did: 'One cannot imagine how much this young man costs me, and with it all, he only gives me disappointments and is no use in my plans.' He even referred to him as a *mauvais sujet*.

The difficulty was that Jerome had to be made useful because he was needed in the pursuit of Napoleon's aim of reorganising Europe by the distribution of thrones among his family. Since there had to be a sufficient number of brothers to fill the number of thrones envisaged, Napoleon was determined that the youngest must play his part. The consequence of this determination had been the creation of the kingdom of Westphalia in 1807, to which Jerome and his wife Catherine, the daughter of the King of Württemberg, were dispatched as King and Queen. The kingdom was intended to stabilise the French position in central Germany and on the Rhine, since it was assumed that Württemberg would, thanks to the marriage, be a faithful ally. Once in his new kingdom, Jerome elected to establish his court at the palace of Wilhelmshöhe near Kassel, and here he and his wife lived until Napoleon's Europe began to fall apart in 1813.

In the intervening years, Jerome, in spite of his previous attitude of indifference, displayed a great degree of maturity in his approach to public affairs. Although his personal extravagances continued as before, he did try to rule wisely and in the interests of his subjects. As always, the problems arose from the conflict of views between Napoleon and his satellite kings, whether they were his brothers or not. In 1807 Jerome was told how to rule 'your people must enjoy a liberty, an equality and a prosperity unknown in the rest of Germany'. But in a few years the King was further told that 'recalcitrant subjects who refuse to see what benefits are being offered to them ... are guilty of anarchism and the first duty of a prince is to punish them'. Unsurprisingly, given Napoleon's interference, Jerome's reign could only be considered a qualified success.[4]

On the Emperor's instructions, Westphalia was obliged to take part in the Russian campaign of 1812, but Jerome had, according to his brother, proved so dangerously incompetent as a commander that the latter wrote 'you are endangering the whole success of the campaign on the right.' In fact this was unfair criticism, for Jerome had achieved his designated objective as planned, that is the capture of the city of Grodno, but he had delayed a further advance because of poor weather and in order to rest his troops. Napoleon, having produced the accusations of incompetence, announced that Jerome's command was now made subordinate to Marshal Davout, which so enraged Jerome that he resigned, refusing to serve under a marshal. Napoleon regarded his resignation as the equivalent of desertion in the face of the enemy, though he did in fact legalise Jerome's action retrospectively, perhaps realising that he had been too precipitate in his earlier criticism.

Whatever his faults, Jerome was loyal to his brother, though in 1814, on the question of the defence of Paris, he acquiesced in Joseph's crucial, and disastrous, decision to abandon the capital. He immediately rallied to Napoleon during the Hundred Days, and at Waterloo displayed great courage both at Quatre-Bras (where he was wounded) and in the attempt to take Hougoumont, a scene of appalling carnage. He further proved his loyalty by refusing to withdraw from the battle, continuing fighting even after Napoleon had himself left the field.

When the second abdication came, Jerome and Catherine, having abandoned the idea of seeking refuge in America with Joseph, put themselves under the protection of her father the King of Württemberg, but pressure by the Allies on the King meant that his protection proved too constraining. With the death of the Emperor in 1821, the couple were able to join *Madame Mère* in Rome. Although Jerome displayed little or no interest in keeping a possible restoration of the dynasty in the public eye, he and Catherine were affected by the activities of Louis' two sons, who were determined not to accept the political inactivity of the older generation. Napoleon Louis and Louis Napoleon became involved in the insurrectionary movements of 1830 in the Papal States and, as a result, Jerome and his wife were forced to leave Rome. They moved to Florence, where Catherine died in 1834, leaving two sons and a daughter. Within a few years of her death, Jerome had married a very rich Florentine widow and resumed his normal extravagant and somewhat aimless existence. As far as the Bonapartist cause was concerned he was simply known to be a member of the family, with little or no interest in its dynastic future. Indeed what really exercised him after 1830 was finding a way to be able to return to France with the agreement of King Louis-Philippe.

For the most part the members of the imperial family, dispersed and demoralised, pursued a policy of aggressive inertia. When faced with the task of maintaining the rights of the dynasty, their attitude might simply have snuffed out any hope of an eventual restoration. This, however, was not to be the case. If the lesser members were inactive, the constant activity of its head and founder ensured that *he* was setting the future in motion, fully confident that he could move it, just as he had the past. Did he remember what Hegel had said of him in 1805: 'It is only from heaven, that is from the French Emperor, that matters can be set in motion'? Imprisoned on St Helena, Napoleon, the great star, was ready for his most important performance, the one which would enable him to project an image specially designed for future generations. By linking his dynasty to the future, Napoleon was taking a gamble, but he had always done that, and who could say it wouldn't work? 'On s'engage, et puis on voit' (You begin and then you see) had always been part of his philosophy of life – you could not know until you tried it. Apart from that, he had for the moment nothing better to do.

His most important task was to create a coherent structure out of the disparate elements which had made up his life and work. In military terms this posed no problem, since he was indisputably the greatest military strategist who had ever lived. The difficulty lay in the field of the political legacy, which needed to be given a considerable 'spin' before being offered to the world outside St Helena, always bearing in mind that the outside world already had, through experience, its own interpretation of the same events. Fortunately for Napoleon, his collaborators proved to be not only those who chose to accompany him to his exile, and who were destined to spread his message, but also the British government. As the great maritime power and nominal protector of St Helena, Britain was entrusted by the victors with the responsibility of keeping the former Emperor prisoner on the island, from which the only escape route was by sea. Since the waters around were constantly patrolled by warships, there was little or no chance of either rescue or escape, apart from which there was a garrison of two thousand men.

Not content with the safety precautions needed to guard their prisoner, the British authorities set about the process of 'desacralising' Napoleon, who, it had already been laid down, was henceforth to be addressed only as 'General Bonaparte'. Any letters, packages or other communications that did not bear this form of address were to be refused delivery, while at Napoleon's residence at Longwood all communications addressed to 'General Bonaparte' were systematically refused. Battle was joined on these and other issues early on, and continued until Napoleon's death in 1821, but in only six years he had more or less achieved what he had set out to do, that is establishing his credentials as the martyr of St Helena. The gratuitous vexations inflicted on him by the British government were of great help to him in achieving his goal; and, although exaggerated to suit his purpose, it must be remembered that there were very real grievances. The constant surveillance, the limitations imposed on his movements, not to mention the debilitating effects of the climate, when added to the whole claustrophobic atmosphere, were factors which conspired to make the imprisonment a torment.[5]

Napoleon was surrounded by a curious mixture of people who made up his 'court', chosen from among those who had offered to share his captivity. This had not been an easy decision, for all who accepted were informed by the British authorities that, if they chose to accompany him, they were to remain with Napoleon until his death. Napoleon's own selection included Marshal Bertrand, former Grand Marshal of the palace, and two former Court Chamberlains, the Count of Montholon, and the Comte Las Cases, who was allowed to be accompanied by his young son. To these were added General Gourgaud and also the wives and children of Bertrand and Montholon. Since Napoleon's doctor refused to go with him, his place was taken by Dr Barry O'Meara, a surgeon in the Royal Navy, whom Napoleon had got to know on the voyage to St Helena. Because of O'Meara's sub-sequent importance in the evolution of what we must now begin to call the Napoleonic legend, it is important to clarify his position in the Emperor's entourage. The doctor has been accused of being simply a spy, whose duty was to inform on his patient and those attending him; and without doubt Lord Bathurst, the English Minister responsible for St Helena, was not displeased to have a naval officer at the heart of things producing first-hand accounts of the prisoner. O'Meara, however, seems to have wanted to see himself as simply a close observer writing to his friend, who was the Admiralty archivist in London, about the events at Longwood. This could never be other than a fiction, given the circumstances, and in the end O'Meara became virtually a double-agent, balancing between French and English, a role which, even as an Irishman, he could not sustain. Ultimately it seems he was led more and more into the French camp until in 1818, suspecting him of actual treason, the Governor, Sir Hudson Lowe, demanded that he leave the island.

It was not the least of the Governor's mistakes, for, once back in England, the dismissed surgeon published his account of Napoleon's treatment on the island in a widely read book which created a sensation. Its publication was the first great victory in the propaganda war which Napoleon waged relentlessly, ostensibly against his captors but basically against the threat of oblivion. In his final confrontation with Hudson Lowe, the last time they spoke directly to one another, Napoleon lost his temper in an outbreak which revealed his real preoccupation, saying: 'What gives you the right to deprive me of my title of Emperor? In a few years your Lord Castlereagh and your Lord Bathurst and all the others, you who are addressing me,will be buried under the dust of forgetfulness ... while the Emperor Napoleon will remain the subject, the glory of history and the lodestar of all civilised peoples.'

Napoleon accomplished the task which he had set himself from the beginning: that is to organise a rewriting of those aspects of his career which could be judged harshly and to contrast these with those areas in which he had excelled. It was obvious that he could take his military stature for granted, though, leaving nothing to chance, he took care to dictate accounts of his campaigns to Grand Marshal Bertrand, to O'Meara and Las Cases. Clearly, in the case of the two last named, he intended that they should publish the 'correct' version he had given them.

The most important part of this exercise was the presentation of Napoleon by himself in the role of builder and reformer, the legist and the great organiser, who saw in all his conquests not just the saving of France and the Revolution but the basis for a great new European states system. 'I wished to found a European system, a European code of laws, a European judiciary. There would be but one people in Europe.' Convinced that the future was with him, Napoleon saw himself as addressing this future by means of what would become the written word, thanks to his faithful recorder Las Cases. It was vitally important that it should be Napoleon's version of events that was accepted so that it could become the gospel as dictated at St Helena.

Sufficiently well informed by a selection of newspapers that reached him on the island, supplemented by various clandestine channels of information, Napoleon knew that post-Waterloo Europe, and France in particular, was full of discontents. The inept and reactionary policies of the various European governments only served to point up what had been achieved by Napoleon, and it seems that the ex-Emperor may have had a faint illusion that he would be returned from exile to reorder affairs. With this in mind, he took care to stress his attachment to the ideas of the Revolution, 'these great and magnificent truths, they will control [the future] and this unforgettable era'. The implication was that he was the man to face the challenge as he had done before. Should he not be in a position to do this, there was his son.

By 1818, Napoleon seems to have realised that he would never leave St Helena alive, so all his efforts were now focused on the edification and instruction of his son, the hope of the dynasty, whom he would try to mould from a distance. Convinced that the restored monarchies were precarious, and that the Waterloo coalition was suffering internal divisions, Napoleon hoped that his son might one day inherit the throne of France or Italy. In the short term, his fear was that the boy would be so totally brainwashed by his entourage at Vienna that Napoleon II would forget who he was. All his French attendants had been dismissed and those who now surrounded him were part of the Habsburg court especially chosen for their ability to eliminate all memories of Napoleon and all knowledge of his achievement.

There was little hope that this scheme would work, and it seems incredible that anyone could ever have thought it possible to remove all knowledge of Napoleon from his son. Count Dietrichstein, his tutor, was obliged to write to Marie-Louise, 'the Prince knows nearly everything about his father and he hides it from us constantly', proof that early on the boy had learnt to keep his thoughts to himself, and how to dissimulate – excellent qualities in a potential ruler.

By the time he was an adolescent, the young man could read the *Mémorial de Sainte-Hélène* by Las Cases, the foundation document of the cult of his father and the seminal work for the evolution of political Bonapartism. Since he was, by general consent, highly intelligent with a good memory and a lively imagination, the Prince was unlikely not to have profited from his reading, exactly as his father had intended. We know from the memoirs of his friend, Count Prokesch-Osten, that they often talked together about these works and about other accounts of what had happened at St Helena, and so the young man was far from ignorant of his father's ideas and his captivity.

Napoleon died at Longwood, on 5 May 1821. In his will, dated 15 April 1821, he set out the reasons for his death: 'I die before my time, murdered by the English oligarchy and its hired assassin [Hudson Lowe]. The people of England will avenge me all too soon.' Neither the positive assertion nor the hopeful premise need to be taken too seriously – they are there for dramatic effect. The *actual* causes of the Emperor's death has become a matter for debate but can be left to those who feel it is worth pursuing it in increasingly intense and envenomed arguments.[7]

Dynastically, the important fact was that Napoleon's death immediately made Napoleon II the head of the House of Bonaparte. The fact that he was a child of ten, and that there was no constitutional mechanism, that is no Council of Regency, did not in any way alter the conviction of the diehard imperialists who now focused all their hopes on him. When Napoleon's will became known, it was clear from article 4 that he expected the succession to be assured, even if only on a theoretical basis: de jure, if not de facto. 'I urge my son never to forget that he was born a French Prince, and never to lend himself to the triumvirate which oppresses the people of Europe. In no way whatsoever is he to fight or harm France. He is to adopt my own device: "Tout pour le peuple français" (everything for the French people).'

All those objects which he had left to his son were items most closely associated with his personage as soldier and Emperor. They included the sword of Austerlitz, the grand collar of the Legion of Honour, the cere-monial sword of the First Consul, and his library. The boy was never to receive any of these bequests, for the Law of Exile of 1816 had stipulated that, since all the Bonapartes were deprived of civil rights in France, they could neither lay claim to anything under French law nor possess any goods. As Louis XVIII had said: 'there is no justice for Bonapartes in France'. But, by depriving the young man in Vienna of his father's legacies, Louis inadvertently underlined the fact that he was a Bonaparte and not an Austrian prince.

For the Bonapartists, the death of the 'Martyr of St Helena' was the signal for the production of a torrent of souvenirs, medals, popular prints, statuettes and all sorts of trinketry which stressed the connection between the ex-Emperor and the people, all destined to underline the difference between the imperial regime and that of the restored Bourbons. At a different level the propaganda effort was carried on by the publication in 1822 of O'Meara's book, *A Voice from St Helena*, which was soon translated into French, and then, in 1823, by the publication of Las Cases' *Mémorial*. These two versions of the captivity, which became the key texts for

Bonapartism, had a degree of success, above all in France, that would have gratified their inspirer. By putting forward an interpretation of the whole Napoleonic adventure, linking it to the Revolution and to the glory which the imperial regime had brought to France, and by stressing the debt owed by the nation at every level to the work of Napoleon, Bonapartism became an alternative to the Restoration settlement of the Bourbons. The result was that when Louis XVIII died, in September 1824, to be succeeded by his brother as Charles X, the foundations of an active Bonapartist movement had been well and truly laid.

It was no longer an affair of iconography, medals or statuettes of the great man, nor was it simply a literary exercise, as a series of plots to overthrow the Bourbons made clear. Organised by disaffected groups, frequently embracing a mixture of Republicans and Bonapartists, and accompanied by attempts to suborn sections of the army, their lack of success nevertheless provided propaganda victories. One such attempt produced popular martyrs, the 'Four Sergeants of La Rochelle', executed for their part in what they and others firmly believed was a properly organised *coup*, to bring about the return of Napoleon II from Vienna and the re-establishment of the Empire.

The most audacious attempt at finishing the Bourbons was the murder of the Duke of Berry, the eldest son of the King's brother. The assassin, Louvel, a fervent Bonapartist, hoped that, by depriving it of an heir, he would end the dynasty, for the Duke of Berry's only brother was sterile, while both Louis XVIII and his brother were too old to produce an heir. Berry was therefore the only one capable of maintaining the dynastic succession, and with him gone there would be a problem, and who could foresee the consequences of a broken succession? This was one plot which might indeed have worked – but for the fact that the Duchess of Berry was pregnant when her husband was murdered. Seven months later she gave birth to a son, hailed by the royalists as the 'child of a miracle'.

More than the miraculous birth of an heir was needed to save the increasingly unpopular Bourbon dynasty, and matters came to a head with the accession of Charles X. The new King, unlike his brother, had no time for concessions to opposition groups, nor a desire to engage in political trimming in order to maintain an already precarious throne. Backed by the ultra royalists, Charles attempted to carry through a series of reactionary measures to strengthen the monarchical element in the constitution. The outcome was a revolution, which broke out in July 1830 and resulted in the overthrow of the restored monarchy. To the Bonapartists it seemed that the moment had come to restore the Empire. Napoleon II was now twenty years old and the political upheaval seemed made for a restoration of the imperial dynasty: for who else could lay a serious claim to the throne of France, and who else had so many indications of popular support?

6

Hope Deferred

Unfortunately for the hopes of the Bonapartists, the Revolution of 1830 – the 'Three Glorious Days' – had not been designed to open the way for a popular decision as to its outcome. It had been made by politicians for politicians, men who were motivated by a fear of the consequences of the ineptitude of Charles X and his government. If the King were to continue a policy of reaction, there was a risk that a genuine popular revolution, with strong Bonapartist overtures, would break out, something which the leading opposition groups were determined to prevent. It followed from this that the leaders of 1830, all well-established politicians, had already mapped out a route which they intended their revolution to take. Since they themselves came from a generation that had felt the effects of the Revolution of 1789, they were firmly resolved to avoid a repetition of the events it had produced both at home and abroad. They were also only too aware that in getting rid of the restored Bourbons they were breaking the terms of the treaties of 1815, thereby giving the Allies the automatic right to intervene in the affairs of France.

Had the Bourbon dynasty, as represented by its elder branch, been capable of ruling within the confines of the constitutional settlement of 1815, it might have survived. Its incapacity, or unwillingness, to do that so alarmed the wealthy and well-established sections of French society that they were prepared to resort to extra-legal means to bring about a change.[1] It was clear to these people that the least acceptable solution would be a restoration of the imperial dynasty. Not only was this associated with 'popular' government, but its reappearance would alarm the European powers. While demonstrations occurred in Paris, the crowds crying alternately 'Vive l'Empereur!' and 'Vive Napoléon II!', mingled with cries of 'Vive la République!', the sober men who had dethroned Charles X had already devised a plan which would stabilise the situation.

As revolutions go in France, 1830 was one of the least violent, being virtually over in three days. The principal actors among the political groups, though not the only ones, were Thiers and Guizot. Both had been in opposition to Charles X, but both were fierce opponents of popular revolution, and, in order to prevent events from getting out of hand, they had a candidate for the throne whom they intended to install as soon as possible. The designated candidate was the Duke of Orleans, Louis-Philippe, who could lay claim to the throne as he represented the cadet branch of the Bourbons. Not only that, he represented the 'revolutionary' branch, since his father had voted for the death of his cousin Louis XVI, and Louis-Philippe had himself served in the revolutionary armies, though he later ended up as an *emigré* and a willing collaborator with England. It was these factors which had led to his being considered by the Allies as a possible alternative to Louis XVIII in 1815.

From 1815 to 1830, Louis-Philippe had been careful to avoid any overt clashes with the reigning branch of the Bourbons, but he was not averse to letting it be known that he was there. In 'conservative' liberal circles he was considered to be a viable alternative, should things go wrong with the restored monarchy. Unlike the senior branch, he was not short of heirs, since he had five sons all in good health. Above all, in July 1830 he was available, he was in Paris and therefore could be presented to the Assembly without delay. In an attempt to save the dynasty, Charles X, on abdicating, had named him Lieutenant-General of France, and Regent for his grandson, something which Louis-Philippe decided to overlook. So he became Louis-Philippe I, King of the French, neither by the grace of God nor the will of the nation, but by a sort of conjuring trick, produced like a rabbit out of a hat. Those who feared real revolutionary disorders, but were not enamoured by the prospect of the new monarchy, were told that, 'if the Duke is not proclaimed at once we shall have the Republic'.

It was the absence of Napoleon II, and the fact that he was so little known in his native land, that handicapped his partisans in 1830. Even more depressing was the fact that no person thought of remembering the names of the other members of the family. Only the name of Napoleon himself roused the masses and was capable of producing a riot at street level. Clearly the family's policy of avoiding any political activity had been all too successful, in that few, if any, expected an action on its part that might help the imperialist cause. The events of 1830, however, forced the surviving brothers to abandon total abstention and to make their presence known. Joseph lodged a formal protest with the Chamber of Deputies about the proclamation of Louis-Philippe, claiming that the chamber had usurped the sovereign rights of the people to choose its dynasty. He further pointed out that the people had expressed their wishes in a plebiscite held during the Empire, the last being in 1815. These wishes had been set aside by force of arms, not by an expression of the popular will, and it was therefore possible to question the validity of this act of *force majeure*. Joseph also wrote to the Emperor Francis at Vienna, to Marie-Louise and to Metternich, asking that the Duke of Reichstadt be entrusted to him, so that he could be formally presented to, and recognised by, the French people.

Lucien approached the Austrian Minister in Florence, putting forward the same arguments, and, after some hesitation, Jerome gave his backing to Joseph. To these protests were added those of Hortense. She had also lived quietly since 1815, devoting herself to the upbringing of her second son, Louis Napoleon, while trying to maintain some sort of relationship with her husband. Now she asserted publicly that the people in 1830 had wanted the Empire and Napoleon II. She later revised her opinion, deploring, regretfully, that Napoleon II was really an Austrian Prince whose mother was cordially disliked in France, and who would never be forgiven for her abandonment of Napoleon I. From Rome came a note of caution, in the opinion expressed by *Madame Mère*. Letizia thought that Joseph's protests and projects were ill-conceived because there had been no preparation of public opinion. She also pointed out that Joseph, writing from America, carried little weight. By trying to negotiate with the Emperor Francis, not a favourite in France any more than his daughter, the Bonapartes risked compromising themselves and the dynasty in the eyes of the French people.

This was in fact a key issue, for the new regime had, in September 1830, revoked the laws of exile against almost all those who had been banished in 1815 but had maintained the laws against the Bonapartes. Undoubtedly the family had hoped that repeal would follow the change of regime, but now all its members found themselves faced with continued exile from France. The strategy must therefore be to work for a change of heart by the new King, and his government, and it was unlikely that this would come about if the government in Paris was irritated by political activity on their part. Jerome, the most overtly anxious for the ending of exile, thought that the protestations of 1830 simply made the family's situation worse and were, in any case, meaningless.

While the older members of the Emperor's family debated policy, the next generation moved from words to actions. Louis' two sons, Napoleon Louis who was twenty-six and Louis Napoleon who was twenty-two, saw their obligations in simple terms. Buoyed up by youthful ardour and illusions, they saw that, if return to France lay in the future, then it was Italy which offered them an immediate field action. Although brought up apart, and differently, the elder by the father and the younger by his mother, the two young men soon discovered a common destiny: to take up the burden of the family.

Napoleon Louis, living with his father in Florence, had married his cousin Charlotte, one of Joseph's daughters. He gave every appearance of being settled into his life of exile, and was occupied in building an industrial fortune based on paper manufacture. There is, however, evidence that he engaged in political activities of a conspiratorial kind, with links to the secret society of the Carbonari. The Carbonari, deriving many of their attributes from freemasonry, were dedicated to the cause of Italian unity – and looked back to Napoleon as the first unificator. Napoleon's kingdom of Italy may have been limited in several senses of the word, but it had existed, and so identified the cause of unification with the family of the Bonapartes.

What remains unclear is whether Napoleon Louis drew his younger brother into contact with the secret society. There is no firm evidence of his joining, though in later years his supposed connection was to impinge sharply on his life.[2] In any event, with or without such affiliation, Louis Napoleon's upbringing by his mother had been much more Bonapartist, and certainly more Romantic, than that of his elder brother. The atmosphere of the Swiss refuge at Arenenberg, where Hortense and her son had lived since 1820 after they moved from their initial home in Augsburg, represented everything on which the Romantic Movement thrived: mountains, lakes, forests and an exiled Prince. Hortense had improved on nature by making her home a colony of Beauharnais and Bonaparte relations, where nostalgia for the fallen Empire added to the charming melancholy which pervaded the atmosphere.

At a more practical level, Hortense, addressing Louis Napoleon, reminded him that 'you and your brother are assuredly heirs of Napoleon after the King of Rome, never weary of hoping'. To keep himself in the family tradition, Louis spent his summer breaks at a military camp as a volunteer, joining the Swiss army at its exercises at Thun. He concentrated on studying

The Later Bonapartes

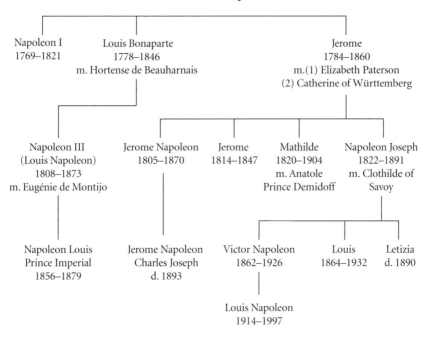

Napoleon I
1769–1821

Louis Bonaparte
1778–1846
m. Hortense de Beauharnais

Jerome
1784–1860
m.(1) Elizabeth Paterson
(2) Catherine of Württemberg

Napoleon III
(Louis Napoleon)
1808–1873
m. Eugénie de Montijo

Jerome Napoleon
1805–1870

Jerome
1814–1847

Mathilde
1820–1904
m. Anatole
Prince Demidoff

Napoleon Joseph
1822–1891
m. Clothilde of
Savoy

Napoleon Louis
Prince Imperial
1856–1879

Jerome Napoleon
Charles Joseph
d. 1893

Victor Napoleon
1862–1926

Louis
1864–1932

Letizia
d. 1890

Louis Napoleon
1914–1997

artillery and military tactics, and was delighted to discover that his commanding officer, Colonel Dufour, was a Napoleonic veteran, so that, through him, he felt he was in touch with the imperial regime.

It was during his service at the summer camp at Thun that he heard the news of the July Revolution, but it was here also that he learned that the change of dynasty had not changed the family's situation. Exile continued, and the ways of exile. So, in November 1830, Louis Napoleon and Hortense set out for Italy on their normal autumn migration. This time, however, the stay in Italy proved to be more eventful than had been anticipated. Louis Napoleon arrived in Rome to see those members of the family who lived there, with *Madame Mère* at the centre of this little court in exile. It included her brother Cardinal Fesch, Pauline and her husband Prince Borghese, together with Lucien and his family, plus Jerome and his wife Catherine. Caroline lived normally in Trieste, then part of Austrian Italy, but, on the news of the Paris revolution, she had moved to Florence to be near to her brother Louis. Joseph was still in America, while Elisa had died in 1826. During Louis' stay in Rome, an insurrection broke out organised by rebels who hoped to overthrow the papal regime, taking advantage of the inter-regnum caused by the death of Pius VIII and before a successor could be elected.

There is a debate as to whether or not Louis Napoleon had links with revolutionary elements in Rome. Certainly the papal authorities were convinced of it, and in spite of protests from his uncle, Cardinal Fesch, he was expelled from papal territory. He immediately returned to his father and brother in Florence, so that when a serious insurrection broke out in central Italy, in January 1831, the two young men were together. This time there is no doubt that they did join the revolutionary movement.[3]

Once it became known that both brothers were involved in the revolt, their father began various moves in an attempt to extricate them from a highly dangerous position that threatened to compromise the entire family. Louis was so horrified that, unexpectedly, he even contacted Hortense directly, begging her to try and rescue their two sons. Austria, recognised by the treaties of 1815 as the guarantor of their maintenance in the Italian peninsula, had immediately responded to the revolts with military intervention and the introduction of martial law. This development put the lives of Napoleon Louis and his brother in danger, not that this worried either young man but, once it was clear to the insurgents that France would not intervene to help them, for fear of launching a full-scale European crisis, the presence of the two Bonapartes became simply an embarrassment. In a last-ditch attempt to persuade the French government that they were not following a Bonapartist agenda, the leaders of the insurrection asked the brothers to retire. Louis Napoleon wrote to his mother, 'they want us to appear as cowards', and went on, quite erroneously, to blame, 'the intrigues of Uncle Jerome and Papa'. In point of fact, Napoleon Louis and he had totally misread the political situation by failing to take into account the possible reactions of the European powers.

The two young men, having been forcibly separated from the main body of the insurgents, were now fugitives from the Austrian army, which by March was in control of the situation and had passed a death sentence on both brothers. Hortense, having been alerted by Louis Napoleon, was now on the move, desperately trying to catch up with her sons, but by the time she reached the town of Forli, where they had last been seen, disaster had struck. She discovered that Napoleon Louis had contracted measles and was already dead, while her younger son was severely ill from the same infection, in an area totally under Austrian control.

The escape of Hortense and her son from Italy is so bizarre and eventful that even a fiction writer would hesitate to commit it to paper. It involved disguises and false passports, and at one-time the Prince lay ill for ten days in a room next to that of the Austrian commander of the port of Ancona. The flight of mother and son, involving frequent perilous journeys, reads like an episode in an historical novel, even though the incidents really happened, but left Louis Napoleon with a permanently weakened constitution. The destination of the fugitives was France, which was reached in mid April, and on 23 April, after fifteen years of exile, the two were in Paris. Hortense made her presence known to Louis-Philippe and asked for an audience, feeling that, even if only temporarily, she and her son were once again at the centre of French affairs.[4]

A hole in the corner interview took place at the Tuileries on 26 April, in the course of which the King expressed his regrets at the necessity of upholding the Law of Exile, while finding a platitude for the occasion: 'The time is not too far distant when there will be no more exiles'. What he made abundantly clear was that the time had not yet come, for the government found the presence of Hortense and her son a threat to the shaky political order which the regime had with difficulty managed to establish. There could be no question of allowing the exiles to remain, for fear that Louis Napoleon's contacts with disaffected sections of French, or more accurately Parisian political society, might lead to a real crisis.

On 5 May, the anniversary of the death of Napoleon I (having deliberately delayed their departure), mother and son became the centre of a demonstration which took place outside their hotel in the Place Vendôme. A substantial crowd, socially mixed in composition, which had assembled around the column surmounted by the statue of Napoleon, cried 'Vive l'Empereur!' until it was dispersed by the National Guard. The result was that on 6 May Hortense and her son were asked to leave France immediately. They set out for England where, after a short stay from May until August, they then decided that they should return to Switzerland.

It was in Switzerland, in July 1832, that they learned of the death at the age of twenty-two of the King of Rome, who had been cut off from all contact with the imperial family since he had been taken from France in 1814. The only member of the family who had actually seen the young Prince since his infancy was Napoleone, Countess Camerata, a daughter of Elisa, who in 1830 went to Vienna determined to see and speak to her cousin. In the event, she had to confine herself to sending him letters and notes, to which he did not reply, but, although she was kept under police surveillance, she was regarded as an eccentric nuisance rather than a threat. She finally managed to waylay the young man and to kiss his hand, at which point he fled. Seemingly, feeling that she had accomplished her mission, Napoleone left Vienna quietly some days later. Apart from this bizarre incident, the Duke of Reichstadt never had any contact with his father's family, and, on his death, he was buried as a Habsburg Prince in their imperial mausoleum at Vienna with no Bonaparte present.

The Bonaparte family, however, had no intention of allowing the death to pass unnoticed. *Madame Mère* had been informed in a letter from Marie-Louise of the death of her grandson, a communication to which she did not reply directly, as an indication of her continued dislike of her former daughter-in-law. As a courtesy, she instructed her brother, Cardinal Fesch, to reply to Vienna via the Vatican, while, for her part, *Madame Mère*, in accordance with protocol, decreed court mourning to be observed by all the Bonapartes.

For the family, the death of Napoleon's son was important because it required rethinking the succession. For this reason Louis Napoleon went to London in the spring of 1833 to meet his uncles, Joseph and Lucien, to discuss the affairs of the dynasty. Joseph, by virtue of the succession established in 1804, was now its head, and he introduced a discussion on the 'new' hereditary settlement as devised by Lucien, designed to supplant the Law of Succession of 1804. The main proposal was that the French people should choose, by universal suffrage, between the three claimants – Legitimist, Orleanist and Joseph Bonaparte! How this was to be done, and what it was meant to achieve, was far from clear except to the uncles, who saw it as a device to remove Louis Napolean from the succession. Both Joseph and Lucien, with the support of Louis, were alarmed by the fact that Louis Napolean clearly saw himself as a legitimate heir, as they considered him to be hot-headed and irresponsible. By his activities in 1830–31 he had brought about his brother's death and had caused the expulsion of all the Bonapartes, except *Madame Mère*, from their refuge in Rome. It is not clear if the young Prince had any foreknowledge of what the 'new' succession law contained, but whatever Louis Napoleon hoped for as a consequence of the death of Napolean II, his position was made clear to him by the uncles. They saw him as a nuisance, and a possible disturber of the family peace.

Angered and disappointed by the indifference and hostility he had met, the Prince felt that he could at least employ his time in England usefully, so he undertook a tour of the manufacturing districts of the midlands and the north. The uncles, happy to see him go, felt that they had dealt with him and that he would no longer be a problem. As for Louis Napoleon, he now had an opportunity to learn about the new world of industry which was beginning to transform England. The tour of 1833 was followed by others in 1838 and 1839. As a result, he ended by being well informed about the nature of industrial growth, for his interests were genuine and went far beyond surface inquiries. He wanted to know how it was that England had become the first great industrial power in Europe, as he had a conviction that France could and should have an equally successful industrial future.

The encounter with his uncles convinced Louis Napoleon of one thing; if no one of that generation was willing to take up the cause of the dynasty, he would have to do it himself. Since the Duke of Reichstadt and his own elder brother were dead, and given that the uncles were actively opposed to any real assertion of dynastic claims, he felt that he had freedom of action. He began by publishing an essay *Considérations sur la Suisse*, on the political and military state of Switzerland, a work which had very little to do with Switzerland but a great deal to do with the importance of hereditary rights. He sent a copy of the pamphlet to Joseph, who replied thanking him formally but without comment.

Whatever the uncles may have thought about him, there was someone who recognised his potential. The Austrian Chancellor, Metternich, had already opined that 'The day of the Duke's death [the Duke of Reichstadt's death], he will look upon himself as called upon to be head of the French Republic.' A close observer of the Bonapartes, Metternich was anticipating, but it is possible that he had read Louis Napolean's book on Switzerland and realised that Louis Napoleon was making his first moves by publishing a reply to the constitution drawn up by Lucien and Joseph by stressing heredity and linking it to universal suffrage. Let the people ratify the choice within the *legitimate* dynasty, that is the Bonapartes, whom they had chosen in 1804 and endorsed on subsequent occasions. By publicly repudiating his elders in this way, Louis Napoleon was also openly proclaiming himself to be the official Pretender. He would not be challenged by any among the younger generation, where there were only two possible contenders, the two sons of Jerome. Neither showed any inclination to become a involved in dynastic matters, largely because of their father, who was determined to come to an accommodation with the existing French government so that he and his family might return to France as soon as possible. This remained Jerome's obsession until he was able to achieve his purpose in 1847, by which time his elder son had died, leaving only Prince Napoleon Jerome as his heir.

Louis Napoleon had now to consider his next move. Realising the importance of becoming more widely known, he turned to literary work, producing in 1836 a manual on artillery. It was designed to focus attention on the author. The fact that a Bonaparte had written a 500 page work on artillery certainly did not go unnoticed in military circles, but, just in case it had, the author managed to ensure that copies were distributed to various regiments in the French army.

Feeling that he had prepared the ground, not just by his publications but by judicious use of friends who acted as his agents in France, the Prince decided to leave literary activities and to try a *coup d'état*. The city chosen for this attempt was Strasbourg, not an accidental choice: it was a garrison town, it was close to the frontier with Germany, and it had a reputation for being strongly Republican and Bonapartist in sentiment. Already in 1831, as a by-product of the 1830 Revolution, there had been an attempt to raise the garrison in favour of Napoleon II.

Louis Napoleon's attempt, made in October 1836, was a total failure and the Prince was arrested, together with many of his leading companions. The government, fearing that any publicity might be counter-productive, decided that the less said, or done, about the affair the better, especially as it had failed so spectacularly. Louis Napoleon was pardoned by Louis-Philippe, who had no wish for a show trial that would give a platform to the Bonapartsts, but he was banished to the United States of America, disembarking in New York in March 1837.

Within the family there were immediate reactions to the Strasbourg affair. Joseph hoped that all the brothers would issue a joint declaration condemning the attempt, but Louis, who had at first been furious with his son, decided it was all due to the bad influence of his mother leading her son astray. Having come to this conclusion, and unpredictable as ever, he swung round and wrote a letter of forgiveness to New York, in which he reconciled himself to his son's ambitions. Lucien was totally condemnatory, while Jerome, much more interested in a quiet life, was at that moment very occupied with a family dispute. This was over the inheritance from their recently deceased mother's will.[5] He contented himself by advising caution, and no family declaration, but he insisted that his daughter Mathilde break her engagement to his nephew, a move condemned by Louis Napoleon's father as 'ignoble'.

Joseph was left to fulminate alone about the attempt, which he condemned as 'this mad attempt which could have compromised us all because it has produced the label "Bonapartism". We absolutely reject such a definition.' It was too late, however, for Bonapartism was officially born as a political ideology at Strasbourg, so that Louis Napoleon's attempt was very far from being a failure. It focused attention on the dynasty, and, although the meaning of the label now attached to it was as yet unclear, it would very soon have a defined programme.[6]

For the present Louis Napoleon was obliged to consider what to do in the New World. Writing from New York to his friend Vieillard (the former tutor to his late brother), he announced his intention of seeing something of the United States of America and then returning to England. In the event, nothing happened as he had planned, because, in June 1837, he received a letter from his mother, who informed him that she was dying of an inoperable cancer. Sending him her blessing, and thanking him for having made her happy in this life, she expressed the hope that they would eventually meet in the next. Determined to be with his mother in her final days, Louis did not hesitate, leaving New York in mid-June on a ship bound for Liverpool. The French government, alarmed by news of his return, refused to allow him any passage through France to Switzerland, although well aware of the reasons for his journey, and persuaded other European states to do the same. Eventually he obtained an American passport, in the name of Robinson, and, having eluded French agents in England, he managed to arrive at Arenenberg while his mother was still alive.

Hortense lingered on until October, her death leaving her son stricken by grief. That this was no passing emotion is shown by the fact that at his death his wallet was found to contain the letter his mother had sent him in New York, which he had carried with him the rest of his life. She had always supported him and, in her will, offered him support from beyond the grave. 'I have no political advice to give my son, I know that he understands his position and all the duties his name imposes on him.'[7]

Hortense's views were in sharp contrast to those of Joseph, who, in a letter to Louis Napoleon, accused him of violating all principles of family and honour: 'You want to step over me during my lifetime and that of your father.' This accusation caused the young man to react sharply: 'When action is required, you turn to the young. Everything has its season, each man, each age fulfils a different need.' The final sentence was both true and cruel: 'When I championed our cause [at Strasbourg] and risked being shot by a Bourbon, you took the side of the executioners.'[8]

Meanwhile, the French government committed a foolish error by publicly threatening the Swiss government that if it did not expel Louis Napoleon they would be forced to take steps. To make their point, they mustered a force of 25,000 men on the frontier between France and Switzerland. This action provided the Prince with a tremendous propaganda victory. He left Switzerland, having issued a dignified protest exonerating the Swiss and making political capital from the illegality of France's bullying proceedings. Having done that, he left once again for exile in England. The English press, and certain members of the English government, advised France not to try the same tactics in England: 'Lord Melbourne's reply to that would be swift.'

Unlike his uncle Lucien, who had been in England as a 'supervised guest' living in the country, Louis Napoleon took up the life of a man about town, establishing himself in London at a smart address in Carlton House Terrace. He acquired a mistress, was welcomed into aristocratic society, and was generally treated with affection and respect. He was received by academic bodies, by the Lord Mayor of London and other dignitaries, including many politicians, all of which gave him status. Perhaps more of a Beauharnais than a Bonaparte, Louis Napoleon had great charm, linked to a fine mind and elegant manners. He appears in Disraeli's novel *Endymion* as Prince Florestan, a dandy and dilettante, but Disraeli missed the point, because he ignored the hours that Louis Napoleon spent in the British Museum Reading Room and in Westminster Library. He also, as he had done on previous occasions, used his time in England to travel through the country, paying particular attention to the industrial regions, where he displayed great interest in methods of production, industrial techniques and, less usually for someone in his position, in the condition of the working people.

All of this was, however, of secondary importance. What really mattered to him was his destiny, for, like his uncle after the battle of Lodi, Louis Napoleon was convinced that he had a political role to play. The only problem was how to put it into effect. As experience had already taught him that he needed to be his own impresario, he now set about the business of self-promotion very methodically.

In 1839 he published *Des idées Napoléoniennes*, a work that underlined his determination to be taken seriously as a political thinker. It was, in effect, an adroit propaganda exercise, being both an appeal to history, vindicating Napoleon I, and a manifesto offering France a new Bonaparte. He argued the cause of the dynasty by identifying it with France and its development since the Revolution of 1789. Only Napoleon had understood what had happened at that time and had been able to control and develop the consequences of this great movement. To do this he had founded a dynasty, 'an hereditary family which would safeguard the interests of all, and whose power rested on the democratic temper of the nation'.

Although the book contained new ideas, it was essentially an elaboration, and a codification, of what had been written and published as a result of Napoleon I's activities on St Helena based, above all, on what Napoleon had himself said. There was no question of a regime that had been despotic. All that Napoleon had done was to protect France and the gains of the

Revolution; and it was to ensure this that he had fought so long and hard to defend them. Putting the interest of the nation above his own personal feelings, he had divorced Josephine and married Marie-Louise, a worthwhile sacrifice, since it had given him an heir and therefore safeguarded the future of the dynasty. Furthermore, if Napoleon's plans had been successful, his son would have ruled over a new and unified European Confederation. Waterloo had ended all hope of that, but it had also reopened the possibility of revolution, by removing the one system and the one dynasty capable of controlling it: 'take care that this [revolution] does not overthrow you'.

It is important to have some understanding of *Des idées Napoliennes*, not just because it went through four editions in France, and sold 500,000 copies, but because it was translated into all the major European languages, including Russian, and was widely read and commented on. As a work of propaganda it was superb, for, as a result, it could no longer be said that Bonapartism had no clear doctrine. It now most certainly had, and it also had the man who claimed to represent it.[9]

The year 1840 turned out to be the one in which the Bonapartes came to public notice in several ways. The death of Lucien produced a spate of articles and commentaries in the press about Napoleon and the Empire, but these were soon overshadowed by the public announcement of the decision taken by Louis-Philippe to bring back Napoleon's body from St Helena. What gave these events added importance was the fact that they took place against a background of an international crisis that involved France in a confrontation with the Waterloo coalition. Having attempted a foreign policy manoeuvre in the Near East, which appeared to the other powers to be an attempt at a new form of empire-building, the four Allies of 1815 re-emerged, determined to put France in its place, which they did by the Treaty of London of 1841. Having talked war, the French government meekly chose peace and, as a result, became deeply unpopular. The press, in particular those papers of a Bonapartist tendency, made great play with the fact that the Emperor was to be brought back to France, but to a France humiliated before Europe.

Inspired by the situation in France, and clearly motivated by the thought that the return of the Emperor's body would give a tremendous impetus to Bonapartist sentiment, Louis Napoleon decided on a second attempt at a *coup d'état* designed to overthrow the Orleanist monarchy. In August, with a handful of supporters, he set sail from Gravesend, sailing down the

Thames on a hired paddle steamer, intending to land at Boulogne, where he expected to find support from the military garrison and, it was rumoured, from certain political figures. It was true that many in political circles had been angered by France's humiliation, and Louis Napoleon assumed that they might be so incensed as to support a possible Bonapartist restoration. Whatever was hoped for, the attempt came to nothing and the Prince was arrested. This time the government was determined not to ignore the affair, which was much more serious than that of 1836, and sent him for trial before the Chamber of Peers, the upper house of the French Assembly.[10]

Louis Napoleon turned the trial into a triumphal assertion of his rights and of his political credo. He offered no defence of his conduct but instead launched an attack on the assembled peers, seizing a splendid opportunity to put forward the dynastic claims of his family, for many of the peers, or their sons, who were sitting in judgement were creations of Napoleon I. Neither Louis Napoleon, nor his able advocate Berryer, were there to argue law; they were there to argue history. Berryer also had his own personal score to settle with the existing regime, for he was a fervent Legitimist and looked on the Orleans monarchy with contempt as usurpers.

Law or history, the verdict was given: Charles Louis Napoleon Bonaparte was sentenced to perpetual imprisonment in the fortress of Ham. By an irony of history, at the very moment in October 1840 when the dead man was being exhumed from his tomb on St Helena, the living one was being entombed for life in a dreary fortress on the Somme. The result was that the government drew few dividends from its attempts to kill Bonapartism with kindness; by adopting its symbols on the one hand while suppressing its living representative on the other, it simply exposed itself either to ridicule or contempt.

On 15 December 1840, Napoleon's body reached Paris, being transferred, with great ceremony, to the Invalides. From the fortress of Ham came a message: 'Sire, do not resent your family's inability to be there to receive you; your exile and your misfortunes ended with your life; ours continues still, but I remember how you caressed me as a child and I hear you say, "You suffer for me, my friend, and I am pleased with you".'[11]

Louis Napoleon always referred to his six years' incarceration as 'the University Years', a *bon mot* that was not meant to be simply an amusing comment, nor was it, for all through this time he studied, wrote and

published, transforming his fortress prison into a sort of St Helena on the
Somme. He relied on friends to supply him with the books he needed for
his literary, historical and political works. In particular, he relied on the
good offices of his god-daughter Hortense Cornu, the daughter of one of
his mother's personal maids, who had married the painter Sebastien
Cornu. Although both she and her husband were Republican rather than
Bonapartist in sentiment, she was devoted to the memory of her former
employer and to Louis Napoleon, with whom she had grown up. Able to
consult works in libraries, and often to arrange for them to be sent to the
Prince at Ham, she became virtually his research assistant. No political
differences were allowed to mar their friendship, which was deep and true,
as their correspondence reveals.[12] In any event, it was reassuring for
Hortense to see that, in his writings, Louis Napoleon defended the
Republican cause, while he for his part was content to do so, convinced
that there was much common ground between the two political tendencies.
In the situation in which he now found himself, he needed to seek out
support from any quarter sympathetic to his predicament and the
Republicans were unrelentingly hostile to the present regime.

Louis Napoleon's publications during this period were numerous and
varied, ranging from a project for the building of a canal in Nicaragua,
joining the Atlantic to the Pacific, to disquisitions on the use of sugar
beet. He also, and this especially pleased Hortense, became a regular
correspondent of a local newspaper that was Republican in its views. The
choice of this paper was not fortuitous. The whole basis of the Napoleonic
dynasty's claim was that its antecedents, indeed the very reason for its
existence, lay in the Revolution. Defined as 'neither red nor white but blue',
a reference to the tricolour flag, the inference was that the dynasty represented neither the red flag of the extremes of revolution nor the white flag
of the Bourbon monarchy. The Prince's aim was, therefore, not immediately
to propose a dynastic solution but to produce something which relied on
political content rather than specific form. The important thing was that
he, as a Bonaparte, should be seen as indispensable in producing a regime
better suited to France than the existing monarchy of Louis-Philippe.

Within the family group, the death of Joseph in 1844 made the way
forward less difficult. Louis Bonaparte had become less critical of his son,
to the extent that they had been, more or less, reconciled. Indeed Louis had
written to him at the moment of his arrest and imprisonment, giving him

his blessing, but, in his usual contrary way, had then ceased to have any
further correspondence with his son. Now, with Joseph's death, Louis
became titular Emperor of the French according to the constitution of the
Empire, and Louis Napoleon therefore became the 'official' heir.

In 1844, Louis Napoleon published what was possibly his most
important work, *L'extinction du paupérisme* (the suppression of poverty)
more important than the *Des idées Napoleoniennes*, because this brochure
proposed a solution to the new problem of what was being called 'the social
question'. As a result of increasing industrialisation, French society was
acquiring a new social group, with the creation of a working class employed
in factories, and this new group, together with the already existing class of
artisans, who had always dominated French industry, existed in deplorable
living and working conditions. In his analysis of the problem, Louis
Napoleon argued that it was an outrage 'that at least one-tenth of the
population is in rags and dies of hunger, surrounded by thousands of
manufactured products which it cannot buy, and millions of the Earth's
products which it cannot consume'. The solution to this was, according to
him, a programme of investment in industry and a vast programme of
public works. This would end a situation where 'we do not over produce,
rather we do not consume enough'. The message was clear: the whole
concept of *laissez faire* must be ended, and so must governmental
indifference to the plight of its citizens. A strong government would make
an end of sectional interests, and would give the necessary impetus to
economic growth by organising a system in which the masses could
participate and draw benefits from its organisation. As a first step, it was
essential to end the censitary franchise based on property and wealth, which
had been the basis of succeeding regimes since 1815, and to replace it with
universal male suffrage. This was a key argument, for it was at this point
that Bonapartism and Republicanism joined forces, both being committed
to the extension of the franchise, though the Republican programme
rejected the plebiscite as a means of popular consultation, largely because
of its association with the Empire.

The great strength of Louis Napoleon's social programme was that it
was easy to grasp, particularly as its author had a gift for clear and well
reasoned exposition of his ideas. As a result, between 1844 and 1848 the
brochure went through six editions, though, as contemporary hostile critics
noted sneeringly, 'his only admirers were to be found at La Villette and in

the Faubourg St-Antoine' (both working-class districts of Paris). These
critics missed the point: the message had reached precisely the audience
for whom it was destined.[13]

By 1845 the groundswell of Bonapartism as a political movement was
becoming difficult for the authorities to ignore, though at this juncture it
seemed still to be under control. At the same time, paradoxically, just as
conditions on the outside seemed to be becoming more favourable for
him, the Prince showed signs of becoming discouraged as the years of
imprisonment began seriously to affect his morale. He wrote to his
correspondent Hortense Cornu: 'Prison is a living death. No one writes to
me. I'm forgotten, and sometimes I'm even happy to be surrounded by
silence'. On top of this, his health had begun to deteriorate. Since 1831 he
had suffered from a weakness in the kidneys as result of the severe attack of
measles during his time as a fugitive. On one occasion, Hortense had been
forced to allow her son to spend a night in the open air in spite of his
condition, and it was this which was to affect his health all his life. To
constant stomach pains were added attacks of rheumatism, brought on by
the cold and the damp of his fortress lodgings. Above all, there was the
general sense of despair that must attack any prisoner, no matter how easy
the conditions of his imprisonment, for some attempt had been made to
make his life sentence easier to bear by allowing him frequent visits by
distinguished people, many of them friends from his sojourn in England.
In particular, a thoughtful prison commander saw to it that there were other
consolations. The young woman who was the Prince's laundress, Eléonore
Veugeot-Camus, became his mistress and presented him with two sons,
Eugène, born in May 1843, and Louis, born in 1845. Nevertheless, even this
relaxation of the rigours of prison life could not compensate for a lack
of freedom.

Suddenly, in 1845, the situation changed because ex-King Louis became
seriously ill and expressed a wish to see his son before he died. Louis
Napoleon immediately made representations to the government, asking for
permission to go to Florence to be at his father's deathbed. His request was
backed up by his father, who wrote to men whom he had known during
the Empire, asking them to use their influence to help his son, so that he
might at least come and see him before his death. The government, seizing
a chance to turn the situation to its advantage, proposed that Louis
Napoleon should make a solemn renunciation of any dynastic pretensions;

in return for this, Louis-Philippe would pardon him. In other words, in exchange for giving up his moral liberty he could have his material freedom.

Louis Napoleon refused this affront to his dignity, but wrote to the King, giving his solemn word of honour that he would return to prison once he had seen his father. The King did not even reply to this letter and, as a result of these failed negotiations, the Prince decided to liberate himself, avoiding any need to compromise his future activities. The escape was carefully planned, based on the fact that, because of building works going on inside the fortress, workmen came and went frequently, and that the guards paid them little attention. As a first step, the Prince's valet, Thélin, obtained a set of workman's overalls to help his master blend in with the others working on the building site. On the morning of 25 May 1846, Louis shaved off his beard and moustache, put on a black wig, and, carrying a plank on his shoulder to hide one side of his face, walked out of his room. His valet went first, so that the guard would pay no attention to the workman who was following him a little distance behind. There was an anxious moment, as a result of the Prince's decision to put a clay pipe in his mouth, the better to fulfil his workman's role. At the final guard post the pipe fell from his mouth and broke but, with amazing self-control, Louis Napoleon stopped, calmly picked up the pieces and walked out of the gate. Once clear of the fortress, the Prince made for the local cemetery, where he had agreed to wait for his valet, who was to bring a small coach to take them to the town of Valenciennes from which they would catch train to Brussels. From Valenciennes, the train would take only fifteen minutes to cross the frontier into Belgium and he would be free.

At Ham the escape was not discovered until the evening, because the Prince's friend, Doctor Conneau, who shared his captivity, had managed to convince the commander of the garrison that his patient had to stay in his room all day because he was ill and should not be disturbed. In the evening, however, the commandant insisted on seeing his prisoner. All he found was a dummy in the prisoner's bed, the prisoner himself being already in Brussels.[14]

In the afternoon of 27 May the Prince arrived in London, where he immediately took rooms at the Brunswick Hotel in Jermyn Street under the name of the Count of Arenenberg. Later in the afternoon, he went for a walk, and in Bond Street hailed the carriage of his friend Lord Malmesbury, who for a moment did not recognise the Prince with neither his beard nor moustache. That evening Malmesbury found himself at a reception, which was also being attended by one of the attachés of the French Embassy, whom his fellow guest informed of his meeting with the Prince. Immediately, a very pale and agitated attaché left the reception.

The same evening, the Prince dined at Gore House, at the invitation of his old friend Lady Blessington. It was an intimate occasion, since the other guests were Lady Blessington's two nieces, the Count d'Orsay and John Forster, the friend and future biographer of Charles Dickens, who knew the Prince from his previous stay in London. After dinner the Prince quite calmly entertained them with the story of his escape, telling it as though it was one of the most natural things in the world to have been condemned to life imprisonment and, after six years, to have escaped from gaol.

His fellow guests were even more astonished by his expressing the conviction that he was on the threshold of fulfilling his destiny, which, in so far as they could grasp it, was to rule France. As he wrote to his cousin, the Marchioness of Hamilton, 'I don't belong to myself, I belong to my name and to my country'. For him, it was only a matter of awaiting the moment that would inevitably come.

7

The Restoration

In a letter to the French Ambassador in London, Louis Napoleon explained why he had decided to escape from his imprisonment. He justified his action by pointing out that escape was the only way for him to see his elderly father who was dying, the government having refused him the possibility of so doing. In the event the Prince never did see his father, who died in Florence on 25 September 1846 while his son was still trying to obtain a passport and permission to go to Tuscany. In his will Louis left his son, 'as a particular mark of my affection', not only all his own decorations and souvenirs of the Empire, but also everything in his possession which had belonged to the Emperor Napoleon. The publication of the will, and this bequest in particular, confirmed the Bonapartists in their acceptance of Louis Napoleon as Emperor of the French, by right of succession to his father.

It was one thing for the faithful to accept the new dynastic succession, but it was difficult to see how it could become the view of the bulk of the French nation. The political structure of the July Monarchy, with its restricted franchise, precluded any means of achieving a parliamentary breakthrough by the normal electoral process. Furthermore, since 1840 the regime appeared to have reached a point of balance, with Guizot seemingly permanently at the head of government, enjoying the full support of the King. A stable parliamentary majority was achieved because the 240,000 electors who were eligible to vote were easily managed by a system of patronage. This system was denounced by its critics as representing 'the principle of Chinese immobility', so ordered as to be virtually unchangeable. Appearances were deceptive. Republicans, Legitimists, who had never forgiven 1830, and Bonapartists, whose memories were even longer, all agitated – not necessarily hoping for a revolution – demanding change, in particular an extension of the franchise. In the late 1840s the crisis caused by bad harvests, economic recession and general discontent began to give a sharper and more menacing edge to political agitation as working people began to involve themselves and to show their strength.[1]

It was now that the small Bonapartist groups began to reap the harvest of Louis Napoleon's literary efforts, particularly his pamphlet on the suppression of poverty. The fundamental strength of Bonapartism lay in its ability to provide a fusion with Republicanism – 'the Republic is in the Empire' – a slogan which made sense to both groups, especially in the demand for the introduction of universal male suffrage. In the thirty odd years since the fall of Napoleon, folk memory had perpetuated and extended the cult of the Emperor, and this collective memory was willing to see in the nephew a promise of a return to the imperial regime. Those readers of Louis Napoleon's pamphlets who inhabited the working-class districts of Paris and other major cities, and who had been so despised by the governing class, were about to show that they had understood what they had read.

For the moment Louis Napoleon was content to wait upon events, for, as he wrote to his cousin Marie of Baden, now Marchioness of Douglas, 'because fortune has twice betrayed me, I feel that my destiny is near fulfilment. I am awaiting my hour'. While waiting, the Prince filled in his time in London very agreeably. He had rented a house at 3 King Street, St James's, an unpretentious but elegant residence. From here he visited the top echelon of aristocratic society, ranging from the Duke of Beaufort and the Duke of Devonshire to the Marquess and Marchioness of Douglas, who were his relations. London clubs opened their doors to him, and some, like the Army and Navy, elected him an honorary member. To complete the picture of an idle man about town, the Prince had a mistress, Elizabeth Ann Harriet, better known as Miss Howard. A beauty, socially accomplished and with a lively wit, she was at twenty-four an attractive catch since, as a result of her progress in her profession, she was a very wealthy woman. Courted by several, she refused all other offers, having fallen in love with the Prince. Alexander Dumas said of her that 'she loved her 'Poleon' as ardently as Desdemona loved Othello', and she certainly gave proof of it.

The picture of an idle and dissipated forty-year old is not an attractive one, and would hardly have served to endear Louis Napoleon to any potential supporters, had it been the whole picture. Always economical in speech, seeming often to be lost in some sort of vague daydream, there are occasional glimpses into the Prince's mind. A friend of his, Colonel Damer, with whom Louis often talked, remarked to a mutual friend, Lord Alvanley, that 'he has a thousand good qualities. But on the subject of politics he is as mad as a hatter'. This remark was occasioned by the Prince's saying quite cheerfully, to the colonel, how much he looked forward to receiving him in the Tuileries before too long.[2]

Louis Napoleon kept himself well informed about events in France, at one level simply by reading the newspapers, and by talking to those who had access to information because of their position in English political society, and who were also his friends. There was also another level of information, supplied by sympathisers in France, many of them virtual agents in the Prince's employ. From 1847 onwards he had the added advantage of having members of the family installed in Paris, for Jerome, together with his son, Prince Napoleon Jerome, had finally achieved his aim of being able to reside in France. He eventually received from Louis-Philippe a promise of a pension of 100,000 Francs, but it came too late, for the overthrow of the Orleans monarchy in February 1848 dramatically changed the lives of all the Bonapartes.

The Revolution of February 1848, not unlike that of 1830, came about in order to prevent something worse. The refusal of the King and his leading ministers to yield to political pressure for an extension of the franchise produced a situation in which even those groups which had been responsible for the monarchy's creation turned against it. The propertied and professional classes had thrown their weight behind Louis-Philippe in 1830, for fear of unleashing a real revolution. Now, in 1848, they found themselves once again confronted by a stubborn monarch who refused to see that only timely concession to public discontents would prevent a serious revolutionary outbreak. Those among the political class who made the first moves did not want to overthrow the established regime, they wanted to reform it, so that it could continue; but, rather like the monarchy itself, they totally misjudged the situation. By the time the King had agreed to make concessions, and had on 24 February been persuaded to abdicate in favour of his grandson, the insurrectionary crowds had demanded, and obtained, the proclamation of the Republic and the establishment of a provisional government.

The news of the proclamation of the Republic reached London almost immediately, though no details were as yet available, since no letters or newspapers had arrived from Paris, but Louis Napoleon did not hesitate. On the morning of the 22 February, accompanied by his friend Count Orsi and his valet Thélin, he caught a train from Charing Cross bound for Dover and the crossing to France. He had acquired an English passport and entered at Calais, unrecognised and without any difficulty. By the 28th he was in Paris, installed in the Hôtel des Princes in the Rue Richelieu, from where he sent a letter to the provisional government of the Republic:

> Gentlemen, the people of Paris having destroyed by their efforts the last traces of the foreign invasion [a reference to 1815], I hasten back from exile to place myself under the flag of the Republic which has just been proclaimed. Without any other ambition than that of serving my country, I announce my arrival to the provisional government.[3]

That evening, crowds demonstrated outside the hotel in which the Prince was staying, thanks to the activities of groups of Bonapartists who had made his presence in Paris known. There had already been marches and meetings in the working-class areas of the city, during which many cried 'Vive Napoléon!', and some had even demanded that he be named head of the provisional government. Alarmed by this, the government sent a deputation to the Prince, saying that, while they had no wish to deprive him of his right to be in France, thereby implicitly recognising that the Law of Exile was not to be invoked, they asked him, given the present state of public disorder, to leave the country. Louis Napoleon left, having made a dignified protest, and returned to London; but the journey had not been fruitless, for he had now ceased to be a legend and had become a positive and living expression of the imperial dynasty. As far as the Law of Exile was concerned, it was in fact only formally abrogated in May 1848, preventing Louis Napoleon from standing in the elections held in the April. This legal obstacle soon turned out to have been a blessing in disguise.

One of his major problems was the lack of any real organisation to maintain and foster his cause. Thirty-three years had passed since the fall of the Empire, and many of those who would have supported the imperial cause in 1830 were either dead or had rallied to the recently defunct regime. Others had become Republican – though this allegiance was eventually to prove a help rather than a hindrance when it came to promoting the Prince's cause. The quick visit which he had made to Paris had one very important consequence, for it enabled the Prince to find individuals who would work for him and who would try to canalise the various disparate currents which made up the Bonapartist movement. Fragmented from lack of leadership, it now needed to be directed.

The main direction of these activities was entrusted to Jean Fialin, the self-styled 'Viscount of Persigny', who had been one of the principal co-conspirators with Louis Napoleon in 1836 in organising the attempted *coup* at Strasbourg. An ex-military man, he had, as a virtual soldier of fortune, pursued a chequered military career, during which he had come to the notice of ex-King Joseph, who gave him an introduction to Louis Napoleon. This proved to be the turning-point of his life, for he found his true home in his devotion to the Bonapartist cause and to its representative. In 1839, having served a light prison sentence as punishment for his participation in the Strasbourg affair, he joined the Prince in London, and it was here, in 1840, that he wrote and published his *Lettres de Londres*, propaganda pamphlets extolling the virtues and capacities of the Prince, comparing him to Octavian, Julius Caesar's nephew who became the Emperor Augustus. Given the strength of his convictions, and his closeness to Louis Napoleon, Persigny willingly took part in the second attempt at a *coup*, that of Boulogne in 1840. This time, as we know, the adventure ended badly for all the leading activists, and Persigny, for his part in the ill-starred adventure, was sentenced to twenty years' imprisonment.

As a consequence of the 1848 Revolution he had been freed, so he was already in Paris when Louis Napoleon arrived on 28 February, and he immediately contacted the latter on his arrival. His zeal for the cause and his determination impressed the Prince, who had no hesitation, in entrusting him with the formation of political groups which would promote the Bonapartist cause in the forthcoming elections.[4]

Persigny would have liked to try for a *coup de force*, but Louis Napoleon, older and wiser now, saw that the way forward was in an alliance with the Republicans, who clearly had a substantial and organised popular support. The alliance would be tactical, but in the short run it was the best move, an analysis which was borne out by the result of elections, held for the first time under universal male suffrage, which gave an electorate of nearly ten million. Unable to be a candidate because of the Law of Exile, the Prince saw with satisfaction that members of the Bonaparte family were elected: Prince Napoleon, the son of ex-King Jerome, Pierre Bonaparte, one of Lucien's children, and Prince Murat, the son of the former King of Naples. All three were elected on their own account without involving their cousin. While it was disconcerting to discover that his relatives could act for themselves, with no need of him, it was reassuring to realise that it was their name, and their connection to the Empire, which had enabled them to be successful. If it had done that for them, what might it not do for him?

The name would, in the event, need to do a very great deal, for several reasons. First, Napoleon had arrived in Paris almost as a tourist, knowing little of the city. Perhaps more dispiriting was the fact that he remained personally unknown outside a very restricted circle of sympathisers. Secondly, all political activity needs to be well financed and the Prince was short of funds. His father's death had given him a capital of some three million francs, but much of this had gone to pay back sums already borrowed. As for his mother's inheritance, that was long since gone. Always generous to a fault, he took care of those who were close to him: for example, in return for his devotion at Ham, he bought his friend Dr Conneau a medical practice for twenty thousand francs. By 1848, the Prince was living on credit, based on his 'expectations', financed by the major banks such as Barings or the Rothschilds, together with loans cobbled together from various financial agencies.[5] This lack of money explains why so much had to be left to his few agents and friends in France, who had to make a great noise by beating loudly on very small drums.

They were successful beyond their wildest hopes because of the magic of the name. Songs, cheap medallions, prints, handbills, small flags inscribed 'Vive le Prince Louis!', even matchboxes with his name printed on them, all cheap, but all effective means of popular propaganda, were widely distributed by his supporters. When the time came for nominations for the partial elections to the Assembly, to be held in early June, the Bonapartist agents were anxious to test public opinion and pressed Louis Napoleon to allow his name to go forward. It turned out to have been the correct strategy, as he was elected in four departments: the Seine, the Yonne, the Charente Inférieure and Corsica. Even more significant was the fact that when he arrived to take his place in the Assembly he was greeted by crowds shouting, 'Vive Napoléon!', and even 'Vive l'Empereur!'

The government was alarmed by this and considered invalidating the election, but were reassured by Louis Blanc, a leading Republican, who said in his speech: 'Let the nephew of the Emperor draw close to the sun of the Republic; I am certain he will disappear in its rays.' Others spoke in the same vein, often being openly contemptuous of the Prince's abilities. As a result, his election was validated by the Assembly. The Prince, perhaps momentarily overcome by the rays of the Republican sun, decided once again to abandon his parliamentary seat. In his speech of resignation, he ended by saying: 'The hostility of the executive power means that I must refuse an honour which it is supposed I have gained by the use of intrigue. But, if the people should charge me with any duties, I should know how to fulfil them.' In his statement it was clear that the devil was not in the detail but in the ambiguity of the phrasing.[6] Once again, Louis Napoleon returned London to await the outcome of events in Paris, events with which he had no intention of being associated, for he had correctly foreseen that in Paris a crisis point had been reached in the relations between the conservative Republican majority in the Assembly and the mass of the people.

The incident which provoked the confrontation was the closure by the government of the national workshops which had been established in the early days of the Revolution. Having decreed the 'right to work', the government needed to provide for the lack of it, for trade was virtually at a standstill. This meant dealing with increasing numbers of unemployed, 14,000 in March had risen to over 100,000 in June, all maintained by what were virtually handouts from the government. On 21 June, a decree was issued closing these workshops and ending all payments, an action which resulted in an outbreak of violence in Paris that lasted until its suppression by General Cavaignac after four days of bloody street fighting.

The government was merciless in its reaction. Fifteen thousand people were arrested, many were condemned to hard labour after a summary trial by councils of war, while over four thousand were transported to Algeria without trial. For Louis Napoleon the June days would provide the catalyst for his triumph. He had not been in any way involved in these terrible events, while those who had perpetrated them had become an object of loathing to large sections of the populace. Whatever its founders had hoped that the Second Republic might be, recent events had changed its actual and future shape for ever.[7]

In the wake of the June insurrection, partial elections to the Assembly had to be held for the new session that would begin in September. This time there were fifteen vacant seats and, in August, Prince Louis declared himself a candidate, pointing out that he 'had remained a stranger to every kind of manifestation and political manoeuvre'. He was elected for five of the fifteen seats, and this time, significantly, topped the poll in Paris. On 24 September, in his fortieth year, the nephew of Napoleon arrived in Paris and took rooms in a hotel on the Place Vendôme. From his window he could contemplate the famous column surmounted by the statue of his uncle, whose genius had been the guiding star of his life and whose achievements formed the basis of his faith in himself as heir to what the dynasty had created.

The Assembly in which the newly-elected deputy took his seat was in the process of elaborating a new constitution, which appeared in November 1848. It provided for a single chamber assembly of 750 deputies, elected by universal male suffrage, and a President of the Republic, also elected by universal male suffrage. He was to be elected for four years but would be ineligible for re-election until an interval of four years had passed. The constitution was so devised that the presidential powers were controlled by the Assembly, and its makers felt that, thanks to careful drafting, every eventuality had been covered. One, however, had been ignored: what would happen if President and Assembly disagreed? Who should prevail, since both were representative of the people's vote? Such a possibility was, it seems, not even considered.

Although the presidency of the Republic was open to any candidate, Louis Napoleon still needed the repeal of the Law of Exile in order to put himself forward. Some deputies revealed themselves afraid of his candidature, but he defended his position in a speech to the Assembly that was considered so inept that it was greeted with laughter. It was decided that this was a Bonaparte who would pose no threat to the Republic. Adolphe Thiers, one of the leading politicians, described him as a cretin, and so, confident in their assessment, the deputies repealed the Law of Exile on 11 October. In early November the Prince put forward his name as candidate for election as President.[8]

Although his uncle, ex-King Jerome, was now installed in Paris, together with his son Prince Napoleon Jerome, Louis Napoleon, as head of the Imperial House, consulted them about his actions merely as a matter of courtesy. He tolerated no infringement of his rights, and, when his cousin signed himself 'Napoleon Bonaparte', he was told that this was an unacceptable pretension. Jerome's daughter Mathilde, Louis Napoleon's ex-fiancée, opened her salon to all those who might be useful to her cousin and at the same time served as his hostess since he was unmarried. Mathilde, who may well have come to regret her broken engagement, was the victim of an appalling marriage to the fabulously wealthy Count Demidov, a Russian noble whose treatment of his wife was so brutal that the Tsar himself had intervened and arranged a separation. Fortunately, Mathilde was left extremely well off financially, something that was eventually to prove useful to Louis Napoleon when funds were badly needed.

In fact money was already required in order to finance the presidential campaign, though when it came to influencing the political groups the Prince was himself the best campaigner. Louis Napoleon had a splendid instinct for electoral politics, that is to say he told his audience what it wanted to hear, and, as a result, he became the candidate of choice. His only real rival, General Cavaignac, was defeated because of his ruthless suppression of the 'June Days' in Paris, which had alienated the left, while the conservative right, mainly monarchist, disliked his unchangeable and unshakeable Republican convictions.

But really it was quite simple. The name alone proved to be worth its weight in gold and carried the day. Louis Napoleon was elected President of the Republic, on 10 December 1848, by roughly five and a half million votes against one and a half million cast for his nearest rival, Cavaignac. The immense majority of the rural voters, two-thirds of the electorate, had voted for the Prince (at some election meetings they actually spoke of him as the Emperor) and the meaning of this was clear. For the first time since the fall of the Empire, the people had expressed their will and it had been expressed in a clear message.

Guizot, one of those who had made the Revolution of July 1830 and who had been a pillar of the monarchy of Louis-Philippe until 1848 overthrew that system, summed it all up. 'This experience revealed the strength of the Bonapartist party, or more accurately, the name of Napoleon. It is no small thing to be at one and the same time a national glory, a guarantee of the Revolution and a principle of authority.'[9] To ratify his election, the new President went to the Assembly on 20 December and took an oath to maintain the constitution and to defend the Republic. He then moved into the Elysée Palace, which had been designated as his official residence, and began to look about him for reliable friends in order to set up his household. Like most successful politicians, his first thought was to reward to those who had been his companions in the days of ill fortune and difficulty. In his case he had little choice, since the political world of Paris was unknown to him except for those few active politicians he had met during the months between February and November 1848. It must be remembered that the Prince was in Paris almost as a stranger, a circumstance that he was determined to remedy as quickly as possible.

He chose to wear the uniform of a general of the National Guard, and he took care to be seen mostly on horseback as he visited the main public buildings of the capital and showed himself to its people. Short in the leg and long in the body, he looked his best on a horse and had an especially good seat. He also used a carriage, dating from the Empire, which had been rescued from the stables at the Tuileries bearing the full imperial coat of arms. The servants in the Elysée Palace wore the old imperial liveries and the President was addressed as 'Highness', and 'Monseigneur'; only the President of the Assembly now called him 'Citizen'.

The imperial connection was made evident in other ways. His uncle, Jerome, was appointed to be Governor of the Invalides, while his cousin, ex-King Jerome's son Prince Napoleon, was sent as ambassador to Madrid. Here he distinguished himself by saying that that the Bourbons should now be thrown out of Italy as they had been France, a view which, not surprisingly, led the Bourbon Queen Maria Cristina to demand his recall. The Prince, known to the family as 'Plon-Plon' because of his childish mispronunciation of his name, had begun his official life as he would go on, being a source of trouble to his cousin. In his evident determination to play an active part in the evolution of the regime, he more resembled his turbulent Uncle Lucien than his easy-going father.

The Prince now made the acquaintance of another relation, his half-brother, the Count of Morny, of whose existence he had only become aware on the death of his adored mother, and which had greatly upset him. Morny, a son of the Count of Flahaut, himself an illegitimate son of Talleyrand, had been born in 1811 as a result of a liaison between Queen Hortense and Flahaut. He had grown up in an aristocratic milieu closely linked to the Orleans dynasty and, as a consequence, he had been very close to the family of the ex-King Louis-Philippe. Now, however, he turned to Louis Napoleon and became one of the most important members of the President's entourage, providing a strong link with the conservative political world whose support was essential to the new President. The people may have had the votes but the elites had the experience of government.[10]

Apart from Morny, the only other possible 'dynastic' help came from the Count Walewski, the son of Napoleon by Marie Walewska, now thirty-eight years old and having pursued a career in the French diplomatic service. Although he had not had any direct contact with Louis Napoleon during the latter's years of exile, he now immediately offered his services. The

President appointed him minister at the grand ducal court in Florence in 1849, and in 1851 he was moved to the kingdom of Naples. In late 1851 he was appointed ambassador in London, the post that he had always coveted, at a moment of crisis in the evolution of affairs in France when an ambassador would need all his skills. The appointment was, in itself, proof of the esteem in which Walewski was now held by his cousin.[11]

There was yet another family member, an illegitimate son of Napoleon, Count Léon, who had no talent except for failure. A marginal existence had led to his imprisonment for debt, and in 1840 he had become a paid agent of the French government, which sent him to London, instructing him to find ways to discredit the Prince. He succeeded, as a result of an insolent act of provocation, in forcing Louis Napoleon to meet him in a duel, though duelling was now strictly illegal, but the police arrived before there was any serious action, cautioned both parties, and decided not to pursue the matter. The question remains, however, as to whether or not Count Léon had been sent to London *specifically* to provoke a duel in which his opponent might be killed. Or was it simply the hope that the English government would expel the Prince as an unwelcome law-breaker?

Whatever the intention, Léon returned to France, where he continued to exist by conducting dubious business affairs and acting as a government agent, but in 1848, showing neither remorse nor shame, he presented himself to his cousin, now President of the Republic. Louis Napoleon displayed great kindness: he paid Léon's debts, and saw to it that he, like all the other beneficiaries, was paid the legacy which had been left to them by Napoleon in his will. Léon was incorrigible, however, and on five occasions between 1851 and 1870 Louis Napoleon rescued this wretched man by paying his debts, though it was a part of his Napoleonic inheritance he could probably have well done without. This particular relationship ended in 1870, when Napoleon III had no more to give.[12]

There was undoubtedly an air of make-do-and-mend about Louis Napoleon's new situation. His salary of 600,000 francs per annum was almost immediately swallowed up by repayment of debts contracted in less happy days, and by the necessary expenditure connected with his position as President. Consequently, his financial situation remained fragile. Forced to turn to the Assembly to ask for money, he received a grant of 1,600,000 francs, as one deputy courteously put it 'to keep him out of the debtors' prison at Clichy'. The debate occasioned by the President's request proved to be a source of much amusement to the deputies, who outdid one another in making derisive comments about the Prince's unhappy circumstances, something the President himself could not fail to notice and remember.

Quite apart from the financial problems that the Assembly had sneeringly and grudgingly agreed to remedy, the Prince's actual living conditions left much to be desired. According to one contemporary visitor, the state of the Elysée was a disgrace:

> the [presidential] apartments are as faded as the President, and the bronze chandeliers, which date from the First Empire, in the same style as those of the English Embassy, make decent lighting impossible, because there are too few lights in the chandeliers and wall brackets, and the candelabras. The furniture is neither splendid nor plentiful; as for the carpets and curtains, the former are threadbare and the latter faded.[13]

In these dismal surroundings the Prince President was supposed to uphold the dignity of his position and to represent the French nation. It was, however, an indication that those who were politically important did not expect the occupant to remain there for long, and so, with this thought in mind, they briskly declined to listen to his requests for refurbishment. For his part, the Prince had no intention of using his own money, as he had much better uses for it; so things remained as they were.

It was not just the state of his lodgings which made it clear that the political elite regarded the position after December 1848 as one that would be temporary, destined to end in 1852 with the election of a new President who could not be Louis Napoleon since the constitution precluded a second term. They omitted from their calculations two factors which were to make a nonsense of their plans for the future. One was the increasing desire of a majority in the country to end the Republic, a desire shared by many of the elite, but for different and anti-populist reasons. The other was the ability of Louis Napoleon to make use of his legal position and his popularity with the masses, something which he knew to exist as a result of his election to the presidency. Little by little he freed himself from the control of the political groups, at the same time successfully exposing their divisions and their increasing isolation. Simultaneously, he proceeded to reinforce his own direct links with his electorate by undertaking tours of the provinces and by publicly associating himself with progressive measures. His increasingly skilful efforts to put the Assembly in the wrong were abetted by the deputies' seeming determination to alienate the masses from the regime. Their campaign culminated in an electoral law of 1850 that disenfranchised some three million voters by the imposition of a residential qualification. Although the measure was quite obviously designed to deprive the more popular elements of the vote, it was also a clear attack on the principle of universal suffrage as established by the constitution. The President accepted the law, but under protest, delighted that the Assembly had thereby provided him with a weapon which could be turned against it, should the need arise. If the constitution could be altered once, why could it not be altered twice? Hence his supporters began a campaign to enable the President to stand for a second term of office, although the constitution forbade it.

The Prince, hoping for a second term, now openly supported the campaign designed to drum up sufficient popular support for this to become possible. As a consequence, petitions flowed in to the National Assembly from all the local councils in France, calling for a constitutional revision. But a majority in the Assembly rejected the appeals: the conservative leaders wanted a Prince Consort not a Prince President. As if to underline their determination to keep Louis Napoleon in check, the same group refused his request for the restoration of universal suffrage, abrogated by the law of 1850. It seemed as if the conservative group was determined to drive the President towards a *coup d'état*, from which they would benefit, for he was a guarantee of order and stability, but from participation in which they would be legally if not morally absolved. It seems quite certain that Louis Napoleon would have preferred a prolongation of his powers by legal means, hence his campaign to bring about a revision of the constitution in his favour, but in the long run it was equally clear that he would not shrink from a confrontation with the opposition. For some months he had been making his own preparations by placing his men in key positions, so that, if and when the moment came, the *coup* would be swift and, he hoped, bloodless.

There was a further reason for his hostility to the conservative group, whose leaders appear to have been planning the installation of a son of ex-King Louis-Philippe as President in 1852, a manoeuvre made possible thanks to the arithmetic governing the election to the presidency. The law of 1850 had reduced the number of voters from 10,000,000 to 7,000,000, but the constitution demanded that the President be elected by at least 2,000,000 votes, which now meant a third and not a fifth of the electorate.

In the event that no candidate obtained the required number of votes, it fell to the Assembly to nominate the President. In preparation for such an eventuality, two sons of Louis-Philippe were expected in France, the Duke of Aumale and the Prince of Joinville. As no less a person than Queen Victoria wrote to her uncle, King Leopold of the Belgians: 'It seems that poor Joinville had some mad idea of going to France. The candidature of Joinville was, from every point of view, totally unreasonable and led Louis Napoleon to pursue a desperate course'. [14]

The 'desperate course' to which the Queen referred was that taken by Louis Napoleon, once he had finally abandoned all hope of a peaceful resolution of the conflict between himself and the Assembly. In fact, by mid-November little choice was left to him but to make his *coup d'état*, for apart from the constitutional impasse, he was faced with financial ruin. Both the Prince and Morny, who was deeply implicated in the preparations for the *coup*, had not only run out of funds but had also been refused credit, so that on the eve of 2 December 1852 Louis Napoleon had exactly 6000 francs in cash. These he gave to General St-Arnaud, whom he had chosen to lead the military part of the operation, to distribute among the soldiers.

Clearly the *coup* was in dire need of cash to facilitate its success, but just how the money was raised has remained a subject for debate. One of the main contributors was Miss Howard, who sold her jewels and mortgaged her property in England in order to help her 'Poléon'. Others contributed smaller sums, including his cousin Princess Mathilde, who was the only member of the dynasty to participate in a positive fashion, since neither her father, ex-King Jerome, nor her brother, Prince Jerome Napoleon, made any move to assist Louis Napoleon. As far as the banks are concerned, it seems that Barings must have helped, for in 1852 they were repaid the sum of 814,000 francs, but it seems certain that none of the French banks was involved, largely because all their sympathies lay with the dethroned dynasty.

On the evening of the 1 December, 1851 the Prince President was holding his customary Monday reception at the Elysée Palace. As usual he mingled with his guests, with whom he remained until just after 10 o'clock. His withdrawal was unobtrusive, but it was of great import, for he had gone to launch 'Operation Rubicon', the long-awaited *coup*, which was scheduled for the early morning hours of 2 December. The date was chosen deliberately, for it was the anniversary of the coronation of Napoleon in 1804 and also that of his great victory at Austerlitz in 1805, two key moments in the history of the imperial dynasty.[15]

It all went surprisingly easily. The main opposition leaders were arrested, most of them woken from their beds and quietly transferred to the prison of Mazas. The army offered no resistance, a success that owed less to the distribution of 'beer and sausages', as Marx claimed, then to the effect of the name Napoleon: 'Your history is also mine. There is between us in the past a shared glory and a shared misfortune.' So spoke the Prince in his proclamation to the army. In any case the French army had, by 1851, become so accustomed to changes of regime that many may really have thought one more would make little difference. Nevertheless, it is quite clear that if the army *had* wished to act differently then everything would have gone badly wrong; once again the name made all the difference.

On the morning of 2 December, Parisians awoke to find that everywhere there were placards with a proclamation from the Prince, dissolving the Assembly, ordering the holding of new elections with a full, restored franchise, based on the universal suffrage of 1848, and proclaiming martial law. In the proclamation, the Prince announced that his action would be submitted to the judgement of 'the one sovereign that I recognise in France, the people!' At ten o'clock he rode out from the Elysée, to be greeted by the cheers of the crowds lining the streets, and, on entering the Place de la Concorde, was surrounded by cries of 'Vive l'Empereur' and shouts of 'to the Tuileries!' But the Prince had as yet not decided on a change of residence, for it is by no means sure that, even at this stage, he had decided on a restoration of the Empire. For the moment he therefore confined himself to a tour of the streets, even though popular clamour made clear what was wanted, for very few cried 'Vive la République!'.

Among the professional politicians there could be little opposition, partly because the key men had been arrested, but largely because all attempts to rouse the people made by those still at liberty failed dismally. Here and there a few barricades were erected, but they were poorly defended by the small groups who manned them. One young Republican deputy, Baudin, was killed in a skirmish with troops, but he was the only member of the Assembly to lose his life in defence of the constitution. Everything in fact appeared to be going smoothly until, on the evening of 4 December, a group of insurgents, accompanied by a crowd who had apparently come along to watch events, was fired on during a panic reaction on the part of some of the soldiers. This was the fatal moment, destined to haunt Louis Napoleon and his regime until its end. Some four hundred died, while the soldiers lost twenty-six dead with some two hundred wounded. The figures are both shocking and tragic, and were to be indelibly associated with Louis Napoleon's name, but set in the context of nineteenth-century political convulsions in France they were relatively low.

Events in Paris, however, were soon overshadowed by serious disturbances in the provinces, and it was these insurrectionary outbreaks which produced the greatest acts of repression. The motives behind these movements were often confused, but for the conservative majority in the countryside, particularly the landowners, it was simply a revolt of the 'Reds', and they proceeded to suppress it with ferocity, using the presidential *coup* as an excuse to settle their own scores. Many of those who were most active in the 'hunting out of the Reds' liked neither Louis Napoleon nor his *coup d'état*, but they seized their opportunity and then blamed the President for the repression.

For the victims of these measures it was not merely a question of prison or exile; it was also the ruin of their fortunes, their reputations and their employment. Worse still was the effect on the families of those who had been proscribed, who were frequently ruined on the simple basis of guilt by association. All these people were to form a hard core of irreconcilable opponents of the regime for the whole of its existence.[16]

True to Napoleonic tradition, the new regime submitted itself to the promised plebiscite on 28 December. The result was a resounding success for the Prince President: 'more than seven million votes have absolved me', he proclaimed. The figure of those who had voted to approve his action was exact, but the use of the word 'absolved' is interesting, for Louis Napoleon had a bad conscience about what had happened on the night of the 2 December, and above all, what had happened on the 4th. As the Empress Eugénie once said, while talking about her husband after his death, 'it was for him a cannonball that he dragged at his feet all his life'.

The measure of his sense of guilt was shown by his immediate attempts to mitigate the consequences of what had happened, particularly with regard to those who had been arrested and summarily tried. Where possible, he granted individual pardons, and he set up a commission to consider all the sentences which had been passed during the period of violent repression. As a consequence of this review, nearly five thousand people were pardoned, but the problem was not so easily solved. Many of those who had been arrested were literate and well able to air their grievances in publications which were implacably hostile to the regime. Their continual refrain was that nothing should be forgiven or forgotten; and, with writers of the calibre of Victor Hugo among the critics, there was little chance of pardon for the regime.

In January 1852, the new constitution was promulgated. Unsurprisingly it closely resembled the constitution of the Consulate promulgated in December 1799 and ratified by plebiscite in 1800. It established a nominated Senate and a Legislative Body elected by universal male suffrage, and it provided the President with a ten-year tenure of office.

This change of regime had not necessitated any creative constitutional thinking, for, as the President had said in his proclamation:

> I did not have any pretension, so common in our time, to substitute a personal theory for the experience of centuries. On the contrary, I looked for examples in the past which could be followed, what men had produced them, and what good had come from them … In a word, I said to myself, since France has for fifty years been maintained by virtue of the administrative, military, judicial, religious and financial organisation of the Consulate and the Empire, why should we not also adopt the political institutions of that period?[17]

The Prince was reminding the country of his title deeds, but in fact the new constitution also contained elements of his own political thought as expressed in his various writings. The regime was not simply to be a backward-looking pastiche of what had gone before: 'one must not merely copy what has been done, for imitations do not produce resemblances'. What needed to be underlined was the fact that Bonapartism, and a Bonaparte, belonged to the present. As he had written: 'Put yourself at the head of the ideas of your time, these ideas follow and support you; follow behind them and they drag you along, oppose them, they will overthrow you.' Louis Napoleon was announcing that he was in tune with the ideas of his time and that he proposed to be at their head.[18]

Nowhere was this more evident than in the acceptance of universal suffrage as the basis of the regime. Louis Napoleon saw his authority as being an exercise of *personal* responsibility, hence article five of the constitution: 'The President of the Republic is responsible to the French people, to whom he has always the right of appeal.' This remained a fundamental basis of the regime throughout its existence – sometimes summed up in the Bonapartist slogan: 'Tout pour le peuple et par le peuple' (everything for the people and by the people). It remains to this day a fundamental doctrine of latter-day Bonapartists.

While the plebiscite was inherited from the Consulate, there was a fundamental difference between the regime of uncle and nephew, since the latter depended not just on plebiscitary appeals but also on regular elections to the Legislative Body, so that the political climate was constantly being tested. Because the masses had been enfranchised, it was essential that the regime apply itself to restoring economic stability as a first step in improving social conditions: 'In the budget, one must find support for a system which will have for its aim the betterment of the working classes.'

As a means of restoring the economy, a vast programme of public works, particularly the construction of railways, was undertaken, the necessary capital being raised by granting concessions to groups of financiers, both French and British. Meanwhile, building works were begun in Paris, including the huge new market complex of Les Halles, allocated a grant of 19,000,000 francs, to serve the immediate needs of feeding the population of the city. The impression created was of a regime that was dynamic, reformist and aware of the needs of all its citizens, and this impression was reinforced by a series of decrees, issued in January 1852, setting out plans for road and canal building, and the establishment of a nationwide electric telegraph system. A highly centralised governmental structure needed swift and sure means of communication with the Departments. As a further indication of economic plans, an enquiry was ordered into the state of France's major ports, their capacity, facilities and, most importantly, their possible expansion.

In his desire to press forward his plans for major social reform, the Prince President provoked a political crisis by alienating three of his principal collaborators who objected to his order that the possessions of the Orleans family in France should be sold within a year. Although quite within his rights, four men, Morny, whom he had named Minister of the Interior, the banker Achille Fould, who was Minister of Finance, Eugène Rouher, the Minister of Justice, and Pierre Magne, Minister of Public Works, all resigned in protest. Quite unmoved, the President then went on to confiscate the private fortune of ex-King Louis-Philippe, which should, in fact, already have been merged with the crown estate in 1830.

The money thus made available amounted to many millions of francs, which the President immediately allocated for the building of orphanages and workers' housing in Paris and other major cities. It also went to the foundation of mutual benefit societies designed to facilitate loans for the working people. The resignation of the four ministers revealed their latent sympathy for the Orleans monarchy, and also, perhaps, a lack of confidence in the new regime. Whatever it was, all four eventually returned to office.

The better off sections of society accused Louis Napoleon of taking a cold and calculated revenge on the fallen dynasty, and Parisian wits were able to make use of a play on words in order to mock the President: the word *vol* means 'flight', but it also means 'theft', so 'Le premier vol de l'aigle' could be read two ways. Flight or theft, the beneficiaries were simply grateful for the way in which the money had been used.

As the year advanced, and the regime established itself, *the* great question began to be the subject of debate and speculation – if and when the Empire would be restored. The question of a restoration of the Empire was one that concerned not only France, and the French people, but also needed to take into account the possible reaction of the other European powers to such an event. The *coup d'état* had been accepted because, in the aftermath of the revolutionary movements of 1848–49, most European governments feared the instability of a quasi-revolutionary regime, and, rather like the conservative groups in France, saw Louis Napoleon as a guarantee of order. As a result, the *coup* had been welcomed by such diverse political figures as Lord Palmerston and Tsar Nicholas I. It was made clear to France, however, that the basic structure of the European state's system was based on the treaties of 1815, and so, while a stable France under a capable President was one thing, a restored Empire under a Napoleon was something else. Might not a restored imperial regime be tempted to reassert France's real place in European affairs and so threaten the status quo?

Louis Napoleon was keenly aware of the necessity to make clear his intentions, remembering the alacrity with which the Waterloo coalition had reacted in the crisis of 1840–41, when it seemed that France was attempting to operate a 'forward' foreign policy. The subsequent climb-down had damaged the prestige of the Orleans monarchy enormously, and it was obvious that great care must be taken by the new regime to avoid any possible recurrence of that situation. Tsar Nicholas, while accepting the *coup*, told the French ambassador, by way of a warning; 'Stay away from the

Empire'. The same message had come from London, in a different form: 'The Powers hold the treaties of 1815 as being a final settlement.'

Nevertheless, and in spite of a possible hostile reaction abroad, by the autumn of 1852 it seemed inevitable that the Empire would be restored. In order to gauge the state of public opinion, the Prince President had gone on an extensive tour of the provinces and had everywhere been greeted by crowds, triumphal arches and civic receptions, all indicating a desire for the return of the Napoleonic regime and the dynasty. Since there seemed to be genuine enthusiasm within the country, Louis Napoleon now turned to reassuring foreign governments.

On 9 October he was in Bordeaux, a city that had always been hostile to the Empire, because its trade had been ruined by the Napoleonic wars. It had been the first major city to proclaim the Bourbons in 1814. It was, therefore, not by accident that Louis Napoleon made his most important speech there. He announced his proposed conquests: 'We have vast uncultivated lands which must be brought into use, roads to build, ports to enlarge, rivers to make navigable, the system of canals and railways to finish, opposite Marseille a vast kingdom to assimilate to France [Algeria]. These are the conquests I am considering ... ' 'There are those who say the Empire means war, I say to you "the Empire means peace".'[19]

After Bordeaux there could be no further hesitation. On 16 October the President arrived in Paris to be greeted virtually as sovereign with cries of 'Vive l'Empereur!', the next step on the way being the address from the Senate proposing the acceptance of the imperial title. The change had to be ratified by plebiscite, which was held on 20 and 21 November, on the proposition: 'The people wishes the re-establishment of the imperial dignity in the person of Louis Napoleon Bonaparte, and his descendants direct, legitimate, or adoptive, and grants him the right to regulate the succession to the throne in the Bonaparte family as set out in the senatus consultum of 7 November 1852.'[20]

In the plebiscite 7,824,129 voted 'yes', 253,145 'no' and 2,062,798 abstained. Perhaps the most interesting comment on the event came from the Republican Jules Ferry, an irreconcilable opponent: 'One day the rural population showed that it could "want". The peasant wanted to crown his legend and his word made the Empire. His word was free, passionate and sincere and he repeated it three times, with even greater enthusiasm in 1852 than in 1848 or 1851.' Excluded from the political process by successive regimes since 1815, the mass of the newly enfranchised had expressed *their* preference with, as Ferry remarked, 'enthusiasm'.[21]

On 1 December the Empire was proclaimed, with Louis Napoleon as Emperor, to be known as Napoleon III. Certainly the reign of Napoleon II had been, as the new ruler said, ephemeral, but it had been legal, because the Emperor had been proclaimed by the Senate in accordance with the constitution then in force. Dynastically, therefore, his successor was correct in recognising it as such and in considering himself to be the third member of the dynasty to reign. Nevertheless, Napoleon III made an important point by saying: 'My reign does not date from 1815, it dates from this moment when you [the Senate delegation] made known to me the votes of the nation.' This would always be a dynasty with a difference.

8

The Empire Restored

The Empire once re-established, there was no further talk of its ruler being a 'cretin', or an 'adventurer'. Guizot, writing to an English friend, pointed out that the masses were able to accept the Empire because it represented order, stability and the fulfilment of the Napoleonic legend. For the upper class of society, however, the aspiration was for a short-lived regime that would restore order and stability and then disappear: 'This government, even as an Empire, remains what it is, a power established on a very broad base, but from which the top of society is, and wishes to remain, separate.' He went on to say:

> This man has an extraordinary mixture of boldness and of patience, of fatalism and prudent calculation. He believes in his star and he will follow it, and in the depths of his soul he is absolutely resolved to follow it until the end. Unlike his uncle, he has not an inexhaustible fund of ideas nor an insatiable drive in his character; he is rather slow and indolent; he likes pleasures and he likes his leisure. He will enjoy his situation and he will do and say today what he must do, so that Europe will not be disturbed by him, and he will hold back as long as possible the moment when he must seriously compromise himself in order to realise his dreams. When one is a fatalist one can for a time struggle against the destiny to which one feels oneself called, but sooner or later one yields and even drives oneself towards it.[1]

Once the Empire had been restored the problem of the succession to the throne had to be dealt with promptly, since Napoleon III was unmarried and therefore had no direct heir to ensure the continuity of the dynasty. It seemed clear that, his father having already renounced any claim, Prince Napoleon Jerome should be considered as heir until such times as his cousin should have a son, but Napoleon III did not want to accept this. Even before the proclamation of the Empire, angered by his cousin's open opposition to the *coup d'état*, he had written to ex-King Jerome: 'Your son does nothing to merit such a high destiny. I tell you with total frankness that as long as your son does not show himself fit to govern France he will not be included in the succession to the throne.'[2] It was not considered fitting, however, that the new regime should begin with a dispute about the succession and so the constitution left a margin of manoeuvre whereby the new Emperor could choose his successor from either his direct, legitimate or adoptive descendants. This safeguarded family peace, at the same time maintaining the principle of heredity.

Neither King Jerome nor his son was satisfied with this state of affairs. The King, in a public gesture, resigned from his presidency of the Senate, while his son, following his normal practice, had a fit of sulks. The Emperor was obliged to write to them, reminding them that they had an obligation to the family:

> Now it is not a question of saving the situation but of establishing a dynasty. I therefore adjure you to pay great attention to what you say and to hide the disappointment which you must feel. When one bears our name and is at the head of government, there are two things to do: to satisfy the interests of the most numerous class of people and also to draw to oneself the upper classes.[3]

Evidently, the best solution to these problems of succession would be an imperial marriage followed by the birth of an heir. Since he already had two illegitimate sons, the Emperor might reasonably hope that he would have a legitimate one.

Before anything else, however, there was one loose end which needed to be tied: what was to be done with the faithful Miss Howard. His companion of many years, financial contributor to the expenses of the December *coup*, and still attached to her Prince, she could not simply be lightly discarded. The lady had, in any case, no intention of going without a fight and there were several scenes between the Emperor and her, one of which ended, she said, when 'God Almighty fell asleep on the sofa while I sobbed'. All ended moderately well: the money was repaid, and with it she purchased the château of Beauregard, a handsome property near Paris. Then on 24 January 1853, less than a week before his marriage, Napoleon III issued letters patent creating her Comtesse de Beauregard. She died there, almost forgotten, on 16 August 1865.

This problem having been disposed of, all that now remained was to find a suitable lady who could be at one and the same time Napoleon's Empress and the mother of his children. Given the circumstances of the succession problem, it is understandable that Napoleon III did not want any delay.

The fact that the marriage took place on 30 January 1853, within a few months of the restoration of the Empire, conceals the difficulties in actually finding a wife. Discreet soundings were taken in European court circles to ascertain if any Princess was disposed to risk a marriage to a French sovereign. Beginning with Marie-Antoinette, recent brides had not been fortunate, and on this occasion only two possibles displayed any enthusiasm: one was related to the former Swedish ruling House of Vasa, the other was a German Princess, Adelaide of Hohenlohe-Langenburg. Neither was a princess of the first rank, and both were Protestants, though in the event, these problems turned out to be academic, since neither candidate was prepared to accept the offer. Fortunately, Napoleon III, who had expected a rebuff, and indeed may have hoped for one, had already made his own choice.

The future Empress, Eugénie de Guzman, Countess of Teba, had already met her suitor when he was President of the Republic. She and her mother, the Countess of Montijo, had been introduced to Louis Napoleon as a result of their acquaintanceship with Princess Mathilde, an introduction which the latter certainly lived to regret. The daughter of a Spanish nobleman who had been an officer in the army of Napoleon I, and who had also held a post as Chamberlain in the Imperial Court, Eugénie had grown up in an atmosphere of Bonapartism, her father having always remained faithful to the dynasty. Educated in France, she was, as Napoleon III said, 'French at heart not only by upbringing but by the memory of the blood which her father shed in the service of the Empire'. As a further justification of his choice, the Emperor pointed out that new principles required new attitudes and these did not include 'trying to insinuate oneself at any price into the families of the older European dynasties. Rather one should not forget one's origins, maintain one's own identity and adopt unhesitatingly before all Europe the position of parvenu, a curious title when one has arrived there thanks to the vote of a great people.' As for Eugénie: 'gracious and good, she will, I am convinced, bring back to the same role the virtues of the Empress Josephine'. It was a delicate reminder to his Bonaparte relations that he was also a Beauharnais.[4]

On the evening of 29 January 1853, the civil marriage between Eugénie and the Emperor took place in the Tuileries. He had invited selected members of the family as witnesses to the ceremony, which was held in the great Hall of the Marshals, but even careful selection did not prevent exhibitions of ill-bred behaviour. When the time came to greet the newly-weds, Prince Napoleon bowed to the Emperor but pointedly ignored the Empress, while Prince Pierre Bonaparte saluted neither the one nor the other. For Eugénie it was a splendid introduction to family life among the Bonapartes, which she might have reflected had not improved during the period when the family was no longer reigning.

The next day saw the religious ceremony at Notre-Dame, which again as in 1804 led to family difficulties. Princess Mathilde was obliged to travel in a carriage with Eugénie's mother, since she detested both her brother Prince Napoleon and her father ex-King Jerome and refused to travel with them. As she was not fond of Madame de Montijo either, it is little wonder that she arrived at the cathedral in a state of high discontent. Had she, during the carriage ride, meditated on how she might have been the prospective bride and Empress, had she not broken her engagement in 1836? Since, however, all the members of the family made no attempt to hide their feelings of antipathy to the marriage this meant that her behaviour was in itself not particularly remarked on, but Mathilde was to prove unrelenting in her hostility to Eugénie.

The ceremony was magnificent, and Lady Augusta Bruce, writing to Queen Victoria's mother (who passed the letter on to the Queen), having described the splendour of the interior of the cathedral, added 'a sort of national prejudice made me attribute the grace and dignity of the scene, for what there was of either came from her, to the blood of *Kirkpatrick*!!!' That is, to the Empress's Scottish Grandfather. Lady Augusta was herself a Scot.[5]

It is often suggested that the marriage contracted by Napoleon III was a *mésalliance*, though in fact Eugénie was herself a grandee of Spain and an heir to considerable estates, but it was not her social position that had attracted Napoleon III to her; it was, quite simply, her beauty. Although it is true that beauty is generally a matter of opinion, Eugénie *was* striking looking with auburn hair and blue eyes, together with a fine complexion, and in an age when *décolletage* mattered her shoulders were said to be superb. This was combined with an elegant carriage and a vivacious manner, at times sometimes too vivacious, leading to her making occasionally indiscreet comments when she was Empress. What is worth noting is that those who were initially hostile to Eugénie rarely changed their opinion of her during the next eighteen years, and some cases, only death ended an enduring aversion to her. As a result of this sustained hostility, she has generally had a bad press, not only among contemporaries but also among later historians of the Empire. There seem to have been various reasons for this. As far as the Bonaparte family were concerned, she could not hope to win. Prince Napoleon had already given his view by saying, 'One does not *marry* Mademoiselle de Montijo', a comment that had angered the Emperor.

During the whole of the reign, Prince Napoleon's sister Mathilde continued to wage her own campaign against the Empress, while assisting her brother in his vendetta by making her *salon* in the Rue de Courcelles a centre of hostile comment and calumny. Criticism had begun immediately, and the evening of the civil wedding had already provided an occasion for bad behaviour. The Princess said of the departure of the imperial couple on their honeymoon: 'Each one of us [members of the imperial family] returned home worn out and with a heavy heart; we felt that the Emperor was lost to us.' It was hardly an enthusiastic send off, but perhaps it was marginally less offensive than the disgraceful behaviour of the previous generation at the wedding of Marie-Louise.

Eugénie herself had no illusions about the interpretations of her character. In later life, in exile in England, friends tried to persuade her to protest at the continued campaign of denigration waged against her. She replied, 'My legend is established; at the beginning I was the frivolous empty-headed woman, and then I became the fatal influence, and remember that legend always triumphs!'

There is no doubt that Eugénie was often too outspoken, sometimes being so overborne by the force of an idea as to express her views too vehemently. The Emperor once said to her: 'Eugénie, you don't grasp ideas, the ideas grasp you.' The fact that the Emperor was determined to make her his active partner in the running of the Empire, and his insistence on this joint public role, while it heralded the invention of the modern concept of monarchy, put the Empress in a prominent position, her role being officially recognised after July 1856 when she was designated Regent.

From the very beginning the Emperor, making use of what became a highly developed railway system, travelled widely throughout France, on most occasions accompanied by the Empress. She herself on several occasions acted on her own, as when she visited areas stricken by an outbreak of cholera, and also in the work which she undertook to bring about an amelioration of the conditions in which young prisoners were held. As her later life would show, she had a strong and determined personality, but it cannot have helped to make her popular in a masculine society that she displayed symptoms of feminism. Perhaps, in many ways like her husband, she was too modern for her time; what is certain is that the traditional image of a silly, vain and bigoted woman will not stand up to examination.[6]

Her immediate task was to come to terms with the Bonaparte family, not only because she was now related, but also because there had to be a court and they must inevitably form part of it. Napoleon III did his best to limit access to the court to the most immediate members of the family, something which had been made easier by the fact that so many of the older generation were dead, or else had never been considered to be part of the intimate family of the Emperor. Only two members, the Prince Napoleon and the Princess Mathilde, were given the status of Imperial Princes (*Princes Français*) with a separate civil list and, in the case of Prince Napoleon, the right to sit in the Senate and to be assigned an official residence in the Palais Royal.

As far as the rest were concerned, when he felt it necessary the Emperor maintained them through his privy purse, showing to them in many instances a generosity far beyond their worth. It is said that on one occasion Prince Napoleon accused his cousin of having inherited nothing from the great Emperor, to which Napoleon III replied, 'yes, the family'. In an attempt to control some of the more wayward members, such as Prince Pierre Bonaparte and Marie Letitia, both descendants of Lucien, the Emperor forbade them *entrée* to the Tuileries. Pierre's character was so violent, and his public behaviour so appalling, that he was denied all access to the court, eventually joining the Foreign Legion. In the case of Letitia, who had married an Irish baronet, Sir Thomas Wyse, her refusal to accept the Emperor's decision that she confine herself to being Lady Wyse, not invoking imperial pretensions by calling herself Bonaparte Wyse, led to her being expelled from France.[7]

In addition to the Bonaparte relatives, there were also descendants of Josephine's family, the Tascher de la Pagerie; then there were the Murats, descendants of the former King of Naples, and also those who were the issue of what were known as 'the Italian marriages', the Primolis and the Bacciochis, some of whom held honorary positions at court. To an extent, and inevitably, the presence of the names of the First Empire at the court of the Second seemed to underline the fact of continuity between the two regimes. But presence did not imply influence and such posts as were held by these people, with the exception of Prince Napoleon, were purely honorary. It can be assumed that Napoleon III had not forgotten that so many of those close to his uncle, and in positions of power, had deserted him when the crisis came.

Although court appointments carried no political weight, it was essential that a functioning court structure be set up in order to make certain that everything ran smoothly. This led to the re-establishment of the *Maison de l'Empereur*, modelled on that of Napoleon I, which itself had recreated certain features of the pre-revolutionary system. As director of the newly-established household the Emperor appointed Achille Fould, a banker whose financial expertise would obviously be of use in the organisation of what could well turn out to be a costly affair. Napoleon III was determined that, from its inception, his court would not only be new but would be a new *type* of court. He was an innovator, not merely a man of his time as has been pointed out but frequently one who was ahead of it, and so he was determined to avoid the rigid exclusivity which was the hallmark of the traditional European court structure. As a result of this conscious decision, the court of the Second Empire was conceived of as a public spectacle which would not only shine in the eyes of the French people but would also become the envy of people's less fortunate than they. The court, and by extension the city of Paris, would become the focus of all Europe, and even of a wider world, for the Emperor, conscious of the huge changes in the speed and ease of travel, foresaw an influx of visitors not to just from the Old World but also from the New. There was no point in people flocking to Paris if there was nothing to see or do when one got there, and so the court would be open as well as brilliant.[8]

As well as the civil, there was also the military household, which was responsible for overseeing the personal safety of the sovereign. It was in fact this military household which became most familiar to the mass of people, who, by the nature of things did not see the civil household, which only operated within the palace. The population of Paris, and visitors to the capital, were impressed by the military reviews at which they could see the crack regiments, including, since 1854, the restored Imperial Guard and also the *Cent Gardes*. These wore a magnificent blue and silver uniform and were picked for their stature, the minimum height being six feet. They were also picked for their looks, since many of them were involved in court ceremonial, including lining of the grand stairway at the Tuileries during balls and official receptions. These were the occasions which enabled them to display for hours the rigid immobility for which they became famous throughout Europe. From its beginning, the Second Empire resembled a splendid military pageant, with colourful regiments whose uniforms were ornamented with sabretaches, aiguillettes and gleaming leather. Even the ordinary infantrymen managed to look exotic on ceremonial parade, though the baggy scarlet trousers of the Zouaves tended to make almost everything else look dull.

The palace household, rarely seen except by those who had access to the court, was no less splendid, though necessarily less exotic than the military. The household was divided into various sections, all theoretically under control of the Minister of the Household. The palaces of the Tuileries and St-Cloud each had its own prefect or governor who maintained a small staff of his own, while officers like the Master of the Horse were responsible for providing carriages and the necessary transport when the imperial family or the household had need them. There was also the Chief Huntsman (*Grand Veneur*), hunting being as always one of the favourite royal pastimes, whose duty it was to organise the imperial hunts, particularly during the autumn at Compiègne.

The 'Legitimist' nobility, that is those who had remained loyal to the elder Bourbon branch that had been deposed by the Revolution of 1830, kept away from the court, just as it had kept away from that of Louis-Philippe. Their attitude was that the whole affair was shabby and second-hand, quite apart from its illegitimacy, because the forty-year gap between the First and Second Empires had, in their opinion, increased the impos-sibility of these people being able to perform their court functions properly and with dignity. One unbiased observer, who remarked favourably on the court, was Queen Victoria. During her visit in 1855 she wrote to her Uncle Leopold of the Belgians: 'everything is beautifully *monté* at court, very quiet and in excellent order; I must say we are both much struck with the difference between this and the poor King's [Louis-Philippe's] time when the noise, confusion and bustle were great'. Victoria was not one to be impressed by second best and, although perhaps the imperial court was more successful in mounting great set-pieces than in its day-to-day running, it does seem to have functioned effortlessly and above all with great brilliance.[9] If, however, one looks at contemporary courts, such as those of

Russia or Austria, where a more traditional pattern of behaviour and etiquette was the fossilised norm, then, measured against them, the Court of the Tuileries might indeed seem to be governed by a spirit of careless frivolity and even disorder.

By altering the perspective, it can be convincingly argued that a 'democratic monarchy' with, at its head, an Emperor elected by and directly responsible to the people had need of a different set of values from those prevailing at St Petersburg or Vienna. Unlike his fellow sovereigns, Napoleon III reigned by the grace of God and the will of the people, to whom the constitution made him directly responsible, a point which he never forgot. Given that the people had put him there, the Emperor saw it as his duty to be seen as the people's sovereign, not just in the matter of governing but by his behaviour as a sovereign who must associate the people with all aspects of his life. In playing the role in which the ruler is seen not only to be ruler but also responsive to the general life of the subjects, Napoleon III may be credited with being the founder, or certainly one of the founders, of modern monarchy. It was the same sort of thinking which made him involve the Empress in carrying out public duties. Sovereigns must not only rule but be seen to be at one with their people.

One of the ways in which dynasties reinforce their links with their people is by continuity and by the production of heirs. Although the Emperor had married for love, it was expected that the union would, as soon as possible, produce a child who, ideally, would be male. In April 1853 the Empress miscarried and as a consequence remained extremely unwell for months, and there was a further disappointment in 1854. It was an alarming omen for the imperial couple, but on 16 March 1856 Eugénie fulfilled her duty by giving birth to a son, thus securing the future of the dynasty. *The Times* noted sombrely that, 'since Louis XIV no direct heir had ever succeeded to the French throne', but no one paid much attention to these gloomy prognostications, so great was the universal joy in France at the birth of the Prince Imperial.

There was one snag, however. The birth of the Prince had been so difficult (the Empress had been in labour for eighteen hours) that no further child could be hoped for, since the doctors had advised that further pregnancies should be avoided. All the more reason therefore to rejoice at the birth of a healthy boy, for the Prince was robust as an infant, making it an event of great dynastic significance, not least because it removed Prince

Napoleon, the Emperor's cousin and heir designate, from immediate hope of the succession. This served to increase the dislike felt by the Prince for the Empress, a dislike which envenomed not only personal but also political relationships, for Prince Napoleon henceforth appeared to take a delight in publicly opposing the Emperor's policies and also, equally publicly, in quarrelling with the Empress. His official residence at the Palais Royal became a virtual 'court of disaffection', while his sister, Mathilde, ran her salon as a second centre of hostility. Both, by their unconsidered actions, were to do much harm to the regime and to the dynasty.

None of this could obscure the triumph of the Prince's baptism, which took place in Notre-Dame on 14 June 1856, a long delay having been neces-sary because the Empress had been so weak after the birth that she was unable to leave her bed for months. The Pope had agreed to be godfather and sent a legate, Cardinal Patrizzi, to represent him at the christening, although the ceremony itself was performed by the Archbishop of Paris. The godmother was the Queen of Sweden, also unable to be present in person, who was represented by Princess Stephanie Louise Napoleon, Grand Duchess of Baden. The child was christened Napoleon Eugène Louis Jean Joseph. After his name in the baptismal register of the imperial parish of St-Germain l'Auxerrois, the Emperor wrote 'Son of France', thus curiously reviving the custom of the *ancien régime* because, as he said, 'when an heir is born to perpetuate a national institution that child is the whole country's son: and this name will serve to remind him of his duties'.

The occasion was a splendid one, remembered afterwards as one of the high points of the Empire. The route of the procession from the Tuileries to Notre-Dame was crowded, and the appearance of the imperial family was greeted with cries of 'Long Live the Emperor, Long Live the Empress, Long Live the Little Prince!' In the procession there were twelve state coaches, each drawn by eight horses, with the carriage containing the imperial heir preceding that of the Emperor and Empress. Eugénie was dressed in pale blue and wearing all the crown diamonds, while the Emperor was resplendent in the uniform of a general of division. Count Hübner, the Austrian Ambassador, thought that, 'the Empress was more beautiful than ever', and Lord Cowley, the English ambassador, said: 'I do not know that I have ever witnessed a finer sight than the baptismal ceremonies'. Prosper Mérimée, a long-time friend of Eugénie's family, wrote to her mother in Madrid: 'The Empress was in great beauty, the Emperor also looked very impressive and when, after the ceremony, he held up the child in his arms to present him to the multitude the enthusiasm was genuine and great.'[10]

The city of Paris offered as a gift to the Prince a cradle which was fashioned in the shape of a Viking boat with the imperial eagle at its prow, while above the infant's head the city of Paris, personified by a young woman, held aloft the imperial crown. The Pope's gift was a spray of golden flowers, as a complement to the golden rose that he had already sent to the Empress, as a special mark of papal goodwill.

The ceremonies of the marriage, and then the baptism of the Prince Imperial, were important because they replaced a coronation. Napoleon III does not seem to have felt the need of a public coronation, as had been felt by Napoleon I, who had wanted such a public gesture both to French Catholics and to the Pope as evidence of his reconciliation with the church. At the same time, his coronation had been placed firmly within the limits of the Concordat of 1801, as underlined by the anomalous position of the Pope during the ceremony, and by Napoleon's oath to uphold the revolutionary settlement which took place during the ceremony. In that sense, the coronation of 1804 was essentially a political gesture, legitimising not only the dynasty but also the Revolution.

By 1852 when, on the face of it, a coronation might have seemed to be a natural consequence of the restoration of the Empire, there was much less political need for a public gesture. After all, the Concordat had been functioning for over fifty years and the need for dramatic reconciliatory gestures between Pope and Emperor had passed. Napoleon III did broach the question of a coronation with Pope Pius IX but negotiations proceeded slowly and fitfully, marked by a lack of enthusiasm on both sides. It would be unwise to say that this indeterminate situation arose as a result of hostility; rather it came about because neither party wished to push the matter. The Pope indicated a general desire for a revision of the 1801 Concordat, but was mindful of the fact that he owed his position in Rome to Napoleon III. When Pius had been evicted by the Republican revolutionaries in 1848, who had gone on to proclaim a Roman Republic, he had appealed to the Catholic nations of Europe to restore him to his temporal estates and it was Louis Napoleon, as President of the Republic, who had dispatched troops in 1849 to restore papal authority. Although well aware that gratitude is a commodity generally in short supply, not least in international affairs, he could reasonably expect some sort of recognition of his action on the part of the Pope. In France itself he had also, as President, helped the passage of an educational reform, known as the *Loi Falloux*, which had strengthened the church's position in the public educational system. For the moment there was no real cause of tension between Emperor and Pope, and it was clear that the new sovereign had no intention of seeking a quarrel about ecclesiastical affairs. The church would be given its place and, in return, was expected to throw its weight behind the imperial regime. The Te Deum sung in Notre-Dame after the 2 December 1851 was an early example of this type of cooperation. The 15 August, the Feast of the Assumption of the Virgin and also the birthday of Napoleon I, was declared to be *the* public holiday of the Empire, and provided an annual opportunity for church and state to celebrate jointly.

Since it was intended that the church would, without question, give its public blessing to the dynasty, even if there were no official coronation, the marriage and the splendid baptismal ceremony of the Prince Imperial stood proxy for an official crowning. By agreeing to be godfather to the Prince Imperial and by sending the Empress a golden rose, which was a personal gift that the Pope bestowed on Catholic sovereigns, Pius had given public recognition, in a sense his papal blessing, to the new regime.[11]

What gave greater lustre to the festivities surrounding the birth and baptism of the Prince Imperial was the fact that these events coincided with the signing of the peace which marked the end of the Crimean War. This was a multiple triumph for Napoleon III, not least because the peace conference had been held in Paris pointing up the return of France to the mainstream of European diplomacy. The Emperor could also compliment himself on having cracked the unity of the Waterloo coalition by fighting as the ally of England against Russia. When the euphoria surrounding all this apparent triumph had dissipated, things began to seem less simple, but for the moment all was well, and Paris, with its glittering and seemingly endless imperial fête, became the capital of Europe, and even the world beyond.

During most of the reign of Napoleon I, Paris had been the capital of a country which was almost continually at war. During the Second Empire peace was the normal state of affairs, occasionally interrupted by some military activity, but nothing resembling the continual wars of the Revolutionary and Napoleonic eras. It therefore was possible to undertake a massive programme of rebuilding in the capital, something that the Emperor had in mind from the moment he had come to power. To assist him in carrying out his projects he had found the man he needed in Baron Haussmann, who had proved that he could be both ruthless and highly efficient as prefect of the difficult Department of the Var. He had then proved equally efficacious at Bordeaux. In 1853 Napoleon III rewarded his talents and ambition by appointing him Prefect of the Seine.

Napoleon made it plain that for him the problem of Paris was not simply one of creating prosperity for its inhabitants; rather it was one of transforming and embellishing the city in such a way as to make life better for its inhabitants while simultaneously making it worthy of the new France. Paris would become a European capital to which all would look with envy and the desire to emulate its splendours. He was to achieve most of this, though he was to receive little thanks for it from the Parisians, who in large part remained hostile to his regime. During his reign successive elections resulted in the defeat of governmental candidates by supporters of the opposition groups, either Republicans or Orleanists, looking either to the future or to the past but united in their dislike of the Empire. This hostility did not in any way deflect him from his purpose, so that by the time the regime fell in 1870 Paris had been altered forever and bore, and indeed still bears, the mark of Napoleon III. The Third Republic, anxious to prevent the idea that the Empire had achieved anything worthwhile, above all any idea that Paris (or indeed France) owed anything to the fallen dynasty, preferred to attribute the transformation of the city to Haussmann. The personal involvement, and decisive impetus given by Napoleon III to the entire project, was systematically played down, though later historians are more generous in their assessment of the Emperor's contribution.[12]

His achievement had been saluted by no less an enemy than Victor Hugo, writing from his exile in Jersey in1867 after many of the major transformations had been completed: 'This city does not belong to a people, but to peoples … the human race has a right to Paris. France, with perfect detachment understands this.' And indeed the rebuilding of Paris was not designed simply to provide a city for tourists or for pleasure, although both these groups were to be catered for; it was to show Europe that France had already achieved, and was continuing to pursue, economic strength and growth. The Paris exhibitions of 1855 and 1867 echoed the Crystal Palace Exhibition of 1851 and were meant to show that France was capable of rivalling Britain in economic development. There was a great upsurge in the French economy during the Second Empire, thanks to governmental policy, including the all-important opening up of the banking system, to make it more flexible. Banking was 'democratised', by opening it up to the small investors, tempted by the prospect of gaining interest on even modest deposits, producing a flow of cash that was needed for investment in industry. To this was added the money raised by direct loans, launched by the government, which again were open to even the small investor, and it was this availability of capital that really enabled the modernisation of the country. The growth of the railway system, coupled with the development of roads and canals, facilitated the expansion of heavy industry and industry in general. The ability to transport agricultural products quickly from one area to another increased consumption, brought with it increased rural prosperity and finally put to rest the age old fear of famine. This resulted in a general increase in the standard of living throughout France, though it would be unwise to exaggerate what this meant in the lives of ordinary people. Nevertheless, the voting figures across the country seem to indicate a sustained level of contentment, so there must have been among contemporaries a degree of satisfaction.

Using Britain as an example, Napoleon III, and the economists who advised him, believed that the introduction of free trade would enormously strengthen the French economy, since only by opening up French industry to greater competition would it be galvanised into accepting the new methods of production. It was the pursuit of this policy that led, in the first decade of the regime, to the development of the infrastructure, so that by 1860 France had reached a point where the country could compete with the greatest economic power of the age. The outcome was the signing of the free trade treaty of 1860 with Britain, as much an act of faith as of policy, for it provoked great opposition among French industrialists. But events proved that the conviction of the Emperor and his economic advisers was justified, since the economy, deprived of its protective barriers, continued to grow and expand. In spite of this success, there remained a hard core of protectionists, who formed a nucleus of opposition to the regime, which was to find political expression.

One consequence of this was to make Paris more and more a commercial as well as a political centre, so that alongside the long-established artisanal trades, furniture-making and printing for example, new industries were established, associated as with so much of the economic expansion with the growth of the railways, so that the engineering industry became a part of the capital's industrial life. This produced an increase in population, as people were attracted by the possibility of employment, something that in turn urged on the rebuilding programme, because it was necessary to clear away the appalling slums and to begin building proper housing for the workers.

Houses, however, were not enough. What was also needed was clean water and clean air, and above all a system of sewage disposal which would end the outbreaks of cholera that had afflicted the city, together with other European capitals, in the earlier part of the nineteeth century. Always interested in English opinion, the Emperor asked Edwin Chadwick, a public health expert who was visiting Paris, what he thought of the improvements that had been made in providing air, light and water for the populace, to which he replied: 'Sir, it was said of Augustus that he found Rome brick and left it marble. May it be said of you that you found Paris stinking and left it sweet.'

Chadwick's enthusiam reflected his own interests in public health, but the transformation of Paris had produced much more than clean water and efficient sewers. It was thanks to all the urban improvements that the city became a fitting backdrop to the one area in which the Empire's success was unchallenged: its reputation for the brilliance and splendour of its court and its society. The Tuileries palace, having been dubbed 'the first salon in Paris', had fulfilled a prophecy that Lord Malmesbury had made in March 1852. In the course of attending a court function, he had commented on the air of unreality which surrounded the pageant, for he felt that not every-one had quite mastered their allotted roles. He went on to say: 'but, when each actor becomes acclimatised by time, it will be a magnificent court, with a sovereign who will command the attention of all Europe'. The rebuilding of Paris provided a suitable setting for the imperial show, and there were also the other great stage sets, the palaces at Compiègne, Fontainebleau and St-Cloud, all of which were used to enhance the dynasty's prestige. Those who were received at court found that the Emperor's ease of manner and his charm seduced all who came in contact with him, while the Empress's beauty and her sharpness of intellect (some-times too eagerly exercised) in no way detracted from her graciousness as a host. The stuffier European courts might at one time have classified

Napoleon and Eugénie as 'other persons who may be invited', but in Paris, secure in the knowledge that its court was the envy of Europe, no one worried about this.

In any event, the imperial dynasty had no need to feel in any way inferior amongst crowned heads. It needs to be remembered that since the fall of the First Empire in 1815 the Bonaparte family had, by marriage, extended and enlarged its connection with all the major royal houses of Europe. As a result Napoleon III, in spite of his unorthodox line of succession, could claim kinship with the majority of European rulers. The Habsburgs, the Wittelsbachs and the royal Houses of Baden and Württemberg, even the Romanovs, all had links with the Bonapartes. To these Napoleon was to add a connection to the House of Savoy, as a result of the marriage of his cousin Prince Napoleon to the Princess Marie Clotilde, daughter of King Victor Emmanuel of Piedmont. Through the Beauharnais connection, the descendants of Eugène tied the family to the royal houses of Portugal, Brazil and Sweden.

Acceptance by dynastic Europe was sometimes uneasy, but Napoleon's Empire was a fact of life to which most rulers adapted. Determined to make friendship with England the keystone of his foreign policy, as being the surest way forward in Europe, he began by inviting Prince Albert to a meeting at Boulogne. It was a chance for the Prince to form an opinion of his host, which turned out to be favourable, though Albert deplored the Emperor's constant cigarette smoking. The prize was won, however, for an invitation came for the imperial couple to visit England in 1855 as guests of Queen Victoria. A state visit to the hereditary enemy would do wonders for the prestige of the regime and the dynasty.

The Queen, alarmed by the prospect: wrote in her diary 'These great meetings of sovereigns, surrounded by very exciting accompaniements, are always very agitating', but in fact the encounter was a great success. Napoleon III deployed all his charm (Lord Clarendon said he wooed the Queen) and put everyone at ease, avoiding any comment on the banquet held in the Waterloo Room, and ended by being invested with the Order of the Garter. At the end of the six days, the visit had assumed the atmosphere of a family gathering based on the personal relations established between the two sovereigns. When the time came to part, both couples were genuinely sad – the only cheering thought was the return visit to Paris planned for August. It was an early example of summit diplomacy, which features so largely in our own age, and it seems to have been remarkably successful. At least it gave the illusion of achievement, which was useful in reassuring public opinion that all was well between France and the rest of Europe, but there can no doubt that good relations with England were important and this visit did make a difference.[13]

As agreed at Windsor, the Queen and Prince Albert, accompanied by their two elder children, arrived in Paris in August 1855 for the state visit. The city was already *en fête* because of the Universal Exhibition, which was so to impress Prince Albert that he visited it three times during his stay. From the moment they arrived, the royal couple were shown what had been achieved by the regime, their route from the station taking them along the great new boulevards, one of which the Emperor asked the Queen's permission to name the 'Avenue Victoria' in honour of the visit.

No effort was spared to make the visit successful and memorable, and it worked. The Queen said: 'How beautiful and enjoyable is this place'. Even the visit to the tomb of Napoleon I in the Invalides, on the arm of Napoleon III, 'My dearest friend and ally', was an unqualified success. At the end, the Queen summed it up in a simple phrase: 'we parted with mutual sorrow'. Indeed, so reluctant was the Prince of Wales to go that he asked the Emperor if he might stay. *He* was never to forget Paris. In this case there is no doubt that personal diplomacy, in spite of subsequent political vicissitudes, did form the basis of a real, warm and lasting friendship between the two royal couples.[14]

Perhaps this is the moment to ask what Napoleon III, as ruler, hoped to achieve? He wanted above all to create a society at peace with itself, to put an end to the dismal series of failed regimes which had been tried in France from 1815 to 1848 and which had only served to reinforce the impression given to other powers of the country's second-rate status. He saw that to achieve this there must be a reconciliation between masses and classes, something that could be brought about, he believed, by increasing the general prosperity of the country. By giving to the less well off in society a better and more secure life they would have a reason for maintaining stability, while under the rule of the only dynasty that could lay claim to inherit the traditions of the Revolution civic peace could be attained. The task of the third Napoleon was, therefore, to add economic prosperity and social peace to the administrative and legal stability bequeathed by Napoleon I. The Emperor was under no illusions about the difficulties which confronted him in pursuing these goals: a sceptical, and frequently hostile, elitist political class confronted sections of an embittered working class, all too aware of the previous actions of this particular group; a situation that made class reconciliation a daunting prospect.

In order to achieve this reconciliation it was essential that the existence of popular Bonapartism be recognised and encouraged by measures destined to show the mass of the people that the regime did not automatically side with the wealthy and powerful. At a local level, people were trained to look to the prefects for solutions to problems and not to the local notables who were accustomed to being in control. The emphasis was on the existence of a direct line from sovereign to people that must be seen to be effective in bringing local affairs to the attention of the government – that is, in the popular mind, to the Emperor. Clearly these feelings were reinforced by the participation in elections and, when necessary, plebiscites. What the mass of the French people were learning during this period was how to exercise the political power conferred on them by universal suffrage, a process which refutes the accusation that the regime was both reactionary and repressive.

Accused of dictatorship, the Emperor's reign gave the lie to the accusation; had he been a dictator he could have achieved a great deal more, but at the possible cost of social breakdown. That is why at no point, except for the first few months of 1852, did France lack representative institutions and a legal system, nor was it deprived of an opposition. The governmental machine was ruthless, but it felt itself, with reason, to be faced with a potentially revolutionary and frequently violent society. What Napoleon III hoped was that firmness applied in the short run would lead ultimately to a relaxation, a 'liberalisation' of the more authoritarian aspects of the regime, and the extraordinary feature of the Second Empire is that the Emperor *kept* his promise to work for an increasingly liberal regime. The word needs qualification, for the 'liberals' in this context were a composite group of Orleanists and Republicans, who, while they clamoured for parliamentary government and political freedom, were fiercely opposed to the social and humanitarian aspects of the government, that is to the Emperor's most cherished policies.

It was precisely because he was aware of the intentions of the conservative groups in politics that Napoleon III had tried to make liberalisation a gradual process that moved at his pace and in his time. What hindered the carrying out of this scheme was the lack of any committed Bonapartist group willing to give him wholehearted support in his reform projects, since the convinced Bonapartists saw any concessions to parliamentary liberalism as a weakening of the regime. Because the government depended on a majority in the Legislative Body, to get its business done, Napoleon III and his ministers were forced into a difficult balancing act between opposing groups in order to get their policies accepted. For the Emperor, and for the future of the dynasty, the most worrying development was the openly expressed opinion by leading conservatives that the time had come 'to get rid of him'. It was precisely this attitude which confirmed the Bonapartists in their hostility to the reform programme, since they suspected that any increase in the influence of this 'liberal' group would lead to a weakening of the regime. That was indeed its intention.

To the various voices clamouring for or against reform was added that of Prince Napoleon. Far from being a help, he attacked the Emperor for not going farther and faster on the road to democratisation. The Prince saw himself as a real Bonaparte radical even republican in his convictions, and believing in the Consulate rather than the Empire. Unfortunately, his public criticisms were not accompanied by any concrete or constructive proposals, and, in his correspondence with his cousin on the subject, it was apparent that he considered his opinions were so well founded as to be above discussion. In this respect, as in others, he greatly resembled his uncle Lucien, and only extreme patience on the part of Napoleon III made any relationship possible. When it is remembered that the Prince lost no opportunity to demonstrate his hostility to the Empress, even to the point of deliberate rudeness, there was little in his public or private conduct to endear him to the Emperor.

In spite of all the difficulties, Napoleon III persevered: by the late 1860s freedom of the press and freedom of political assembly had been conceded, and in 1868–69 there was a moment of hope that the wider policy would succeed. Emile Ollivier, a Republican deputy in the legislature, whose father had been arrested and deported in December 1851, rallied to the Empire. To the Emperor, this was a justification of his policy and, not without some trepidation, he moved to the 'crowning of the edifice', as he put it, by promulgating in 1870 a new constitution ushering in the 'Liberal Empire'.

Although the new system represented a partial triumph for the conservatives, for Ollivier's ministry was a heterodox affair, the Emperor, in spite of much opposition, had already achieved for the masses some of his aims for that social justice whose outlines he had drawn in *The Suppression of Poverty*, his brochure written in 1844 while he was imprisoned in the fortress at Ham.

General prosperity had brought better standards of living and in 1864 the workers had been granted the right of association, enabling them to present a common front against the employers. In the same year, the repeal of articles of the Civil Code gave to workers the right to strike. Even more surprisingly, under the Emperor's protection, the First International had been allowed to set up its offices in Paris.[15]

By the summer of 1870 it seemed that the restored Empire, together with the dynasty, had succeeded in firmly establishing itself. There was an heir to the throne, a healthy and intelligent fourteen-year-old boy, and the Emperor had crowned his promised programme of liberalisation by promulgating the new constitution to reform the imperial system. This constitution had been ratified by a plebiscite held in the month of May, in accordance with the Bonapartist tradition, and almost eight million voted their approval of the new system, as against the one and a half million who voted 'No'. The interesting point about this plebiscite is that many who took part were new voters, not those who had voted in 1851 and 1852. The dynasty had therefore successfully renewed its union with the people, the basis of its claim to govern. The Emperor was pleased, and a leading Republican opponent, Leon Gambetta, felt that he had indeed every right to be: 'it is a crushing blow; the Empire is stronger than ever'. His view was that of the majority of people both inside and outside France. It proved to be mistaken.

9

Triumph and Catastrophe

In 1870, at the age of sixty-two, Napoleon III had carried through a major reform programme by inaugurating a new constitutional structure that he hoped would consolidate the Empire and secure the future of the dynasty. Unfortunately, in spite of all the efforts he had made, his most challenging problem, that of establishing France's position in the European states system, remained unresolved. The Emperor had always insisted that the control of foreign policy must remain in his hands, the reason being that he was well aware of the difficulties which would arise once he began to probe the weaknesses of the European system established in 1815, designed as a check to French ambition. From the beginning of his reign, the Emperor made plain his conviction that only by drawing England to him in a firm and fully functioning understanding, a real *entente cordiale*, could France hope to regain its position in European affairs. As far as the rest of his policy was concerned, it represented a continuity rather than a new departure, because since 1815 successive regimes in France had sought to break through the restrictions placed on their freedom of manoeuvre by the Waterloo coalition. It was natural that with the advent of a Bonaparte to power large sections of French society, what one might call 'radical' Bonapartist groups, thought and expected that France would play a more positive role in European affairs and, above all, that there would be an end to the tutelage in which the country had been held since 1815.

Well aware that much was expected of him, Napoleon III was also well aware of the risks which a 'forward' foreign policy would entail. The treaties of 1815 certainly restricted the foreign policy of France, but they also, paradoxically, protected France from the threat of further change, since the situation rested on an equilibrium accepted by all the major European powers. It was therefore unlikely that France would be threatened by a major international upheaval, providing that it did not provoke the rest of Europe, hence Napoleon III's statement in 1852 stressing that 'the Empire means peace'.

The Emperor was resolved to achieve the unpicking of the 1815 system by means of diplomacy rather than war, and to this end he maintained two basic principles of conduct in foreign affairs. The first was the alliance with England, which he considered essential in order to avoid France being isolated in Europe. Convinced that England held the key to future developments on the Continent, and also believing that her commercial financial and external interests coincided with those of France, he set himself to convince English statesman that a real *working* arrangement could be established between the two countries.

The second basic factor in Napoleon III's strategy was his belief in the settling of affairs by means of international congresses of the powers. He was convinced that disputes and problems could be solved by discussion and by negotiation, so that states could come together in a peace conference without passing through the intermediate stage of war. To him it seemed that a diplomatic crisis need not necessarily end in armed conflict but could be solved by common sense and concession, destined to serve the common good of all. It was a laudable doctrine, but in the context of the time it was unrealistic. A cynic might well have added that, had France been militarily more powerful, the Emperor would have been less pacific. Whatever the reason, Napoleon III did try to make diplomacy work in this way, to the point where it sometimes led to an appearance of hesitation and inconsistency in the conduct of his foreign policy.

The basic problem for the Emperor was that, while France needed Britain, it was not at all clear to British statesmen that their country had any need of France, except when it suited their purposes. Napoleon III is reputed to have said 'other countries are my mistresses, but England is my wife', and, true or not, the marriage was, like most, full of ups and downs. Napoleon III, however, clung to it.

If the Emperor was to make any progress in pursuing the English alliance, clearly the best way would be to find an enemy against whom a common front could be established, and in the mid nineteenth century Britain's only apparent enemy was the Russian Empire. British statesmen were constantly alarmed by Russian activity in the Near East, feeling that intervention in the large and decaying Ottoman Empire would be followed by Russian expansion into the areas formerly controlled by the Sultan. Well aware of English fears, Napoleon III decided that a joint Anglo-French approach to the problems of the Near East would be popular in Britain and would provide him with the lever he sought to hoist France into place in the European system. It is highly unlikely that he envisaged anything more than joint diplomatic pressure on Russia to bring Tsar Nicholas I to the conference table to discuss the problems at issue. That explains why Napoleon used, as a pretext, the artificial or at best symbolic question of the keys to the Holy Places in Jerusalem, whose custody was disputed between the Latin Catholic and Greek Orthodox Churches. Those who accuse Napoleon III of having gone to war on a frivolous pretext miss the point. He chose to take up the issue precisely because he thought it could not possibly lead to war, in that neither the Tsar nor the Sultan, in whose Empire Jerusalem was, would see the issues as of much importance. He miscalculated badly, forgetting the Tsar's pride, which made him unyielding in his claim to be protector of the Greek Christians, and the reaction of the Sultan, who was weary of being pressured by the Powers and who feared for the security of his Empire. As a result of this grave error of judgement, the protagonists set out on a collision course which led to the Crimean War, and the Emperor, who had set out to find a diplomatic partner in a European Congress, found himself instead with an ally and engaged in a European war.[1]

Not only was Napoleon III engaged in a war which he had not really wanted, it was a war that went badly and which threatened to become unpopular in both France and Britain. Eventually, the war came to an end, neither participant having particularly distinguished themselves militarily, though on balance the French army put up a better show than the English. The whole affair, however, was far from being a wasted effort, since it gave rise to the visit of the imperial couple to England, and the return visit of Victoria and Albert to Paris, occasions which underlined the friendship between the two countries. There was also the fact that the peace conference that finally ended the war was held in Paris, a diplomatic triumph for Napoleon III, whose brilliant stage management of the occasion showed that France was once more at the centre of European affairs.

In spite of the brilliance of the occasion, two things detracted from any real feeling of satisfaction. First, dynastically, the war had been an occasion for an unfortunate incident. Prince Napoleon had gone to the Crimea at his own request, saying: 'When the nation takes up arms, Your Majesty will accept that my place is among the soldiers.' Unfortunately, once at the front he acquired a reputation for not being keen to be under fire, and had returned home, pleading ill health, without the Emperor's permission and against his wishes. The affair was much commented on, especially by the enemies of the regime, and did considerable harm to the reputation of the imperial family.[2] The second, and much more serious result, was that the peace was designed to suit Britain and not France, since England insisted upon a clause closing the Straits to Russian warships and neutralising the Black Sea. Napoleon, who had planned on a reconciliation with Russia once the war was over, now found this to be impossible, since the new Tsar, Alexander II, always insisted on the repeal of what were known as the Black Sea clauses before any other consideration. France, therefore, found itself still constrained in its foreign policy; for to satisfy Russia there would have had to be a breach with England.

There were other, and deeper, reasons for disquiet, something that went to the heart of the regime. The Bonapartist inheritance presumed an 'active' policy, destined to carry on the work of the Revolution by defending the cause of oppressed peoples in Europe, a sentiment which had surfaced strongly at the time of the Revolution of 1848. Like it or not, the dynasty's inheritance, its very title deeds, lay in the Revolution, a package which had to be accepted as a whole. To pick and choose was not really an option. While this undoubtedly represented one of the strengths of the dynasty, it also produced pressures which Napoleon III could not ignore. To pursue a wider policy, without actually alarming and antagonising the whole of Europe, was an extremely difficult proposition. As Napoleon said, in the middle of his reign: 'It's all very fine to have sympathy for the national aspirations of this or that people, but it's the Revolution which, by coming into play, spoils it all. It's because I cannot, and will not, have dealings with the Revolution that I have so many problems nowadays. The Revolution defeats the best causes, destroys the sympathy one might feel, which makes Italy odious to me, while Poland disgusts me.'[3] It was a dilemma that proved insoluble, because, try as he might, Napoleon III could not live down the taint that went with his name, and his motives were always suspect.

The Waterloo coalition had been breached by the Crimean War, since Britain and France had become allies, and the Tsar Alexander was principally preoccupied with the internal reconstruction of his Empire, which the war had shown to be lamentably weak. Taking advantage of the situation, Napoleon decided that the time had come to redraw the map of Italy which, since 1815, had been either directly or indirectly ruled by

Austria. French interests in Italy were based on both political and economic considerations, both in a sense strategic. It was clearly to France's advantage to advance its south-eastern frontier by the acquisition of Savoy and Nice, while the building of railways in the region would give it a strong economic and strategic position in northern and central Italy. To achieve this, Austria must be dislodged from Lombardy and Venetia, ruled by it under the terms of the 1815 settlement, something which would inevitably lead to a weakening of Habsburg influence throughout the entire peninsula. The question was: if France began to threaten Austria's position, would the other signatories of 1815 come to Austria's aid? Having calculated the odds, Napoleon III decided that at the moment this was unlikely. Britain appeared to have little interest in the region, Russia was preoccupied, and resentful over Austria's attitude during the Crimean War, while Prussia had its own grudges against Vienna because of friction resulting from Austrian policy within the German Confederation.

Italy occupied a special place in the Bonapartes' thinking about Europe, because under the Empire part of it had been erected into a kingdom of which Napoleon I had been King, and its existence had been seen as symbol of Italian nationhood. Furthermore, the Bourbons had been expelled from the kingdom of Naples to be replaced as sovereigns first by Joseph Bonaparte and then by Murat (married to Caroline Bonaparte), while Elisa Bonaparte was Grand Duchess of Tuscany. The result was that large parts of the peninsula had become virtually an appanage of the dynasty. After the fall of the Empire, Italy had served as a place of refuge for most of the family, and it had been the scene of Louis Napoleon's youthful escapade when he and his brother had volunteered to help the revolutionary movement in 1830. The family connection was therefore strong, and, in an Italy subjected to extremely reactionary regimes after 1815, there is no doubt that there was a hope among Italian patriots that the restoration of the Empire meant that Napoleon III would do something to help Italian aspirations for unity.

There was a further reason for intervention, arising from the personal hostility which the family were bound to feel against Austria, whose conduct in 1814 and 1815 had made of it the virtual nemesis of the dynasty. The behaviour of Marie-Louise, and the subsequent treatment of Napoleon II at the Austrian court at Vienna, had only served to strengthen the already strong feelings of dislike. These factors led Napoleon to consider moving against Austria in order to dislodge it from the Italian peninsula. To them was added a further complication, namely the growth of revolutionary movements in Italy. The existence of these movements, which seemed to be capable of promoting general instability, alarmed the European powers, who rightly suspected that the restoration of the imperial dynasty had given new life to old hopes.[4]

Well aware that he was suspected of being one of the causes of unrest in Italy, Napoleon III decided that a further round of personal diplomacy might help to calm the situation. In August 1857 he and Eugénie made a personal visit to the Queen and Prince Albert at Osborne. The atmosphere was cordial and relaxed. But that was all that the encounter achieved. There was no extension of the *entente*, and British Ministers were not convinced that the Emperor sought peace and stability. There was an unforeseen consequence in that the visit strengthened the friendship between the Queen and the Empress. Victoria noted 'she is very well informed, well read, much more serious than people give her credit for', adding, 'I am sure the Emperor would do well to follow her advice'. The Queen's views are not to be taken lightly since she did not give her friendship or respect without good reason.[5]

In September there was a meeting with the Tsar at Stuttgart, but Alexander was convinced that the alliance with England had just been reinforced by the visit to Osborne and was not prepared to negotiate on anything. Continuing his tour the Emperor went to meet Franz Joseph of Austria, but this meeting was so personal rather than political that it did not even take place in Vienna and ended in an exchange of courtesies. If, as seems possible, Napoleon III was hoping that he could bring about a European conference, in which there could be a general discussion – preferably of the 1815 settlement in its entirety – he was disappointed.

In any case the whole situation was brought sharply into focus by a practical demonstration of the seriousness of the Italian revolutionary movements. In January 1858 an attempt was made to assassinate Napoleon III as he drove with the Empress to attend a performance at the opera in Paris. The narrowness of their escape was a frightful reminder not only of their human vulnerability but also of the fragility of the regime, for had they died the heir to the throne was only two years old. This was the third serious attempt to kill the Emperor and, as in the other two, the perpetrators were Italians. This most recent outrage was the work of Count Orsini, who had been moved to his action by the hatred he felt for Napoleon III, because of his failure to help the Italian national movement. French public opinion, enraged by the attempt, was further inflamed when it became known that the bombs which had been thrown by Orsini had been made in Birmingham, and that the whole conspiracy had been hatched in London. An outburst of Anglophobia put Anglo-French relations under severe strain at all levels, particularly when one of the conspirators arrested in London was acquitted at his trial.[6]

The Emperor, who incidentally had wanted to pardon Orsini and his accomplice, and had only yielded to his ministers' demands for their execution when they pointed out that innocent people had been killed, made strenuous efforts to restore good relations with England. In trying to repair the damage done to the *entente*, and as a public demonstration of his fidelity to the alliance, he invited the Queen and Prince Albert to visit France hoping that once again a meeting between the sovereigns would dampen down hostility on both sides of the Channel.

The meeting took place at Cherbourg in August 1858, and both couples tacitly agreed to make the maximum number of public appearances together, the Emperor escorting the Queen while the Empress was escorted by Prince Albert. The crowds, initially cool in their reception, gradually thawed, largely because the imperial couple worked hard to demonstrate that all was well between the visitors and themselves. It all ended on a happy note, not least because it was known Napoleon III had offered passage through France to troops being sent to India to suppress the Mutiny. By going overland by rail to Toulon, the sea voyage would have been considerably shortened.

The meeting with the English royal couple could, however, be no more than an interlude, because it was clear that the Italian question had to be tackled, particularly after the sharp reminder given by Orsini of the threat posed to the Emperor's life. Napoleon III had already had desultory discussions in 1856 with the Prime Minister of the kingdom of Piedmont, Count Cavour, about possible French intervention, but these had remained inconclusive. As a result of Orsini's attempt, Cavour now realised that he had a weapon which he could use to push Napoleon into action. He stressed how dangerous the activities of the revolutionaries were, an argument to which the Emperor was susceptible, realising that if the movement really got under way it would give Austria an excuse to intervene, as in 1830, in order to suppress them. Such a move would provoke a real crisis for Napoleon III; at home, French popular opinion would clamour for intervention against Austria; and this might very well lead to a serious international situation if Austria invoked the 1815 settlement and looked to the other signatories for support.

An international war was exactly what Napoleon III did not want. Austria must be isolated and for this reason his agreement with Cavour depended upon the *Austrians* threatening Piedmont, thus putting themselves in the wrong. Napoleon may well have hoped that the existence of such a threat would enable him to find support for the European Congress which he wished to call to deal with the 'Italian Question', but unfortunately not everyone would accept that there was any Italian Question, and so the Emperor's game of diplomacy without war failed.

He had now no option but to go forward, though no longer really completely in charge of events, since he had handed over to Cavour the decision of whether or not to provoke a war with Austria, and this carried serious risks. When the Emperor had come to an agreement at Plombières, he had made it plain to Cavour that he had a very limited view of what 'Italian unification' would mean. Piedmont would acquire Lombardy and the Veneto from Austria, there would be a middle kingdom which would be ruled by Prince Napoleon, who would marry the daughter of the King of Piedmont, and the Papal States would be left intact, as would the kingdom of Naples. It was intended that this rearrangement would replace Austrian by French influence throughout the peninsula, while, at the same time, enlarging the Piedmontese kingdom.

The government in Vienna, well aware of Napoleon's manoeuvring and weary of the diplomatic game, was finally provoked into action by the mobilisation of the Piedmontese army, which had been put on a war footing. Austria demanded that Piedmont withdraw its army from the frontiers of Austria's Italian provinces. Since the agreement had stipulated that Piedmont must be the victim of an Austrian attack in order that France should come to Piedmont's aid, this ultimatum resolved Napoleon III's dilemma and opened the way to war with Austria.

On the morning of 4 May 1859, the Emperor issued a proclamation, designed to allay the fears that his policy was producing in Europe generally, and in the Italian states in particular, in which he disclaimed any revolutionary intent: 'We are not going to foment disorder nor to disturb the power of the Holy Father, whom we have replaced on his throne.' Rather more imprudently, he went on to speak of Italy being freed, from 'the Alps to the Adriatic', an aim that seemed to be in the best Napoleonic tradition, and on 10 May the Emperor left Paris to take command of the army.

A large crowd surrounded the Tuileries Palace, and the whole route from there to the railway station, where the Emperor was to take the train, was lined by a cheering crowds. The Place de la Bastille was full of people crying 'Vive l'Empereur!', and in the Faubourg St-Antoine the horses were detached from the carriage, the people pulling it themselves until the arrival at the station. Napoleon III would never again be as popular as he was on that day, at a moment that provided a demonstration of how the strength of the dynasty lay with the people, who identified it with the great days of the First Empire when France was thought to have defended the interests of other nations. This was a simplistic view, but it was nevertheless deeply felt and it needed to be taken into account in any analysis of the links which existed between the dynasty and the people, as well as the implications for both parties.[7]

Since the Emperor had gone to command the army, the Empress Eugénie became Regent, a task which she was to fulfil successfully, in spite of carping from ex-King Jerome, who made it plain that he considered her to be quite unfit to be so. His son, Prince Napoleon, who as part of Napoleon's Italian plan had married the daughter of the King of Piedmont, was given command of an army corps, the Emperor hoping that he would distinguish himself in the campaign more than he had done at the Crimea. The military campaign resulted in two French victories, the first at Magenta on 4 June and then at Solferino on 24 June, this second victory being followed on 11 July by a sudden French demand for an armistice, although the Austrian army was far from being totally defeated.

The armistice of Villafranca came about because Napoleon III had little choice. If the war was popular at home, there is no doubt that this Italian adventure, which seemed a prelude to a new era of French expansion, had alarmed the other European powers. Austria's defeat, and the consequent unpicking of part of the 1815 treaty system, had, it was felt, begun to alter the whole balance of power in France's favour. Such a shift was viewed with real apprehension and it led to a movement by Prussia to rally to Austria's support, in spite of their internal differences about the running of Germany. Prussia was not a power to be ignored; so, well aware of this, the Emperor decided to bring the war to an immediate end. Another reason for seeking peace was the fact that the French army, although victorious, had suffered serious losses and was being ravaged by sickness, for the hot summer weather had produced an outbreak of cholera.

Because the armistice terms envisaged the cession to Piedmont of Lombardy only, while Austria was to keep the Veneto, Napoleon III agreed to forgo his originally promised reward of Savoy and Nice, but extraneous events pushed both Cavour and the Emperor further than they wanted to go. There were insurrectionary outbreaks in many of the Italian states, whose leaders clamoured for union with Piedmont. Cavour, enraged by what he saw as a betrayal by Napoleon, decided that he would encourage these revolutionary movements and accept union with these states. Furthermore, since he could not acquire Venice, he decided to support Garibaldi in his conquest of Sicily and Naples and the expulsion of the Bourbons. As a result of his actions, the carefully balanced the scheme prepared at Plombières had, by 1860, disintegrated and Napoleon III's plan for a federated Italy was in ruins. Confronted with a united Italy, except for Rome which was occupied by French troops, and for which Napoleon had now become responsible, all he could do was to reassert his claim to Savoy and Nice. Their annexation by France, after a plebiscite, certainly represented a successful reversal of the 1815 settlement, but the price had been very high. Europe had been alarmed, the Italians remained unsatisfied, while the Pope, infuriated by the loss of the Papal States, refused to recognise the new Italian kingdom. By a twist of fate, Napoleon III now found himself having to act as guarantor of the safety of what remained of the papal possessions against further encroachments by the Italian state.

At best it had all been a limited triumph, but the feeling among the public was one of rejoicing; the war had been short, there had been no dislocation of trade, and the army had been victorious. It returned to Paris to an almost hysterical welcome, parading under victory arches to cries of 'Vive l'Empereur!' and 'Vive l'Armée!' From 1859 the head of the Emperor on the coinage was crowned with the laurel wreath of the victor, a tangible reminder of what came to be considered the high point of the Second Empire.

Napoleon III, who was not much given to enthusiasm, only too well aware that his Italian policy had not gone according to plan, and that he had indeed upset the European balance, decided to try another round of personal diplomacy. This time, in view of the Prussian reaction to the Italian war, he began in Germany, and in June 1860 he invited William, the Prince Regent of Prussia, to meet him at Baden, whose Grand Duke agreed to act as host. Prince William, who had no intention of allowing Napoleon to separate Prussia from the rest of the German states, accepted only on condition that all the other German sovereigns attended the meeting. The result was that, on his arrival at Baden, Napoleon found himself surrounded by all the German rulers: the Kings of Württemberg, Bavaria, Saxony and Hanover, the Grand Dukes of Hesse-Darmstadt and Saxe-Weimar, plus the Dukes of Nassau and Saxe-Coburg-Gotha. At first glance this meeting appeared to resemble the famous encounter between his uncle and the German Princes at Erfurt in 1808, but then France had commanded without question, while Kings and Princes had been only too eager to please. Now France was regarded with suspicion but not feared, and the Emperor was forced to seek cooperation rather than being able to impose his will.

Napoleon III realised this, and seeing that nothing of substance was likely to emerge from the meeting, turned it into an exercise in public relations, hoping that appearance would conceal reality. He used his charm and affability on all whom he met, he paid calls on all the sovereigns at their various hotels, and was seen in public with them. He then returned to Paris empty-handed. Left with little choice but to continue a policy of conciliation, he tried again with William, now King of Prussia since his brother's death in 1861. In October of that year, the King came to Compiègne as the guest of the Emperor and the Empress, who deployed all their charm in an attempt to woo him into a declaration of support for France. William, however, was disinclined to anything other than exchange of courtesies, once again making it quite clear that any attempt to detach Prussia from the rest of Germany was a fruitless exercise. This was particularly unfortunate, since relations with England, at a political level, had been affected by the Italian war. While acting as Regent, the Empress had written to the Queen pointing out that the Emperor hoped to localise the war, and asking that both she and Albert should use their influence in Germany to achieve this. The Queen replied in a friendly but negative fashion, making clear the distinction between personal feelings of friendship and affairs of state. In fact she had already written to the Prime Minister, Lord Derby, pointing out that the French should be aware of the united action of England with the other powers, since this would have, she hoped, 'a most wholesome influence on the French government'. There could be no doubt, therefore, that the Emperor had begun a process of change which he would find difficult to control without achieving military preponderance, and which risked isolating France in Europe.[8]

It was possibly the realisation that he depended so closely on Britain that led Napoleon III into a an extraordinary enterprise, namely the decision to mount a joint Anglo-French expedition to intervene in Mexico. This came about as a result of a discussion in the autumn of 1861 between Lord John Russell and his counterpart, Thouvenel, the French Minister for Foreign Affairs. The problem under discussion was Mexico, whose chronic governmental instability had led to the failure of successive regimes to honour the debts they owed foreign investors. The crisis came in 1861 when Juarez, the latest victor in the perpetual civil war, unilaterally suspended for two years on all payments on foreign debts, and it was at this point that Britain initiated discussions on intervention. The British bond-holders, together with those of France, who were Mexico's largest creditors, had formed a pressure group demanding decisive action by their governments to recover the money. Anxious to cooperate, Napoleon attempted to extend the alliance to include Spain, hoping that this would draw the two countries closer together, which would benefit France politically and economically. Palmerston was quite willing to support this, because it meant that he could then keep a close eye on the Emperor's Spanish policy, and finally the three powers agreed to mount an expedition to Mexico. There is no doubt that one of the factors influencing European attitudes was the civil war which was now raging in the United States, giving the Americans no time to enforce the Monroe Doctrine. Furthermore, it was held by most Europeans that the Confederate States stood a good chance of winning, and if this should be the outcome then the whole balance in North America would be altered.

Napoleon III was also interested in the possibility of growing cotton in northern Mexico, as this could provide an alternative source of supply now that the Confederate states were blockaded and the export of cotton limited. The problem with the expedition was that each participant had different aims: Napoleon III had an ambitious policy which implied establishing a French presence in Mexico, while Britain was simply interested in collecting money. The Spanish, no doubt remembering earlier episodes, were not at all anxious to have to participate militarily in any way; as soon as the coast of Mexico came in sight, they simply abandoned the enterprise and returned to Cuba. The British made plain their intention of giving the Mexicans a fright but of not intending to land troops in great numbers. As a result, only the French landed in force.

By 1862, Britain had concluded a separate agreement about the money with Juarez and, while indicating that there was no wish to hinder any project of Napoleon, withdrew totally from the affair. The view in London was that if the Emperor was busy in Mexico he would be less trouble in Europe.

From then on France was alone, and Napoleon III, weakened both politically and militarily, sank deeper and deeper into a quagmire which he had completely failed to foresee. In an attempt to stabilise the situation, an Empire was established under the auspices of France, the throne being given to Maximilian, the brother of Franz Joseph of Austria. But by 1866 the whole scheme lay in ruins and Napoleon III decided that he must withdraw: the victory of the North in 1865 had altered the balance in the Americas while in the summer of 1866 the victory of Prussia over Austria had altered the balance in Europe. Faced with these realities, Napoleon could no longer maintain a large and costly expeditionary force in Mexico, so French troops were withdrawn, leaving Maximilian to his fate. The inevitable happened. When in 1867 the news of the shooting of Maximilian at Queretaro by the triumphant revolutionaries reached Paris it was seen not only as a blow to the honour and prestige of Napoleon III but as a further demonstration of France's weakness.[9]

During the Mexican affair, the Emperor had attempted to use the alliance with England as a means of finding a diplomatic solution to his increasing European problems by once again attempting to organise a European Congress, 'to settle outstanding questions', for which he appealed in 1863. The idea was rejected by all the Powers (Queen Victoria dismissing it as, 'an impertinence'), a severe setback for Napoleon, for whom the European situation had worsened. The threat came from Prussia, which had decided to reorder affairs in the German Confederation to the detriment of Austria. If this brought about Pussian dominance, a decisive change in the balance of forces in Europe would occur. In such circumstances a weakened France would be severely disadvantaged.

The outbreak of an insurrection in Poland in 1863 produced an upsurge of popular feeling in France in support of the Poles, and it was felt that the dynasty should fulfil its historic role by intervening on behalf of the insurgents. This brought sharply into focus the ambiguous nature of Napoleon's position: if he intervened he would identify himself in the eyes of the European powers with support of revolutionary causes. At home, failure to help the Poles would be considered a failure to live up to the Napoleonic inheritance. Fully aware of the dilemma, and even more conscious of his military weakness, the Emperor was obliged to limit himself to protests about the treatment of Poland. Since any real intervention was out of the question, the protests were treated with contempt in St Petersburg, and their only effect was simply to antagonise Russia still further.

More alarming was the public support given to Russian policy by Prussia, whose government certainly had no interest in making life difficult for a fellow occupier of Poland, and its support drew the two Powers closer together. The appointment of Bismarck as Minister President of Prussia in 1861 meant that from now on Berlin would pursue an aggressive policy within the Germanic Confederation with a view to weakening Austrian influence. In this context, the drawing together of Russia and Prussia represented a check to Napoleon III's diplomatic hopes. A further setback to French policy came when Prussia, now certain that Russia would not raise any difficulties, inveigled Austria into a joint declaration of war on Denmark in 1864 as a first step in the planned reconstruction of the German Confederation. By its action, Austria fell into Bismarck's trap, but Napoleon III, now seriously alarmed, was unable to persuade Lord Palmerston to accept a joint intervention on behalf of Denmark, in spite of much talk and bluster on the part of the British Prime Minister.

Tension between France and Britain had been growing ever since the French had undertaken the construction of the Suez Canal, which it was feared would greatly enhance France's strategic and economic position in the Mediterranean and the Near East. Above all, there was the fear of a French threat to the trade routes to India, already recognised as the key to British imperial expansion.

Faced with a virtual breakdown in Anglo-French relations, and with his failure to succeed in calling a congress, Napoleon III decided that the only thing to do was to deal directly with Bismarck, in an attempt to gain some sort of diplomatic initiative, and in the summer of 1865 the two men met at Biarritz.[10] The problem with the meeting was that Bismarck knew what he wanted, while Napoleon III was only hoping to find out to what he could achieve by negotiation with the Prussian Chancellor.

Bismarck wanted to be sure that there would be no interference by France in the war which he now planned against Austria, so his aim was to test the possible reactions of the Emperor to such an eventuality. He found, as he hoped, that there was little chance of active intervention by France in the event of war; in fact, it became clear to Bismarck that Napoleon envisaged himself acting as mediator in the event of such a conflict, a role which would restore his prestige without any need for military involvement. As a further inducement to non-intervention, Bismarck indicated that Austria, under Prussian pressure, would cede the Veneto which it still held, providing France kept Italy neutral. Possession of this province by the kingdom of Italy would help to complete the work of unification begun in 1859 and, as Bismarck skilfully pointed out, this would ease Napoleon III's conscience about an unfulfilled pledge. In return for its cooperation, France would achieve a rectification of frontiers; but Bismarck was vague on this point, although it seems that Luxembourg was mentioned. Unfortunately, and very foolishly, none of this was written down. When the time came for an implementation of Napoleon's plans, Bismarck was able to deny any specific commitment. The Emperor commented bitterly, 'I trusted Bismarck and he betrayed me'. It was to prove a fatal mistake.

As had happened before, military events made nonsense of Napoleon's diplomatic subtleties. Austria was so totally defeated by Prussia at the battle of Sadowa in July 1866 that any attempt at mediation by France would have been rejected out of hand by Berlin, especially as it was known that such mediation would be a paper exercise with no military back-up. In Paris there was a great debate about intervention but never any real question of this being possible, because France had not the military capacity. The debate about intervention produced an astounding example of irresponsible behaviour by Prince Napoleon, who told a confidant that he could reassure Bismarck about the Emperor's intentions: 'They'll make noises, but they won't go to war. Tell Bismarck to have no worries on that score; let him amuse the Emperor with evasive comments, and let him annihilate Austria once and for all.'[11] This reassurance must have been well received in Berlin.

For Napoleon III, who did not, as his cousin did, have the luxury of encouraging France's enemies without having to worry about the consequences, the defeat of Austria was fatal. It not only revealed France's weakness but also underlined the extent to which Prussia had become a major power, and a military force, with nothing to hinder the reconstruction of the Germanic states system with Berlin at its centre. The end result was the creation of the North German Confederation with Prussia at its head.

Early in 1867, within a few months of the Austrian collapse, the Emperor together with the Minister for War, Marshal Niel, produced a substantial programme of military reforms in an attempt to strengthen the army, which badly needed a complete reformation in its structure and armament. Although it was clear that, without greater military strength, France's situation in Europe would become more and more perilous, opposition in the legislature defeated the plans for military reforms. As a result, the army remained well below the level it needed to be to confront the newly enlarged and well armed Prussian state.

As a consequence of the weakened position in which he found himself, from now until the catastrophe of 1870 the Emperor's foreign policy was one of expedients and compromises. The result was to demean him in the eyes of Europe, while simultaneously underlining the feebleness of 'court diplomacy' faced with a reality of Bismarck's 'blood and iron' tactics. Perhaps in the spirit of a man threatened with bankruptcy who throws a lavish party to confuse his creditors, Napoleon III, confronted with these difficulties, organised a second Great Exhibition in Paris in the summer of 1867. Once again the capital played host to the major and minor royalties of Europe, including the Tsar and the King of Prussia. Queen Victoria, in mourning since the death of Prince Albert in 1861, did not attend. Neither did the Emperor of Austria, on whom recent military defeats weighed heavily and who preferred to nurse his grief at home. If this gathering of sovereigns in Paris represented an attempt to revive a policy of 'business between sovereigns', it failed. In political and diplomatic terms nothing came from the meetings. Given the absence of the Austrian Emperor, and an unfortunate incident when a young Polish revolutionary attempted to assassinate Tsar Alexander II, this is hardly surprising.[12] It is doubtful if Napoleon III really expected anything of consequence to emerge, but, clinging to the hope that Britain would always be with him, he had taken the unusual step of sending Eugénie to visit Queen Victoria at Osborne in July 1867. Although the visit was not official, it had a serious purpose, which was made clear by the discussions between the two women about the problems facing France. The Queen listened sympathetically, even criticising Prussia's militarism, and urged caution on both sides, but that was far from a concrete demonstration of support for France by the British government.

Given that constitutional proprieties hampered Queen Victoria, the Emperor thought that a less constitutional monarch might be more responsive, and with this hope he and the Empress set out in August 1867 on a state visit to Austria to meet the Emperor Franz Joseph at Salzburg. The journey was so organised that they passed through several German states on the way. They hoped to find that there was pro-French feeling on the part of the south German sovereigns, who, it was thought, would be alarmed by the rise of Prussia. All these rulers however, with the exception of the King of Bavaria, confined their greetings to the minimum demanded by courtesy, an indication of how far anti-French attitudes had developed.

More reassuring, at least superficially, was the welcome at Salzburg. Franz Joseph met the imperial couple, accompanied by his wife the Empress Elizabeth, and there was a huge round of banquets, receptions and country excursions. There is no record of any serious business being discussed by the two Emperors, but whatever there was is unlikely to have been of much substance. Napoleon III found that his host was constrained by the new constitutional structure that had emerged as a result of the defeat of 1866. In the field of foreign policy the Hungarians now had a voice, and well aware that it was Bismarck's victory which had brought them their independent status in the new state of Austria-Hungary, the parliamentarians in Budapest were determined resolutely to oppose any diplomatic moves which might seem to threaten Prussia. The resulting axis between Berlin and Budapest prevented any real hope of a rapprochement between Paris and Vienna and completed the virtual isolation of France in Europe.

Alarmed by this isolation, Napoleon III made an effort to recoup some of his lost prestige by attempting to achieve by negotiation what he dared not attempt by force, conceiving a plan for the purchase by France of the grand duchy of Luxembourg. The territory belonged to the King of Holland, who was quite willing to part with it, and its purchase would have strengthened France's eastern frontier. It would also mean the withdrawal of a Prussian garrison, which had been installed there since 1815 as a visible reminder of France's defeat, and its removal would, therefore, be popular. A bloodless diplomatic *coup* would also enhance the prestige of the dynasty.

Bismarck at first seemed indifferent to the transaction, and all appeared to be on the point of settlement, when suddenly the Prussian Chancellor unleashed a vicious press campaign, reinforced by his own parliamentary speeches, in which he denounced this shameful cession of 'German land'. As a result of Bismarck's *volte-face* the Luxembourg transaction became public, and Napoleon III had no option but to submit the question to an international conference. The conference produced as a solution the neutralisation of Luxembourg. Although this meant the withdrawal of the Prussian garrison, it deprived Napoleon III of the territory he had sought and with it the frontier rectification in France's favour. The only bright moment in all of this was that Britain had worked on France's behalf in order to bring about the international conference. The incident was closed, but it represented a turning-point in Franco-Prussian relations. Henceforth the Emperor was convinced that Bismarck would seek, and would find, a means of going to war with France.

To add to all of these diplomatic problems there was the fact that the Emperor himself was ill. He had been for several years in severe pain and finally agreed to a medical examination. This resulted in a diagnosis of a kidney stone for which the only remedy was a surgical operation, a highly dangerous proceeding. The Emperor realised that if anything went wrong he would leave the Empire with a Regency, because the Prince Imperial would not attain his majority until 1874. There seems little doubt that Napoleon realised that he must hold on to power, avoiding the operation, until the Prince was of age; he could then abdicate in his favour. In the meantime, he intermittently suffered the severe pain brought about by his condition. While this may or may not have affected his intellectual judgement (contemporaries held conflicting opinions), it certainly limited his physical activity.[13] If it came to a war, the Emperor would be severely handicapped.

There was one moment of imperial glory in the middle of all these sombre months when, in September 1869, the Empress set out for Venice on her way to the grand opening of the Suez Canal. Eugénie went on the imperial yacht, *L'Aigle*, calling at Athens and at Constantinople, where she was received by the Sultan and given an enthusiastic welcome by the French community. In November she arrived at Alexandria, made a visit to Cairo, and spent a fortnight sailing on the Nile before reaching Port Said. There she was met by her cousin Ferdinand de Lesseps, the triumphant engineer of the canal. The ceremonial opening took place on the morning of 17 November and the imperial yacht took the head of a flotilla of fifty vessels, immediately followed by that of the Khedive of Egypt. Then, in close order, came the yachts of the Emperor Franz Joseph, the Crown Prince of Prussia and Prince Henry of the Netherlands. The opening of the Canal represented a tremendous achievement in what it presaged for worldwide communications, and it was also a triumph for France and for the imperial regime that had been responsible for backing the project. It was fitting that the Empress Eugénie should have had the honour of opening the canal, but it would have been better if the Emperor himself had been able to be present.[14] Unfortunately, it was a measure of the difficult period through which the regime was passing that Napoleon was obliged to stay at home.

Eugénie returned to Paris in December 1869. Napoleon had already informed her of the results of the general elections which, in the capital, had not been reassuring for the government, since several leading opposition candidates had been elected. The Emperor refused to be upset by the results in Paris, commenting to the Empress that, whether it was Peter or Paul who was elected, the result was much same. He was shaken, however, by an event which was totally unexpected and which reflected badly on the imperial family. In January 1870 Prince Pierre Bonaparte, a cousin of the Emperor who had always been forbidden access to the court because the Emperor considered him to be unsuitable, shot and killed a Republican journalist called Victor Noir. There is no doubt that the journalist in question had given enormous provocation by writing savage and scurrilous attacks on the imperial family, and it is true that the actual course of events leading to the shooting were far from clear, but whatever the circumstances, it was indisputable that the man was dead and that it was Pierre Bonaparte who had shot him. The result was an attack by one of the most savage critics of the regime and the dynasty, the journalist Rochefort, who, taking advantage of the relaxed press laws, produced an article attacking the dynasty and denouncing the Bonaparte family as 'a band of bloodstained assassins'.

Traditionally, political funerals in Paris were occasions for demonstrations. The new government of Ollivier was afraid that the Republicans would take advantage of the funeral of Victor Noir to produce a popular demonstration which could lead to riots. It was to be a test of the government's ability and resolution. In this case it was the government which triumphed, largely because a heavy-handed police presence was avoided, and the leaders of the opposition took good care to stay away. There is no doubt that it was their successful handling of this affair which helped to establish the ministry and helped it to win the plebiscite in May. Unfortunately, at his trial, which was held in a provincial town to avoid any possible recurrence of trouble, the jury acquitted Prince Pierre, thus further discrediting the dynasty, although the Emperor made plain his feelings by 'advising' Pierre to leave France.[15]

It was not, however, events within France's frontiers that would bring about the fall of the dynasty but the consequences of an *impasse* that had its origins in 1868 in Spain. There was a cruel irony here; it was the growth of national consciousness in France after 1789 which had helped to produce Bonapartism and the dynasty, and now it was to be the consequences of an outdated dynastic quarrel that finally destroyed it in the crisis of 1869 and 1870.

In 1868 the Queen of Spain, Isabella, whose political incompetence combined with a certain laxity of morals convinced her ministers that she was unfit to rule, was forced to abdicate. Isabella took refuge in France, where the Emperor, hoping that he could avoid entanglement in Spanish affairs, offered her hospitality as a gesture of solidarity between sovereigns.

The problem was that Spain needed to be provided with a King, since those who had carried through the deposition of Isabella were determined on a monarchy and wanted to avoid a republic. What they needed now was a suitable candidate for the throne. Several were considered, but for various reasons were rejected; of the two front-runners, Napoleon III did not wish to see an Orleanist prince on the throne, while the former King-Consort of Portugal, who was also approached, proved unwilling. To break the deadlock, and to make an end of the affair, the Emperor pressed for the succession of Isabella's son Alfonso. The boy was a minor, and there would have to be a Regency, but at least he would provide dynastic continuity, and at the same time put an end to the embarassing business of trying to find somebody who was willing to wear what the English Foreign Minister Lord Clarendon described as 'that crown of thorns'.

It was at this point that a totally new candidate appeared, a Prince from the Catholic branch of the House of Hohenzollern. Leopold, the Prince in question, had some qualifications as a candidate: he was a Catholic and he was even descended directly from the families of the de Beauharnais and the Murats, and was married to a sister of the King of Portugal. It seemed at first glance that this might make him acceptable to France, whose proximity to Spain traditionally gave it an interest in Spanish affairs, but in fact there was nothing acceptable about it and Bismarck, together with others in Berlin, was well aware of this. At the first whisper of Leopold's appearance on the scene, the French ambassador in Berlin, Count Benedetti, was instructed to let it be known, officially, that this candidacy by a Prussian Prince would never be accepted by Napoleon. The firmness of the French reaction was probably inevitable, but it was also highly dangerous, because it meant that, if and when he sought to provoke France, Bismarck knew that he had exactly the excuse he needed. In the immediate term, the affair was simply allowed to drop, but, as soon as Bismarck became aware of the problems in France brought about by the establishment of the new constitutional and governmental structure, he reopened his campaign to persuade Leopold that he ought seriously to consider becoming King of Spain.

This time, the Prussian Royal House became directly involved in the affair, and on 15 March, at a crown council held in Potsdam, a decision to accept the candidature was taken, making it official Prussian policy. In view of subsequent denials by all concerned that the King of Prussia had ever been directly involved in events, it is worth noting that at this council not only was the King present but also the Crown Prince of Prussia, Prince Leopold (the candidate) and his father Prince Anton. Representing the Prussian general staff were Generals von Roon and von Moltke, and, perhaps most importantly, Bismarck himself. He was later to describe the occasion as 'a simple family dinner', a version which given the guest list was a gross understatement.

While all of this was going on, the French government remained totally unaware of the decisions being taken in Berlin. Bismarck, in a gratuitously insulting fashion, began by informing other European sovereigns of the Prince's acceptance before telling Napoleon. By taking steps to ensure that Queen Victoria was informed of the candidature, a move intended particularly to offend the Emperor, Bismarck made the provocative nature of his policy quite clear, and it is a measure of how confident he felt that he scarcely bothered to conceal it. Convinced, quite correctly, that nothing would come of Napoleon's attempts to form an alliance with Italy or Austria-Hungary, the Prussian Chancellor prepared to spring his trap. On 2 July 1870, the candidacy of Prince Leopold was made known publicly to all the European courts. The French government reacted immediately by asking for a clear and positive statement from the Prussian government as to their attitude to Leopold's acceptance of the Spanish throne. In Berlin, the French emissary attempted to see Bismarck but was told that the Chancellor was unwell, so he was reduced to seeking an interview with the First Secretary of the Foreign Ministry, who pretended to be totally ignorant of the whole business. This was a flagrant lie.

When this exchange became known in Paris all the political groups, together with virtually the entire press, broke out in a clamour of hostility to Prussia, demanding that their government take a strong line. Confronted with this, Napoleon and his ministers were obliged to react quickly and sharply. As the court, together with the Emperor, had moved to the palace of St-Cloud for the summer, it was there that the response to the Prussian candidacy was decided upon at a time when the government's problems were exacerbated by having to confront a populace that was being carried away on a wave of bellicosity and hatred of Prussia.[16] Although the Emperor clearly did not want war, as evidence from all sides makes clear, the British ambassador in Paris reported that 'he feared that, in this matter the French government were following, not leading the nation'. It was generally felt in European capitals that France had been unfairly provoked and that the answer would be to withdraw the candidature. In that way, France would have achieved what it wanted, which was indeed the case. But the Emperor was not convinced that things were so simple: he had seen exactly what the game was, saying, 'it is clear that if the candidature were out of the way, peace would be assured. But how can you imagine that Count von Bismarck who has engineered all of this to provoke us, will let the opportunity slip?'

The Emperor was in fact correct (as Bismarck admitted in 1894 when he published his memoirs), but now in the summer of 1870 the Chancellor suffered an unexpected check to his plans. Since most European nations felt that France had been a victim of provocation, and that the candidature should be withdrawn, on 12 July it was. This was a tremendous diplomatic triumph for the French. Unfortunately, the French government, determined that the affair should be over once and for all, now asked for guarantees that there would be no renewal of the candidacy. Bismarck seized an opportunity to inflame the situation once again, one which came about by chance, because King Wilhelm of Prussia was taking the waters at the spa town of Ems. The French ambassador had approached William while he was taking his morning walk, asking the King to discuss the matter, only to be courteously informed that there was nothing further to discuss. From Ems, the King sent a telegram to Bismarck in which he reported his encounter with the French ambassador, in a seemingly innocuous fashion, but giving Bismarck permission to publish the despatch. Armed with the King's permission, Bismarck proceeded to alter the telegram, by the simple removal of some words, as to make it appear to the Prussians that their King had been insulted by the French ambassador, while, to the French it seemed that the French Ambassador had been insulted by the King. Bismarck then released the amended text to the press in both Paris and Berlin hoping, as he said, that it would be 'the red rag to enrage the Gallic bull'.[17]

10

The Débâcle

The trap which Bismarck had set worked only too well. As early as the 13 July public opinion in France was extremely alarmed by the news of the Prussian candidature, so when Bismarck's newspaper article appeared it further inflamed public passions. The Emperor drove through streets in Paris crowded with people demanding war, and crying, 'Down with Prussia!' and 'On to Berlin!' Given the Emperor's credo, that he was responsible to the people, it seemed impossible that he could remain indifferent to these manifestations, whatever his own deeper feelings might be. There was also the inescapable fact of his dynastic inheritance weighing in the balance, since it would be unacceptable for a Bonaparte to turn away from a challenge, as Louis-Philippe had done in 1840–41. To these factors must be added the confusion caused by the new constitution which made the responsibility for taking decisions a more complex process than it would formerly have been. As a result, when the council met to decide on what action was to be taken in the face of Prussian provocation, there was a great deal of indecision. The Emperor himself hoped, apparently until the last moment, that a way out could be found by means of an international congress.

Everyone knew that the Emperor did not desire war; even in Berlin they knew that, and so the provocation by Bismarck had to be effective.[1] Given the state of public opinion prevalent throughout France, as reports from the prefects and the imperial procurators showed, it was ultimately considered impossible to put forward Napoleon's idea of an international congress to resolve the crisis. Ollivier, who at first had backed the idea of a congress, realising that this would no longer be acceptable is said to have told the Emperor that, if he took such a proposition before the chamber, the crowds in the streets would 'throw mud at our carriages and we would be shouted down'. So, on 19 July, France declared war on Prussia, making it technically the aggressor. Its old-fashioned, poorly equipped and badly commanded army set out to face the strongest military machine of the age.

There was no great public departure as there had been in 1859. The Emperor, accompanied by his son the Prince Imperial, who was just fourteen, left for the army from the small private railway station adjacent to the palace at St-Cloud. This enabled them to go round Paris and join the main line to Metz, without coming in contact with the crowds demonstrating in the capital.

Before leaving for the front the Emperor had nominated Eugénie as Regent, but of course the position of Regent was not as it had been on the previous occasions when the Empress had exercised these powers. Now, she would have to operate within the new constitutional structure which envisaged that she would simply be kept informed by the ministers and could take no decisions on her own.

As it turned out, and as the events unrolled, the Regent became the one person who was unsurprised by the extent of the coming disasters since she had been kept informed by the Emperor of the real state of affairs. On reaching Metz, he had written to her saying that he had found that nothing was ready and that there was total confusion at army headquarters. More alarmingly, he went on, 'We haven't enough troops. I believe we are already lost'; information that she neither could, nor would, pass on to the ministers.[2]

Napoleon said 'enthusiasm is a fine thing, but sometimes rather ridiculous', and when he arrived to join the army at Metz he indeed found little to inspire enthusiasm. In a proclamation to the troops, couched in terms hardly calculated to reassure them, he warned that 'the army we will be facing is one of the best armies in Europe', and that the war 'would be long and difficult'. He proved to be quite wrong: while it was certainly difficult, it was also very short. A month of campaigning sufficed to bring about a series of faulty manoeuvres and defeats, ending in a situation whereby the Emperor, together with his army, found himself trapped in the town of Sedan, with no other resource but capitulation.

On 2 September the Emperor climbed on his horse, something which must have given him extreme pain, because he was suffering from an attack of the stone, and set out to look for death on the battlefield, going towards where the fighting was hottest. This time his 'star' had deserted him and he found no way of escaping what was now his destiny, and so, for the last time, he exercised his authority as Emperor. Wishing to avoid what he now considered would be a useless massacre, he surrendered his sword to the

King of Prussia, 'since I have been unable to die in the middle of my soldiers'. The Emperor, the Empire and the army all collapsed at one and the same time in the same débâcle.

Perhaps the most extraordinary thing about the end of the Second Empire is the speed with which the regime disappeared. Between 3 September, when the news of Sedan reached Paris, and 4 September, when the regime was officially replaced, only thirty-six hours had elapsed. Clearly there needs to be an explanation for this, and there is in fact a simple one. It resulted from the forward planning of those who had been in opposition to the Empire and who seized their chance to end the regime. In a foretaste of things to come, one opposition deputy, on hearing the news of the first defeats, summed up their attitude, saying publicly, 'the armies of the Emperor have been defeated!', only to be reminded by another, more patriotic, deputy that they were also the armies of France.

Alerted by the Emperor's information, as news of the first defeats in early August reached the Empress at St-Cloud, she immediately understood the importance of what had happened. Convinced already that future of the dynasty was in doubt, she felt it was now her duty to do everything to save the country. In an editorial, *The Times* said quite unambiguously 'it is clear that the dynasty has ceased to rule in France', but Eugénie was determined that it was her duty to try and rescue something from the wreckage.

On her return to Paris she immediately contacted Emperor Franz Joseph and the King of Italy, asking them to intervene on the side of France by bringing diplomatic pressure to bear on Berlin to agree to end the fighting. She was unsuccessful, but she remained determined not to abandon her responsibilities: since the Emperor had appointed her as Regent, her duty was to remain at her post until relieved of it by him. She was above all determined not to emulate the conduct of the Empress Marie-Louise, who had proved hopelessly incapable at the moment when Napoleon I had most needed her in 1814. Unfortunately, she was to find, just as Marie-Louise had found in 1814, that those hoping for the overthrow of the dynasty and the regime were more interested in pursuing this objective than in saving the country.

The Empress clung to the hope that she could rally support from the political groups in the crisis facing the country, but the bitter truth was that only a handful of deputies remained loyal, for as the situation deteriorated self-preservation became the dominant thought even among governmental groups. She decided to recall the chambers, in the hope that public debate would produce a coalition of the 'moderate' opposition, but in fact all it achieved was that the conservative groups, who feared a popular revolution more than they feared the end of the regime, overthrew the ministry of Ollivier and set up a new one.

The most alarming feature of all this was that it was done without any consultation with the Emperor, who remained with the army. It was achieved by bringing pressure to bear on the Empress, who yielded to the argument that a change of ministry was necessary for the better prosecution of the war. This was a clever move, because it pushed Eugénie into exceeding the terms of her Regency, which did not authorise her to constitute a new ministry on her own initiative, and it therefore opened the way to further breaches of the Regency statutes should the need arise.

The new ministry, headed by General Palikao, attempted to remedy the deficiencies in men and supplies at the front, and to make preparations for an eventual siege of Paris, something which now appeared to be inevitable. Meanwhile, in the chamber, as the news worsened the opposition became bolder and the ministers began to think that the only solution to the political problem would be the return of the Emperor to Paris. It was felt that his presence would rally support and would worry the opponents of the regime, who had good reason to fear the Emperor's political skill. The opposition groups immediately realised that their plans to remove the dynasty had to be brought to fruition before the Emperor's return made the project more difficult.

They first tackled the Regent and, given the political situation in Paris, it was easy to persuade Eugénie that the Emperor's return would appear as if he were abandoning the army, unthinkable in a Bonaparte, and that it might also possibly unleash a civil war that could only profit the enemy. The force of these arguments made the Empress an opponent of the Emperor's return and thus, unwittingly, an accomplice of those working for the overthrow of the regime. The opposition were in a dilemma. On the one hand, they did not want the Emperor, but they *did* want an army in or near Paris in order to prevent a revolutionary outbreak that would upset their plans for the 'legal' creation of a new regime. They were determined that any governmental change should be accomplished without popular intervention, and by the effective neutralising of a substantial degree of residual support for the Empire, which certainly existed, above all outside Paris. The seven and a half million voters who had indicated their satisfaction with the Empire in May had not all disappeared.

The leader of the opposition coalition, which now included all but the extreme Left, was Adolphe Thiers, who saw the answer to the problem in the shape of General Trochu, an opponent of the Empire but an arch conservative and an opponent of revolution. Thiers convinced the general that he must go to army headquarters at Châlons, seek an audience with the Emperor, and ask to be named military governor of Paris. This appointment would give him control of all the troops in the Paris region and would provide the conservative opposition with the reliable military force they would need to suppress any revolutionary outbreak. On arrival at Châlons the general found that he had an unexpected ally in Prince Napoleon who, for his own reasons, had already made plain to Napoleon the impossibility of remaining in his present situation. He pointed out to his cousin:

> By leaving Paris you abdicated from government. At Metz, you gave up the military command. Unless you go to Belgium you must reassume one or the other. It is quite out of the question to reassume [military] command. As far as the government is concerned, it would be both difficult and dangerous because it means you must return to Paris. Name Trochu Governor of Paris, entrust him with the defence of the city and let him return some hours before you do and inform the population.[3]

The Prince then went on to reveal his plan: the Emperor should not return to Paris but to St-Cloud. There he should abdicate in favour of his son and appoint a new Regent. The Prince was polite enough not to name the new Regent, but it was quite clear that he had in mind his own replacement of Eugénie.

Was this a serious attempt to save the dynasty – or was it simply an expression of personal ambition? It was certainly of little immediate help to the Emperor, who, torn by various arguments, decided finally that he could not 'separate his fate from that of his army', and so Trochu left for the capital to take up his post, armed with full military powers as Governor of Paris. As for Prince Napoleon, the Emperor, who was far from losing all his political sense, dealt with him by sending him to Florence to persuade his father-in-law, the King of Italy, to come to France's assistance.

In Paris Eugénie was now confronted by Trochu, whom she distrusted and disliked, believing him to be disloyal to the dynasty. The general

protested his loyalty, and swore to die on the steps of the throne if the
dynasty should be threatened, but his subsequent actions were fully to
justify Eugénie's mistrust. She was wearing herself out, trying to do what
she felt to be her duty; that is, maintaining some semblance of legitimate
power around which the country could rally, and her situation had in it
both an air of greatness and a sort of futility. As one commentator noted,
'she was personally respected; one spoke of her with a sympathy which
bordered on admiration, but that was all. The feeling she inspired did not
go beyond her own person and did nothing for the government which, as
Regent, she was to represent.'[4] The only thing could have saved the situation
even at this late stage would have been a spectacular military victory, but in
the circumstances in which the French army found itself, despite having
fought bravely and well, this would have required a miracle.

In Paris, the news of Sedan became public on the morning of
4 September, although the Empress had been informed by telegram on the
3rd at about five o'clock in the evening. She had sent immediately for
Trochu, in order to discuss with him the military implications and what
steps were necessary for the defence of Paris, on which the Germans were
now moving. On receiving the Empress's message, Trochu replied that he
was unable to come to the Tuileries, 'because I have not yet had my dinner',
a clear indication that he now considered the Regent to be of no importance
whatsoever.

In a rowdy session in the chamber the loyal supporters of the regime
protested that they were seeing a repeat of the treason of 1815, but they
were shouted down, and the conservative opposition fearful of letting loose
a street revolution, for mobs were gathering, now determined that the 'legal'
transfer of power must take place. To achieve this, the Empress must
formally abdicate as Regent, handing her powers to the Legislative Body, a
provisional government could then be proclaimed and this would
circumvent any uprising. Eugénie believed that a better solution would be
to rally round her in the face of the enemy invasion, but the emissaries
from the Legislative Body convinced her that she was an obstacle and not a
source of strength. Showing remarkable clarity and understanding of the
situation, insofar as it affected the dynasty and herself, the Empress said,

> If the Legislative Body think that I am an obstacle, or that the name of the Emperor
> should be an obstacle and not a strength, in order to dominate the situation and
> to organise resistance, let the Legislative Body pronounces the overthrow of the

regime. I shall not complain of this. I can leave my post with honour for I shall not have deserted it.[5]

In this way she could claim to have yielded to an act of force while bequeathing to the Legislative Body responsibility for the abdication and its possible aftermath.

Having fulfilled her obligations, the Empress now felt it was time she looked to herself, particularly since the mob appeared to have taken over the streets and General Trochu had openly abandoned any pretence of loyalty and military protection. In these circumstances, the few remaining persons in her entourage urged Eugénie to flee, which, towards four o'clock in the afternoon, she agreed to do, saying simply, 'I yield to force and to violence'. She had no fear of death; what she feared, she said later, was to find herself subjected to indignities in the streets: 'I saw myself with my skirts dragged up. I could hear the terrible cries for, you know, the *tricoteuses* left behind their descendants.'

Of her household, the Empress was now left with only her reader, Madame Lebreton, for she had sent away the little group who had remained with her in the palace, and she gave orders that the palace guard, who had remained faithful and at their posts, were on no account to fire on the groups of rioters who had already broken into the gardens. Cries of 'Death to the Spanish woman!' could now be clearly heard by the small group in the Empress's apartments, indicating that the main entrances to the Tuileries were not safe to use. It was decided that the best way to leave would be via the Long Gallery which joined the Tuileries to the Louvre, and which led eventually to the Place St-Germain l'Auxerrois, where all appeared still to be calm. Two officers now appeared and insisted on joining the Empress, Admiral Jurien de la Gravière and Lieutenant Louis Conneau, the son of Napoleon's old friend and doctor. The small party also included the Italian ambassador, Count Nigra, and the ambassador of Austria-Hungary, Prince Richard Metternich, and it was these two who stayed with her, when, on reaching the door of the Louvre, Eugénie ordered everyone else to leave, keeping only Madame Lebreton and the two diplomats. She was afraid that those accompanying her would be set upon by a mob if they were found to be her escort.

Astonishingly, the square was virtually deserted, and all the surrounding streets were so quiet that Nigra succeeded in finding a hackney carriage into which he handed the two women, carefully avoiding any signs of deference. The problem was that neither of the two fugitives had any idea of where to go. Having unsuccessfully tried several places, including the home of a senator who declined to receive them, the Empress had an idea that they should go to the house of her dentist, Dr Evans, an American, and there they at last found shelter. Evans was out, but his manservant admitted the 'two ladies' to wait for him in the library. There, to his astonishment, on his return Evans found the ladies to be the Empress and her reader.

On learning of the Empress's desire to make for England immediately, Evans promised to help them leave Paris. It was agreed that they should spend a night with him and leave the next day for the Normandy coast, where Evans's wife had gone for a holiday, providing an excuse, if necessary, for his travelling with the two ladies. From there it was hoped they could find some way of getting to England.[6]

After what turned out to be a hazardous journey, for at one point the Empress was recognised, the fugitives finally reached Deauville, where Evans handed the two ladies over to his wife, who arranged for them to have a meal. He himself wandered round the harbour, looking for a boat that could make the passage across the Channel. On seeing a small yacht, the *Gazelle*, flying the English flag, he went on board and introduced himself to the owner, Sir John Burgoyne, to whom he explained the reason for his call. Burgoyne was not enthusiastic. As a serving officer in the British Army, he feared political complications; he was even more anxious about the possibility of a severe gale indicated by a falling barometer. He did consult his wife, however, who said immediately, 'there is no problem. Bring the Empress on board'.

Having got the two ladies and Evans safely on board, Burgoyne set sail, although the wind was already at gale force and the sea raging. As a result the crossing was frightful, for in the open sea they found themselves at the mercy of a storm so violent that it sank a large man of war on the same night. Eventually they reached the port of Ryde on the Isle of Wight, last visited by Eugénie in 1857 in very different circumstances, when she had come with the Emperor to stay at Osborne as guests of the Queen and Prince Albert. Her reception this time was less than regal, for at the first hotel they tried the proprietor refused to admit them, so bedraggled and unprepossessing was their appearance. Eventually they found rooms in the York Hotel, but the management installed them in the attic which normally housed the servants.

Having arrived safely, Eugénie's main preoccupation was to find news of the Emperor and of the Prince Imperial. From the newspapers, which Evans had bought, she learned that the Prince Imperial was safe and had ended up at Hastings, while at the same time she learned that the Emperor was a prisoner in Germany. The Prince Imperial had been saved because, towards the end, the Emperor had sent him via Belgium under the charge of his personal equerry with instructions to take the boy to England. In spite of her extreme fatigue, Eugénie set out at once for Hastings, where she found her son installed in the Marine Hotel. After several days they left there because they were the object of constant, if respectful, curiosity.

In a desire for privacy and peace, the Empress concluded that the only solution was to rent a house, preferably near London, that would make it easier for anyone who wished to come from France to join her. She found a house, Camden Place, near Chislehurst in Kent. It belonged to a Mr Strode, who had known the Emperor during his exile in England in the 1840s, and who was more than willing to let the house. The Empress, having signed the lease, moved in on 20 September. There was now nothing more she could do except wait upon events.

Within a short time she was joined by a faithful few: Doctor Conneau and his son Louis, the Duc de Bassano and his wife, and, to her great pleasure, Marie de Larminat, one of her ladies and a firm favourite of the Prince Imperial. These were soon joined by some of the servants, including the Emperor's cook and the *maître d'hôtel* from the Tuileries. To this tiny 'court' came Rouher, the former Minister of State, who quickly became a key political adviser, having always had the confidence of Napoleon III. He was to become the essential link between the exiles and political developments in France, maintaining contact with the Bonapartists who remained loyal to the dynasty.

In October Eugénie found herself confronted by her old adversary Prince Napoleon, whose mission to Italy had been fruitless, and who had left his wife and their three children with her father, the King of Italy. He had come to London to see his mistress, Cora Pearl, who was installed in a house in Lancaster Gate, and also to confront the Empress by paying a visit to Chislehurst. On arrival at Camden Place he wasted little time in niceties and demanded that the Empress give up the Regency and entrust it to Marshal Bazaine, who was besieged in Metz with the last viable military force still (in theory) loyal to the Empire. Bazaine would then go on to proclaim the Prince

Imperial as Napoleon IV, and Prince Napoleon would act as Regent until the boy came of age in 1874. The Empress exploded with rage at what was in fact an outrageous proposition, and a violent quarrel took place, which Prince Napoleon reported to the Emperor in a letter attacking the Empress. Napoleon replied saying sorrowfully: 'How sad it is to see, in the position in which we now find ourselves, these family dissensions.'[7]

Although there were good reasons why the Empress should be outraged by Prince Napoleon's proposal, for whatever her exact status as Regent she was indisputably the guardian of her son, it was clear that various questions remained to be considered. What *was* to be the role of the dynasty? Did it, indeed still have one? The Empress's Regency was now virtual rather than actual, except in so far as she still felt it was her responsibility to try and end the war and avoid a punitive peace with annexations. To that end she had written to the Emperor Franz Joseph, and to Tsar Alexander II, asking them to use their good offices with the King of Prussia. Alexander replied courteously and meaninglessly. More to the point was the reply she received from the King of Prussia, who explained that the annexations of Alsace and part of Lorraine were necessary in order to provide a jumping off ground in the event of a future Franco-German conflict.

In a strange way the war of 1870 can be seen as the last of the Napoleonic wars. The swift movement and the destruction of the enemy's forces were all in the traditions of Napoleon I, except that this time history had been stood upon its head for the victim was France. The collapse had been so total, surprising even the victorious Prussian army, that even Bismarck was unsure of how to proceed. He considered it possible that the dynasty might still have a part to play.

The provisional government in Paris wanted desperately to make peace but was the victim of its own *coup d'état* of 4 September, for with the dynasty gone it seemed to the bellicose radical elements that the time had now come to fight a victorious 'republican war' by mobilising the nation. The problem for the government was not just that it wanted to end a war, which it considered already lost, but that it was reluctant to mobilise the nation by invoking the revolutionary 'spirit of 1793', for this would mean having to arm large numbers of men. To the conservatives who had overthrown Napoleon III, carefully avoiding popular participation, this was an unappealing prospect. In an attempt to circumvent the war party, they tried for peace in September, sending delegates to sound out Bismarck, only to be faced with an explosion of anger and a near riot among the Paris populace when news of these semi-secret negotiations with the Germans leaked out.

The problem was further complicated by the fact that the German army, that is to say the Prussian high command, also wanted to make an end of the war, and they too were looking for a negotiator who would be 'sensible', and who would accept the need for peace even on harsh terms. These terms, which had already been agreed on in August, were simple: they consisted of the annexation of all of Alsace and part of Lorraine, plus a swingeing indemnity. Bismarck had already tried to use Napoleon III, by offering him terms which he made appear to be less harsh than those that the Prussian army really intended to apply, but the Emperor was well aware that Bismarck would like to use him and he would not allow himself to be duped again. As he wrote to the Empress:

> Bismarck would like to treat with us and bring us to sign a disastrous peace. How should one conduct oneself in these circumstances? I begin by saying what one must not do. So long as the fate of Paris has not been decided, nothing must be said or done which have would appear to damage the national defence in the interests of the dynasty. Secondly, I have no need to tell you how determined I am not to sign a peace which would not be favourable [to France].[8]

On 29 October, Bazaine surrendered at Metz, thus putting an end to the last surviving imperial army force of any consequence. The dynasty had now absolutely no further significance. As if to underline the change of status, the Empress set out on 30 October to visit the Emperor in his captivity. Napoleon III was installed in the palace of Wilhelmshöhe, near Kassel, a palace that had been the favourite residence of his uncle Jerome while he was King of Westphalia, and which had then been called Napoleonshöhe. It may, or may not, have consoled the captive nephew to find the furnishings unchanged – including a portrait of his own mother, Queen Hortense, together with other souvenirs of happier times.

Eugénie left after a visit of only twenty-four hours. It had been an interlude of marital reconciliation and, one supposes, mutual comfort, something that is borne out by the letters exchanged between the couple at this time of anguish. They reveal a great degree of understanding and forgiveness on both sides, coupled with simple plans for the future. Of political matters there is almost no talk – how could there be? They had no role to play, and now must wait upon the outcome of events as they developed in France, since it was clear that the Emperor would not be released until a peace was signed.

The surrender of the garrison at Metz had tipped the military balance more heavily in Germany's favour and it became clear, even to the hotheads in the Government of National Defence, that the war really must come to an end. As a result, Bismarck concentrated on the more amenable representatives of the government with whom, at the end of January 1871, he signed a treaty, granting the French an armistice in return for the capitulation of Paris. The armistice was offered so that elections could be held throughout France in order to produce a properly constituted government which could then formally make peace. On 17 February the new National Assembly, issued from the elections, nominated Thiers as 'Chief of the Executive Power', and then on 1 March 'confirmed the overthrow of Napoleon III and of his dynasty, and declared him responsible for the ruin, the invasion and the dismemberment of France'. From his exile, the Emperor protested at the actions of the Assembly, denouncing their proceedings as without any legitimacy, since they had not been elected to decide on the nature of France's government but to make peace with the Germans. As was to be expected, with the exception of faithful Bonapartists, no one in France paid the slightest attention to Napoleon's protest, while abroad, although there was evidence of personal sympathy, no European sovereign showed any inclination to support the imperial cause.

The measure of the Emperor's lack of importance had been evident for some time. Bismarck had long since given up any pretence of negotiation with him, for the game was over and Napoleon could now be regarded as a discard. In Paris the peace preliminaries had been concluded and so Bismarck withdrew his opposition to the Emperor's release from captivity. On 19 March the Emperor left Kassel railway station en route for Dover via Ostend. At the Belgian frontier he was met by his cousin Princess Mathilde, to whose effusive welcome he displayed his habitual reserve and impassivity, showing that he had recovered his personal equilibrium. It is just possible that the enforced rest imposed on him by his captivity had produced an improvement in his health.

On the afternoon of 20 March, among the passengers disembarking at Dover was a short, stoutish man who looked unwell. He came slowly down the gangway and seemed surprised to see that a considerable crowd of people were waiting on the quayside, and that on seeing him the men raised their hats and cried, 'Long Live the Emperor!', while some of the women threw flowers. The man stopped, showing both surprise and emotion, for observers noted that there were tears on his cheeks. It was Napoleon III, who had once again come to exile in England and was so moved that, unusually for him, he allowed his feelings to show. Among those waiting were the Empress and the Prince Imperial, both of whom the Emperor embraced affectionately and tenderly. Then the family group made its way through the crowd, including civic dignitaries, to the station to board the train that would take them to Chislehurst.

This hotel had the advantage of a passageway which connected directly to the railway station, so enabling visitors to avoid crowds if they wished. At the very moment the imperial family entered the passageway a group of people could be seen advancing from the other end, evidently heading for the cross-Channel steamer which was going back to Belgium. It was the Orleans family returning to France. Confronted with this ironical situation of meeting in a narrow corridor, who would give way to whom? After a momentary hesitation, the Empress saved the day by drawing a little to the side and making one of her famous curtseys. For his part, the Emperor raised his hat, whereupon the Orleans Princes bowed slightly, and the two groups passed one another in silence.

The arrival of the Emperor at Camden Place not only reunited the family but also made it seem more like 'a court in exile', although Napoleon III had himself tried to avoid this, saying, 'I do not want to play at being the sovereign and I do not want to have about me the simulacrum of a court. In England I shall be simply a private citizen'. It was, however, inevitable that the faithful should group themselves around the exiles, and to those who had originally joined the Empress were now added others, including some former ministers. There were constant callers at Chislehurst, Sunday being the favourite day for making the pilgrimage, since many attended Mass with the imperial family in St Mary's church. In the afternoon there was a reception at Camden Place that was open to visitors, during which the imperial family circulated among those whom loyalty or simple curiosity had brought under their roof.

The English royal family made clear its intention to maintain friendly personal relations irrespective of political developments when, a few days after the Emperor's arrival, the Prince of Wales called, bearing an invitation from the Queen, who wanted to receive the family at Windsor. She had already visited the Empress shortly after the latter's arrival at Camden Place but now wished to demonstrate her sympathy and friendship with the exiles. Her feelings appear to have been perfectly genuine, in spite of the opinion expressed in a letter to her daughter the Crown Princess of Prussia in September 1870 saying that 'nothing annoyed dear papa more than the abject court paid to the Emperor and the way in which we were forced to flatter and humour him, which was short-sighted policy and spoilt him'.[9] It seems from this that the Queen was clearly able, as always, to draw a fine distinction between personal feelings and political loyalties.

The visit to Windsor took place on 27 March and the Queen noted in her diary:

> I went to the door with Louise and embraced the Emperor *comme de rigueur*. It was a moving moment when I thought of the last time he came here in '55 in perfect triumph, dearest Albert bringing him in triumph from Dover, the whole country mad to receive him, and now! He seemed much depressed and had tears in his eyes but he controlled himself and said 'it is a long time since I saw your Majesty'. He led me upstairs and we went to the Audience Room. He is grown very stout and grey, and his moustaches are no longer curly as formerly, but otherwise there was the same pleasing, gentle and gracious manner.[10]

Some days later, on 3 April, the visit was returned, the Queen driving from Chislehurst station to Camden Place, accompanied by Prince Leopold and Princess Beatrice. She noted in her diary: 'at the door stood the poor Little Prince Imperial, looking very much better, and inside the Emperor and the Empress with their suite ... The heat in the room was overpowering ... Left again at a quarter to five. Felt very tired and sad.' The visit was important in that it was a public demonstration of the friendship which existed between the two sovereigns, even if one of them no longer represented anything but himself. There was one small problem, far from affairs of state, which needed to be dealt with – namely the temperature of the rooms at Camden Place. The Emperor could not bear the cold, so all the rooms were heated to boiling point, to such an extent that a few weeks after Napoleon III's arrival a porcelain stove exploded with the heat. The Queen let it be known (discreetly) that she detested overheated rooms, to which the Duke de Bassano, as master of the household, replied (discreetly) that the point had been taken, and that indeed the Empress herself suffered from the overheating of the house.

These visits could be classed only as expressions of friendship and could not be interpreted as having any political significance. It is highly unlikely that the Queen would have in any way jeopardised her constitutional position by engaging in activities that would leave her open to ministerial or public criticism, though it was not always easy for her to draw a line between public and private. In February 1872 there were national celebrations for the recovery of the Prince of Wales from a serious illness and the Queen invited the Emperor and the Empress to Buckingham Palace so that they could watch the procession to St Paul's Cathedral. When news of their presence at the palace reached Paris, Thiers, still head of the Republican government, threw a tremendous tantrum and demanded that the ambassador in London protest formally to the Foreign Office. The Foreign Secretary explained that he was not responsible for the Queen's guest list. When the Queen herself heard of it, she dismissed the protest as both 'incomprehensible' and 'impertinent.'

The only interesting point in the affair is that it displayed the latent fears of the government in Paris as to Napoleon III's possible future activities, though the most recent threat to governmental stability had come not from any Bonapartist activities, but from the Commune of Paris and its bloody suppression by the government of Thiers. None of this had anything to do with the exiled Emperor, who could only deplore the fearful destruction of large areas of Paris, and express his horror at the repression of the uprising at the cost of some twenty thousand dead. The Republican government had shown that it would be conservative, by its action reassuring those who had feared that 'Republic' might equate with revolutionary and progressives policies. Since this was clearly not going to be the case, what need for monarchy or empire? In fact, in spite of rumours and a certain amount of coming and going between Paris and Chislehurst by former ministers of the Empire, Bonapartist agents and assorted emissaries, there seems to have been little foundation for the view that Napoleon III was planning a 'return from Elba'. While it seemed as if the historic role of the dynasty was always to be called on during a time of crisis and dissolution, what use could a sick man and a boy be? Was there any need for a Bonaparte if others could do what was needed just as well?

Life at Camden Place had the same degree of formality as could be found in any large and well-ordered household, and there was no atmosphere of feverish plotting to bring about an immediate return to the business of ruling France. There is no doubt that the Emperor watched closely the political developments, particularly the Commune and its aftermath, and that he may well have entertained some ideas about a restoration, but for the moment life was lived in a quiet, almost dull, routine imposed by the state of the Emperor's health as much as by any other factor. Although the captivity had done something towards re-establishing his physical condition, Napoleon III was well aware that his medical problem could only be cured by surgery, a prospect which he viewed with disquiet. It was not simply fear of the surgeon which prompted his reluctance, but an awareness of how dangerous the operation for the stone was. Only a little while before the fall of the Empire, Marshal Niel had died from just such surgery, in spite of having had the services of the best surgeons in Paris, and it was precisely for this reason that the Emperor had concealed the report of the committee of surgeons which had examined him in the summer of 1870. The Empress, who knew that he was ill, was fobbed off with the vague reference to 'crises of rheumatism' and remained totally unaware of the real gravity of his condition until an attack in late 1872 which was so acute that finally she had to be told the truth.

Apart from the disquieting problem of the Emperor's health, the life of the exiles resembled that of any group of exiles, 'people's spirits sank, and it became an effort for each one of us to hide our boredom', for, as time passed, the links with the past weakened and the uncertain future seemed to preclude new perspectives. The Empress once compared their situation to the survivors depicted in the famous painting *The Raft of the Medusa*, desperately hoping for rescue.[11]

The Emperor, who had experience of captivity and how to deal with it, decided to approach his exile as a parallel situation and soon established a routine for himself, working each morning in his study dealing with correspondence, or working on his account of what happened in 1870, which was later to be published in Paris under a pseudonym. In the afternoon he received visitors, either seated in his study in his favourite armchair, cigarette in hand, or walking with them in the long hall of Camden Place which ran the length of the ground floor. Sometimes there were visitors from France whose news and views were eagerly discussed, although the Emperor rarely strayed beyond generalities, keeping any confidential exchanges for the privacy of his study.

Both parents were extremely preoccupied with the future of their son, who represented the future of the dynasty, and it was first thought that to improve his English, and to enable him to make friends, he should be enrolled at King's College in the Strand. It proved impossible, however, to continue with this since the Prince was behind in too many subjects and, educationally, little was being achieved. It was then decided that he should enrol at the Royal Military Academy at Woolwich, specialising in artillery as befitted a Bonaparte, and that he should begin in the autumn of 1872. The Prince himself was enthusiastic about the idea, and in November 1872 he put on the uniform of an officer cadet in the British Army. A house was rented for him and his tutor, Monsieur Filon, near the Academy and there he settled down to work steadily and in a manner which both pleased and surprised his tutor.[12]

In the late summer of 1872, the Emperor's illness took a turn for the worse. By October he could hardly bear to sit in a carriage, let alone ride a horse, and by November he was spending days in bed and in great pain. Determined to try and overcome his illness, he went for a short railway journey with his cousin, Prince Charles Bonaparte, one of Lucien's grandsons, who lived in London, but even this proved too much of an effort. When the conversation touched upon the possibility of a restoration Napoleon III simply said, 'It is a pity that I am so ill'. He nevertheless continued to play down the gravity of his condition, writing cheerfully in November to the Prince Imperial, who was at Woolwich: 'My dear child, the consultation took place today and I am very satisfied with the result. The doctors are in agreement that with some simple treatment I shall be well in a month. I embrace you tenderly, your affectionate father.'[13]

The Empress, by now seriously alarmed, decided to call in a specialist and asked Sir William Gull, the Queen's physician, to examine the Emperor. He gave his opinion that an examination of the bladder must be made, and would have to be done under an anaesthetic, for which purpose he recommended that he be joined by his colleague, Sir Henry Thompson, the leading specialist in diseases of the bladder. At this moment Prince Napoleon turned up, and some later commentators have thought it was to discuss the feasibility of making a descent on France as Napoleon I had done. What is clear is that Prince Napoleon quickly realised that nothing could be attempted given the Emperor's physical condition, which must be dealt with as a matter of urgency. The two men had gone on a short carriage ride to see the Prince Imperial at Woolwich but it was clear that the Emperor, though uncomplaining, was in very great pain during the drive.

In December Sir William Gull, accompanied by Sir Henry Thompson, carried out a thorough examination of the bladder and it was decided that there would have to be an immediate operation. The Emperor consented and the first surgery was carried out on 2 January 1873. It appeared to go well, a large stone having been crushed and the fragments removed. But Thompson was worried by the general state of his patient's health and noted that 'The Emperor goes on fairly well, not quite so flourishing perhaps now as yesterday. I regard the case as a very grave one … I shall want all my force, all my resources to get him through, and I may fail. I am very anxious.'[14] Thomson, however, had no alternative but to proceed to a second operation which took place on the 6th and seemed at first to bring great relief to the patient. It was during this operation that Sir William Gull said to his colleague: 'How did this man stay in the saddle for five hours at Sedan? What he must have suffered.'

By 8 January the Emperor seemed stronger and a final operation was fixed for midday on the 9th. That evening he was given chloral to ensure a sound night's sleep and the doctors who took it in turn to be with him in the night were agreeably surprised to find that in the morning he seemed to have no fever and his pulse was regular. Suddenly, at half past ten a change was noticed; the cheeks had fallen in and the nose had sharpened. Thompson immediately took the pulse and found it had dropped almost to nothing. Dr Conneau, who had remained with his old friend through all the operations, and who was no stranger to deathbeds, called for Father Goddard, who was just about to leave the house, having said Mass in the Empress's room. The Empress herself was about to leave for Woolwich to give the Prince news of his father but she was stopped by Dr Conneau, who said there was 'a small crisis'. She ran to the room but Father Goddard was already administering the Last Sacrament and she withdrew until he had finished. She returned to find the end was very near and within a few minutes it was all over. The Emperor died at 10.45 a.m. The Prince, hastily summoned from Woolwich, arrived too late and was left to share his grief with his mother.

The death of Napoleon III was not only a source of sorrow to his widow and son but obviously an event of considerable political importance for the Bonapartist party. Rouher, the leader of the party, and since 1872 a deputy in the National Assembly, received the news, sent to him in a telegram by the Empress, while in the legislative chamber during the afternoon session of 9 January. The deputies noticed him suddenly leave his seat in an obvious state of distress, without knowing the reason, since the evening papers which carried the reports from London were not yet on the street. He left immediately for Chislehurst, arriving on the 10th, to be followed by Prince Napoleon, Princess Mathilde and the Murat family. Other members of the imperial family, Prince Charles and Prince Louis Lucien, grandchildren of Lucien, both of whom lived in London, appeared on the same day. On successive days the leading dignitaries of the former regime began to arrive at Camden Place, so many of them that it seemed like a roll call of the former Empire.

Letters of condolence were received by the Empress from Queen Victoria and from all the other European rulers, including the Tsar Alexander II, the Emperor Franz Joseph and the Emperor William of Germany. For a moment it seemed as if Camden Place had become a real court, with the Empire taking its place once again in the European monarchical system. But this was a court in mourning, a pale and sad reflection of former glories.

The funeral was fixed for 15 January and in the meantime the Emperor lay in state in the hall at Camden Place. His body had been embalmed and he was dressed in the uniform of a French general of division. On the morning of the 14th, the day on which the public would be admitted, the Prince of Wales came with his brother as representatives of the Queen, who feared that her presence would provoke the government in Paris into lodging a protest. She had already written to the Empress to express her own personal grief and distress at the Emperor's death, but it was considered impolitic that any member of the royal family should actually attend the funeral, hence the Prince's visit.

Between the morning and evening of 14th some 20,000 people passed before the Emperor's coffin, for the most part French men and women who had come to pay their final respects. Many wept uncontrollably. When the park gates were finally closed at 9 o'clock that night many hundreds were still waiting hopefully for a chance to enter. The coffin was closed after the family and the household had kissed the Emperor's hand on which were his wedding ring and the ring worn by Napoleon I on his deathbed at St Helena, a stark reminder that both sovereigns had died in exile.[15] The funeral took place in the tiny church of St Mary, with a solemn Requiem Mass celebrated by the Archbishop of Southwark The procession to the church, which was headed by a deputation of Parisian working men, included dignitaries of the former Empire, who walked behind the hearse immediately after the Prince Imperial. He walked alone dressed in mourning and wearing as decoration the star and a red ribbon of the Legion of Honour. Following the Prince came the other members of the family who were present. The church was so small that only two hundred mourners could be admitted to hear the Mass, but many thousands stood outside in the raw cold January day, determined to pay their last respects. Lady Cowley, who was present as the wife of a former ambassador to Paris and a personal friend of the imperial family, wrote a description of the event to be shown to the Queen. 'The funeral was the most touching scene I have ever witnessed. In the church everyone was in tears and the gentlemen who stood beside the coffin were all sobbing. All the pomps and ceremonies at Notre-Dame could never have equalled this scene in the little church of St Mary.'[16]

On 23rd the Queen came from Windsor to condole personally. At Camden Place she was received, as protocol demanded, by the Prince Imperial, looking, the Queen said, 'very pale and sad', adding, 'a few steps further on in the deepest mourning, looking very ill, very handsome, and the picture of sorrow, was the poor dear Empress. Silently we embraced one another and she took my arm in hers but could not speak for emotion.'

The death of Napoleon III marked the definitive end of the Second Empire, although it could indeed be argued that to all practical intents and purposes both had died politically at Sedan. The fact that the Prince Imperial would not attain his majority until March 1874 threw the Bonapartists into disarray, for the dynasty lacked an immediate successor, leaving the Empress as Regent. This situation immediately produced a further disagreement between Prince Napoleon and the Empress, who, having barely had time to mourn, was confronted by the Prince's demand that he should now assume the political education of the Prince Imperial and that the latter should be handed over into his charge. The Empress, seconded by the heads of the Imperialist Party, refused categorically. As a result Prince Napoleon left Camden Place in a sulk, saying that, although his young cousin was charming and as agreeable as possible, 'he remains a child who will do what his mother wants'. It seemed as if nothing could bring these family disputes to an end, in spite of the obvious threat that they posed to the imperial cause and how prejudicial they were for the future of the dynasty.

11

'The Prince is Down!'

The death of Napoleon III inevitably produced serious problems for the Bonapartists, since it came at a moment when it seemed that their political fortunes might be on the point of reviving, thanks to the increasing problems of their opponents. The disparate groups who made up the government, with Thiers at its head, were now starting to break up into their component parts: the two monarchist branches, the Legitimists and the Orleanists, were unable to come to an agreement on fusion between the two Houses, a repeat of the situation in 1848 to1851, and this lack of agreement proved fatal to their cause. The Republicans were divided on the nature of the constitution and argued as to the form that the Republic should take. Thiers had said: 'the Republic will be conservative or it will not be at all', and certainly the brutal suppression of the Commune had calmed fears of the 'reds'. There was a further source of division among the conservatives, which cut across the monarchist and republican differences, and that was the economic policy to be followed by the new regime.

The key issue lay between the supporters of Protection versus Free Trade, that is between those who were convinced that the future of France's industry lay in the maintenance of Free Trade as national policy and those demanding a return to Protectionism. The free traders tended to be Bonapartist in sympathy, given that it was imperial policy which had introduced this system, but when the question was fiercely debated in the National Assembly, it revealed the weakness of the Bonapartists, who were unable to defend their cause with so few deputies in the chamber. It was obvious that their immediate problem was how to increase their numbers in the Assembly, making them a real political power able to fight their enemies within the structure of ordinary politics?

Unfortunately, this was an area in which they were handicapped by their inheritance, and indeed by their whole political outlook. During the Empire there had been no party organisation, though there had been temporary groupings, because Bonapartism was anti-party and the whole idea of

Bonapartism was antithetical to party structure. Party was something that belonged to the opposition groups whose organisation and methods now had to be learned. The history of the next few years turned on the attempts of the Bonapartists to solve this problem, attempts that led them into dangerous political alliances in the hope of strengthening their electoral position; alliances which quite often contradicted the very principles for which, in theory, they stood.[1]

One thing remained as a rallying point and that was the dynasty. The Prince Imperial attained his majority in March 1874, an occasion which enabled the Bonapartists to show that the cause was far from dead. Seven thousand delegates representing Bonapartist organisations came to Chislehurst from all parts of France, together with many other sympathisers, while over three hundred thousand letters were received congratulating 'Napoleon IV' and pledging allegiance. The whole ceremony was accounted a great success, though, as the Empress remarked, it was easy to preach to the converted. It would require more than enthusiasm to restore a dynasty. Making his first real public appearance, the Prince made a very favourable impression on all who saw him. Young, handsome and intelligent, he made an excellent speech, which included all the orthodox Bonapartist doctrines, and while he claimed his hereditary right to the imperial succession, he also declared his wish to submit it to popular approval in the best traditions of the dynasty.

There were notable absentees from the celebration, namely Prince Napoleon, together with those of his supporters who had decided to boycott the whole affair as a mark of their disapproval of the policies being pursued by the imperialist committee in Paris. These absences were noted, but the genuine enthusiasm shown on the occasion helped to prevent any immediate scandal erupting. Prince Napoleon denied that he was motivated by personal ambition but claimed that he alone could represent the 'radical left' aspect of Bonapartism, claiming that his ambition was only 'for the benefit of my country and my ideas'. He nevertheless openly accused the Prince Imperial of being under the influence of his mother, and of inclining towards a conservative and clerical tendency. The Prince was being disingenuous, since he knew perfectly well that for electoral purposes the Bonapartists must take their allies where they could find them. Because the Republicans were unwilling to cooperate, it had perforce to be the conservative sections they would look to for support.[2]

Because of this, the development of the party over the next few years was to be dominated by political manoeuvring made necessary by the search for allies. In the short run, this paid some dividends, since more deputies were elected to the chamber, but the tactical concessions demanded by this sort of 'politicking' was ultimately harmful to the Bonapartist cause. It weakened what had always been its strength, namely a clearly defined political line, and the lack of clarity in their policy, for no one was quite sure now what Bonapartism represented, harmed their chances in the general election held in 1876. It is clear from the figures that many Bonapartists supporters voted Republican because they feared the implications of the alliance with the royalists and the conservative groups. As they saw it, the dynasty had not been established to facilitate royalism in any form but to oppose it.

Here was the first open sign of the fatal schism in the basic doctrine of Bonapartism, whose foundations ultimately depended upon an 'appeal to the people', while at the same time giving them reasons to be *united* behind the dynasty and the imperial regime. What it must never be was a source of dissension. Most harmful of all the signs of disunity were those elections that involved candidates representing different tendencies within the party. The most striking example of this occurred in Corsica in 1876 when Prince Napoleon stood against Rouher, who was the Prince Imperial's choice. Weakened by these endless dissensions, the Bonapartist never achieved sufficient electoral successes to produce a substantial and coherent group in the Assembly. As a result, more and more they came to rely upon the one sure card that they had to play, namely the Prince Imperial, and this they used for all it was worth.

His advantage was that he could represent an imperialist future, untainted by the past, while maintaining dynastic continuity. Too young to have been in any way responsible for the war and the defeat, he could easily be portrayed as the *petit prince* who would restore the dynasty, and with it the regime from which France had benefited from more than twenty years. Throughout France Bonapartist agents distributed photographs, lithographs, medallions and pamphlets, just as had been done in 1848 to 1850, all designed to bring home the message that there was an heir worthy to succeed his father and to take on the dynastic responsibilities.[3] The Bonapartist press continued to extol the advantages of the imperial regime, but at the same time it unfortunately reflected the divisions within the movement, since some papers supported Prince Napoleon and envenomed the debate by their attacks on their opponents.

Some of the party leaders felt that if the masses could be addressed directly, and encouraged to rally again, bypassing the political groups, there was hope of a restoration, but this simplistic approach ignored the problem caused by the memory of the war and the defeat. Knowledge of this paralysed many Bonapartist candidates when it came to elections, because it gave a tremendous weapon to their political enemies, who made good use of it. A further disadvantage was the fact that the country was 'conservative', as the elections of 1871 had shown, and that meant that any stress on a radical social programme, one of the great strengths of popular Bonapartism, could not be used to counter-attack. Too much stress on it would strengthen their enemies, who would denounce the 'threat' to society, while too little simply disappointed their friends.

It was this situation which produced a gradual shift towards the right and led to the emergence of a conservative Bonapartism. Prince Napoleon's prophecy turned out to be self-fulfilling, for a conservative party based Bonapartism was really a contradiction in terms and in the end it proved to be electorally fatal. If the imperial party was not radical, and not interested in the people, then the people must look elsewhere. Inevitably the Republicans were the gainers and little by little they acquired a mastery of the universal suffrage that had, from its beginnings in 1848, facilitated the establishment of the imperial regime.

This is not to say that the party had disappeared or that it was without influence. By 1876 there was a Bonapartist presence in the Assembly: a hundred deputies and some thirty Senators, but they were prisoners of the right-wing groups who had helped to get them elected, and they had no real leader. They had their Prince, but he was an exile, and he had no real political experience, while the steering committee of the party in Paris had no real ideological clout. The odd electoral victory was a poor substitute to for an overwhelming mass movement in favour of the dynasty.[4]

In this climate, of what was, in effect, political sterility, the Prince Imperial decided he must himself do something which would fix him in the popular mind and would show him to the French people. In 1878 a delegation came to Chislehurst, urging Louis to do just that, to arrive in Paris and announce his presence: this would lead to his being hailed by the populace and installed in the Elysée Palace. The Prince listened courteously and then pointed out that a more likely ending to such an enterprise would be his arrest by two policemen who would escort him to the frontier, covered in ridicule. 'No gentlemen, I shall go to France, you can be sure of it, but at the right moment, and it is I who shall choose the moment.'

The Prince was, of course, not simply a Pretender to the imperial throne, he was also a young man in his twenties, full of energy, who seemed condemned to lead a futile existence. He had graduated from Woolwich in February 1874 as a lieutenant, seventh out of thirty-four in his year, and now all he could do was watch his companions, those who had been close to him during his years at the Academy, take up the normal career for which they had trained. He, meanwhile, could go on wearing the uniform of the British army but would remain unable to participate fully in its military life. Obviously his own very particular interests kept him from total inactivity, in that unlike his former companions he had to maintain a close interest in what was happening in France and try to exercise some control over his partisans. Unfortunately, given the nature of Bonapartist politics, which precluded any possibility of taking an initiative, there seemed little he could do except wait upon events. Frustrated by the seeming impossibility of playing a direct role, and perhaps thinking of his father's actions at Strasbourg and Boulogne, Louis came to the conclusion that it would require some personal action on his part to bring him to the attention of the majority of the French people.

In the meantime, his mother, well aware that he was inclined to be bored by the life he was forced to lead, worried about him because, having time on his hands, he willingly accepted invitations to visit the houses of the aristocracy, and was a friend of the Prince of Wales and the Marlborough House set. The Empress did not consider that these circles were suitable for her son, who risked acquiring a reputation for being frivolous, and so she turned to travel, something she had always considered to be a sovereign remedy for most ills, hoping that change would quieten his restlessness.

In the years following the Emperor's death she and her son went to Switzerland to stay in the house in Arenenberg which had originally belonged to Queen Hortense, and which Napoleon III had purchased during his reign in memory of his mother. It had become a 'family' residence, and the Empress had tried to restore it to a condition which made it feel like home, particularly for her son. Apart from these holiday visits to Arenenberg, there were also visits to Italy, where in 1875 they stayed with the 'Italian Bonapartes', descendants of Lucien who had married into the Italian aristocracy, giving Louis the chance to meet his extended family. During the course of the same visit he was received by King Victor Emmanuel, and in Rome he was received by his godfather, Pope Pius IX, a visit that was purely private, but which was immediately seized upon by those who said it was proof of his mother's Catholic influence. The 'radical' group around Prince Napoleon Jerome made great play with the supposed ultra-Catholicism of Eugénie, and its nefarious influence on her son, hoping to discredit the Prince Imperial. In 1878 the Prince visited Denmark and Sweden, this time without his mother, and he was received by the royal families of Denmark and Sweden with full royal honours befitting the heir to a throne. He was very touched by this, for him an unexpected pleasure. As he wrote to the Empress: 'If my father had been at the Tuileries they could not have done more for me'.[5]

These were rare moments, however, in a life which was mostly constrained and monotonous. To be an unemployed soldier with no prospects of a military career, and an unemployed Prince with a doubtful future, meant that there was little to satisfy a vigorous, healthy and intelligent twenty-two-year-old. Not surprisingly, Louis had been looking for a way to break out of his little world, and for a Bonaparte that could only mean one thing: he must find a military career. Already in 1878 the Prince had tried to be attached to the army of Austria-Hungary, using his mother as a means of contacting the Emperor Franz Joseph. The Emperor refused and so Louis was obliged to try and think of another opening which would enable him to appear upon a wider and more important stage. He did not have long to wait.

In 1878 Britain, as a result of its imperialist policies, found that it was at war with the Zulu in South Africa and it was a war that was not going well. In January 1879, at Isandhlwana, a Zulu attack resulted in the virtual annihilation of a column of Lord Chelmsford's force. When news of the disaster reached London in February, there was a demand that the government immediately take steps to avenge this defeat. The government of Disraeli, which was always very attentive to anything which concerned the British Empire, was determined to send reinforcements to the Cape. Convinced that this was exactly the occasion which suited him, Louis wrote to the Duke of Cambridge, Commander-in-Chief of the English army, asking him for a place, no matter what, in the army. He underlined that his request was reasonable, for two of his best friends, Lieutenants Bigge and Slade, together with other officers from his year at Woolwich, had already received the order to go. He felt that that would be impossible for him to turn up at Aldershot, wearing his uniform, while all the others were in South Africa.

The letter received a polite refusal from the Duke of Cambridge, and at this point Eugénie, although in great distress at the thought of what her son was trying to do, was so moved by seeing how upset he was by the Duke's refusal decided that she must try to help. So she approached the Queen, asking her to see if something could be done and, since the Queen was extremely fond of the Prince, something was eventually worked out.

It was the worst of all possible solutions because the Prince was authorised to go to the Cape in uniform, but in a personal capacity, although once he arrived he would be given some sort of job at the headquarters of the army attached to Lord Chelmsford. The result of this ambiguous situation was that nobody was quite clear as to whether the Prince was a civilian or a soldier, and Disraeli, who had done his best to prevent the Prince's departure, feared there might be very disagreeable consequences if anything went wrong.

The Empress was both distressed and understanding about her son's decision. He had told her that he was twenty-three years old and had a name that was too difficult and heavy to bear if he did nothing with it. Here was an occasion for him to exercise his chosen profession and therefore he did not want to let it pass. As she said to her Mother:'What a terrible thing it is to be a born a boy! How many times have I not regretted that I did not have a daughter.'[6]

On 26 February 1879, the Prince went to Windsor to take his leave of the Queen, who was extremely fond of the young man. He wished to thank her for having intervened on his behalf, something which the Queen herself was now beginning to regret, hoping that he would be very careful and not expose himself uselessly to danger, because as she said, 'he is known to be *extremely* adventurous'. On 28 February the Prince embarked for the Cape on board the steamer *Danube*. He took with him Uhlmann, his faithful personal valet, who would install himself at a military base in Durban, and two English grooms Brown and Lomas, who would be responsible for his horses.

Enthusiasm and impatience, two traits which the Prince unfortunately had in plenty, made him find the voyage long and very monotonous. He was also very disappointed that they did not stop at St Helena, as had been at first planned. On 26 March he arrived at last at the Cape. He was given a great public welcome, and installed at Government House as a guest of the Governor, where a great banquet was given in his honour. When he arrived in Durban he had an even greater and warmer reception. As he said to his mother in a letter, 'I was received like a crowned head although I was only in the uniform of a Lieutenant'.

The Prince was certainly flattered and happy to be received as he was by the authorities and to be given a royal reception, but he had not gone to South Africa simply in order to enjoy this sort of life. What Louis wanted was action, and he spoke constantly of contact with the enemy, to such an extent that he worried his superiors, who feared that his enthusiasm would bring him down. On several occasions, while on patrol, the Prince, if he saw any number of Zulu, would draw his sword and charge, prompting one of his commanders to express the opinion that he was becoming a danger to himself and to others. Unfortunately, confusion as to his place in the chain of command meant it was easy for the Prince to circumvent his superiors and so he managed, against the wishes of some, to be involved as often as possible in patrols which he hoped would lead to encounters with the Zulu.

Even more alarming was the Prince's tendency to see these encounters as an excuse for drawing his sword and charging at the enemy. On being questioned as to the wisdom of this behaviour, he said: 'I should always have my sword, not so much to charge as to defend myself if I was surrounded. I should die fighting, and then death would have nothing painful.' It would be unfair to Louis to treat this sort of statement as a sign of an almost adolescent approach to the business of soldiering, because it was grounded in something much deeper and more serious. One of the accusations made against Napoleon III, and repeated ad nauseam by the Republican press, was that he had been guilty of cowardice in 1870, above all, at Sedan. Utterly devoted to his father, Louis had been haunted by the injustice of this, undoubtedly one of the reasons why he was determined to see action was that it would enable him to give the lie to this calumny. He had himself been directly linked to it, for when he fell ill at the Cape with an attack of fever, a hostile French newspaper reported that he was suffering from the usual malady of the Bonapartes – cowardice. Bearing this in mind, it is small wonder that the Prince should look for a way to distinguish himself on the field of battle, even if it meant death: 'I should die fighting, and then death would have nothing painful'.

The invasion of Zululand began on the 31 May 1879 and the following day the Prince was attached to a scouting party in order that he might make sketches of the terrain, something at which he was extremely adept. This small party consisting of six troopers together with a Zulu guide, and was officially under the command of Captain Carey who was the only *commissioned* officer in the patrol. Carey got on well with the Prince because he himself had spent a great deal of time in France, where he had been partly educated, and he spoke French fluently. As the small party was about to leave camp, one of the officers, Major Grenfell, called out to the Prince, 'take care of yourself and don't get shot', to which the Prince replied, 'Oh no, Carey will take a very good care that nothing happens to me'.

The patrol reached a kraal about three o'clock in the afternoon and decided to rest, although there was evidence of recent occupation, presumably by Zulu. No sentry was posted and the patrol then off-saddled and haltered their horses, displaying a surprising lack of care, given the nature of the terrain. A scout returned to warn them that a group of Zulu was approaching, but it was too late, for they had already surrounded the small patrol. When they opened fire, the surprise volley frightened the horses, one of whom bolted, and two troopers were killed outright. As Carey was already in the saddle and galloping away, a trooper called Le Tocq, who came from Guernsey, shouted to Louis, in French, to hurry up: 'Dépêchez-vous Votre Altesse'. Louis ran alongside his horse, trying to mount, but grasping at the saddle holster, which gave way, he fell under the horse's hooves. As a result, the horse trampled on his right arm and at the same moment he found himself alone, since what was left of the patrol was already fleeing across the Donga. It was at this moment that a trooper cried 'Sir, the Prince is down!' Louis, still trying to draw his sword and unaware that he had already lost it, was left to defend himself with only his revolver against the Zulu who now attacked him. He was brought down by assegai wounds, one in the leg and one in the shoulder, and when he sank to the ground was stabbed repeatedly until he was dead.[7]

The following day a search party was sent out to find the bodies; those of the two troopers were naked and mutilated while that of the Prince, also naked except for a gold chain with a religious medallion that he wore around his neck, had not been mutilated. The body had been pierced by eighteen assegai wounds, all in the front, clearly many of them inflicted after the Prince was already dead. The body was wrapped in a cotton sheet and was then taken back to camp. When news reached England, Disraeli neatly summed up the consequence, saying: 'A remarkable people the Zulu. They defeat our generals … and they have settled the fate of a great European dynasty.'

In the immediate circumstances, as far as the army was concerned, some body had to be blamed. Inevitably it was Captain Carey, who had survived and who had been, in theory, responsible for the safety of the Prince. He was indicted and brought before a court martial, accused 'of having when the Prince and escort were attacked by the enemy, galloped away, and in not having attempted to rally the said escort or in other ways defend the said Prince'. Carey pleaded not guilty, and his defence turned upon the confusion as to who had actually been in charge, those of the troopers who had survived said they were not sure who should have given the orders, that is, Captain Carey or the Prince, though they recalled that the Prince had given the order to mount up. It transpired that all the arguments were pointless: the whole court martial subsequently turned out to have been a waste of time, its verdict meaningless, because the whole proceedings were declared to be invalid as the court had not been properly sworn in.[8]

When the news of the tragedy reached England on 20 June, the person most immediately affected was, inevitably, the Empress herself. For some days she was totally speechless and paralysed with grief, but eventually managed to write a few lines to her mother: 'I am without purpose and courage. The weather is cold and I have a fire, but nothing can warm me and my heart is turned to ice.'

In South Africa, the body of the Prince had been hastily embalmed by the military doctors, and had then been transferred to Pietermaritzburg where it lay in the Catholic church, until its removal to Port Natal. Here the coffin was placed on the *Boadicea* which sailed to Simons Bay. The last stage of the journey was aboard the steamer *Orontes*, which arrived at Plymouth on 10 July, before being transferred to the *Enchantress*, a yacht belonging to the Admiralty, that would carry the body and escort to Woolwich reach via the Thames estuary. On arrival at Woolwich, the coffin, borne by eight sailors, was installed in a part of the Arsenal, having been met and blessed

by the Bishop of Southwark. It was then opened in order that the identity of
the corpse might be officially recognised, a duty performed by Rouher, and
it was then brought to Chislehurst with a military escort to await burial.[9]

The Queen had already been to Camden Place on 23 June in an attempt
to comfort the Empress, whose strength and resignation she found, in her
own words, 'beyond all praise'. She now made arrangements to be present
at the funeral, which took place on 12 July, the body being taking to the
church of St Mary where the Emperor was already buried. In order to avoid
offending the French government, it was decided that there should be no
hint of the Prince being given a 'state' funeral, but the Queen was so angry
that eventually two ministers, both of the second rank, attended. The Queen
herself went to Camden Place, together with the Princess of Wales and
Princess Beatrice, while the Prince of Wales, the Duke of Connaught and
the Duke of Cambridge were pallbearers, together with the Duke de
Bassano, the Crown Prince of Sweden and Rouher. The Bonaparte family
was represented by the chief mourner, Prince Napoleon, who was accompanied by his two sons, Prince Victor and Prince Louis, who walked
immediately behind the coffin. There were a few surviving representatives
of the Second Empire, former ministers and prefects among others, but the
government of the Republic had forbidden any serving officers army or
navy to attend. Military ceremonial were performed by the cadets from the
Royal Academy at Woolwich, who, in honour of their former comrade,
marched with arms reversed, while the band of the Royal Academy marched
to the sound of muffled drums. At least it could be said that the Prince had
a soldier's funeral.

Carey was, at the Empress's entreaty, dealt with leniently because, as she
said, getting to what was for her the heart of the matter: 'All I know is that
he has been killed, and that is all'. She asked the Queen to intercede on
behalf of Carey when he came before a second court martial in England.
Carey repaid this generous attitude by publicly blaming the Prince for his
own death and using as his defence the question of who was in charge.
Carey said that he had the impression that the Prince Imperial actually
enjoyed full military status and was therefore the superior officer,
something that he cannot really have believed. So successfully did Carey
pose as a victim that public opinion, aided by the press, found him to have
been made a scapegoat and, in typical fashion, began to see him as an heroic
victim. The Empress, who had been only too willing to find forgiveness,

now found it difficult to accept the fact that he was being transformed into the man of the moment, when, as she said: 'He has no other title to leave to posterity than having saved himself as quick as his horse could carry him, leaving behind him a *comrade* and two men.' What had greatly angered Eugénie, as she told the Queen, was the fact that Carey had tried to blame the Prince for what had happened.[10] Anyway there was nothing more to be done. As Eugénie said: 'Nothing can replace the child who was my whole life since 1870. I had no distractions, no friends, everything was for him and he was everything for me.' She had worthier things to bother about than Carey, who ended his life being cold-shouldered by his peers wherever he went, and who dragged himself from garrison to garrison until he died in 1883.

The Prince's death was of course a tremendous blow to the Bonapartists and the situation was made worse by the fact that Prince, in his will, had bypassed Prince Napoleon and had handed the succession to the latter's elder son, Prince Victor, who was then seventeen. This was a totally arbitrary decision made by the Prince himself; he does not seem to have consulted anyone before he added the codicil to his will, and even the Empress was perturbed at this setting aside of the succession as it had been laid down in the constitution of 1870. She immediately understood that the breach between herself and Prince Napoleon would now probably never be mended, since the Prince remained convinced that Louis' decision was a direct result of pressure from his mother.

The other difficulty was that Prince Victor was still a minor and therefore technically still in his father's charge, something that made relations between father and son more than difficult, and led to the creation of an official split in the Bonapartist group between the 'Jeromistes', those who followed the father, and the 'Victoriens', that is, those who followed the son. There were now two claimants to the imperial succession, and it was immediately clear to friends and enemies alike that the Bonapartist party was so weakened by this situation that the only gainers at a could be the Republicans.

For Eugénie, the loss of her son marked a decisive turning point in her life in which dynastic considerations played little part. For her, the house at Chislehurst had become a sort of living tomb and her one idea was to leave it as soon as possible. There was, however, a practical problem – namely what to do with the bodies of her husband and son, which were still in the small Catholic church of St Mary at Chislehurst. She had first thought of building an extension to the existing church, but this proved impossible because she was unable to purchase the necessary land on which to build; so she decided that another solution would have to be found.

Before taking any final decision, the Empress carried out her resolve to go to South Africa in order that she might visit the spot where her son had been killed, a plan in which she was both helped and encouraged by Queen Victoria. She left England in March 1880 accompanied by a small suite, and having trekked to Itelezi, the place where the Prince had fallen, spent the night of 1 June keeping vigil alone, next to a to a cross which Queen Victoria had caused to be erected there. Once back at Camden Place she found the house, so full of memories for her, to be now unbearable, and began seriously to look for an alternative property to buy. In fact, her personal feelings now coincided with her actual situation, because the owner of Camden Place did not wish either to sell or renew the lease, and so the search for a new house was no longer a matter of choice.

In the autumn of 1880 she found her house, Farnborough Hill, in Hampshire, originally built by Longman the publisher, about thirty miles from London, having been advised of its availability by Sir Linton Simmons, a former governor at Woolwich during the Prince's time there, who had subsequently become a friend of the Empress. What immediately attracted Eugénie to the house was its situation: 'I believe that my dear child, if he could see it, would like it. It is near to the camp at Aldershot where he spent times which he loved to recall, and it's not far from Windsor.' Apart from any link with the Prince, there was a practical point that it would be possible to enlarge the existing building and the house had sufficient grounds, a domain of some 68 acres, which would enable her to carry through a plan of building a church in which to house the bodies of her husband and son. By 1888, after some considerable difficulty with the rebuilding programme and the completion of the church, to which was attached a small monastery, the Empress was able to install the bodies of the Prince and his father the Emperor in what was now known as St Michael's Abbey. The ceremony of the transfer from Chislehurst took place on 9 January, the anniversary of the death of the Emperor in 1873, the two coffins being brought to the abbey on gun carriages, escorted by officers of the Royal Artillery. The officers wished to show by their presence their respect for their former comrade, the Prince Imperial.

Although there is no direct evidence to show that the Empress had decided that the dynasty had little future after the death of her son, it seems clear that, while she went through the motions, she had really little hope of a restoration. She watched with some dismay the activities of her old enemy Prince Napoleon, who in 1883 was misguided enough to try and put himself forward as a possible alternative to the existing regime, stressing his right to imperial inheritance, an attempt which ended in his imprisonment for having conspired against the government of the Republic. True to her own principles, the Empress made the journey to Paris in order to visit him in prison and to demonstrate family solidarity, a gesture that failed to lead to a reconciliation between the two.

In 1886 the Republican government passed a decree banishing from France the heads of any family who had once reigned in that country, naming Prince Napoleon among others, and thereby in a way recognising him as head of the Imperial House. The decree also of course applied to his son Prince Victor, and indeed the entire family decided it had no longer any place within the jurisdiction of the Republic, the only exception being Princess Mathilde, who continued to live her normal life while deftly abstaining from any political action, other than continuing her own campaign against the Empress. The 'black legend' was assiduously cultivated by all those Bonapartists who chose to see in Eugénie the cause of all the disasters, including the most poisonous accusation, originating in a newspaper controlled by Prince Napoleon and totally without foundation, that she was responsible for the war of 1870. By blaming the Empress, it was possible to avoid blaming the Emperor and, by implication, the regime. These internecine calumnies were a great help to the Republican government which concentrated all *its* fire on Napoleon III and the 'shame' of the surrender at Sedan and the loss of territory to Germany.

As for Prince Napoleon, who had so many qualities which could have been of use to the Bonapartist cause, he continued to behave as if he had no responsibilities either to his family or to his dynasty, and in the last years of his life maintained a public and bitter quarrel with his son Victor. Dying in 1891 in Rome, he refused to receive the son he considered to have rebelled against his authority, both paternal and imperial, an act which nothing can justify, and which simply increased the disastrous effect produced in the remnant of the Bonapartist party by this lamentable family schism.

Prince Victor had not the temperament of his father, being quiet and reflective rather than violent and impulsive, resembling more his mother and being perhaps more a 'Savoyard' than a Bonaparte. While his brother, Prince Louis, served in the Russian army, where he reached the rank of General, the white hope of the Bonapartist idea and its imperial claims lived quietly in Brussels. Bonapartism became, for its representative as much as for its faithful, a matter of 'Napoleonism' more and more turned towards the past rather than the present or the future. It was as if this great dynamic force, or what remained of it, and the hopes of the party, or what remained of that, had been put under glass in a museum dedicated to past glories.

From time to time Prince Victor received men who were engaged in politics in France, who were not necessarily Bonapartists but who entertained the thought that the Prince might be 'their man'. In talking to them he made vague proposals, optimistic quite often, and they then took the train back to Paris with the impression that the Republic had little to fear from a Pretender who seemed more interested in collecting relics connected with the family than making an attempt to restore it to political power. In fact, it could be said that he was a Pretender who did not pretend, so that the question of a restoration of the dynasty became of less and less consequence.

Inevitably, the strange amalgam of dissident groups, who might be called 'the Bonapartist tendency', and who aspired to a revision of the constitution of the Third Republic, found a focus for their hopes in General Boulanger. Here was a general who had shown a desire to play politics, who looked well on a horse, and who had captured public notoriety. The dissidents convinced themselves that the General would emulate the young Napoleon and lead their movement to victory, but this psuedo-Bonapartism carried no more weight than the real thing and Boulanger was no Napoleon. As one critic pointed out, 'At your age general, Bonaparte was already dead'. Perhaps impressed by this thought, as well as by the collapse of his movement, the general ended his life by committing suicide at the grave of his mistress. This 'Napoleon of the Music Halls', as Boulanger had been dubbed, had simply served to underline the fact that the idea of Bonapartism, like the dynasty, had outlived its usefulness.[11]

Would it have been different if the Prince Imperial had lived? We have to remember that at the time of the Prince's death in 1879, the Republic had managed to establish itself. Although like all regimes it went through crises, there is no indication that a desire for restoration of the imperial regime was growing. Indeed, with the passage of time, it was declining. It must also be remembered that the Prince Imperial had not at his disposal such a good hand to play as his great uncle had held on the Eighteenth Brumaire, nor as his father had on 2 December. One had been a victorious and popular general, master of an army ready for anything, surrounded by young, ambitious and devoted partisans. Above all, he was assured of the complacency, even the help, of members of the Directory, who constituted the legal government. Even more useful, his brother Lucien was President of the Council of Five Hundred, one of the organs of government, and in a moment of crisis this proved to be of supreme importance. As for his father, Prince Louis Napoleon, when he decided to make his move was already President of the Republic, elected by a majority vote of the people. As one commentator put it, 'it is easy to take a fortress in which one is already installed and of which one is already the commander'.

The Prince Imperial had none of these advantages, in fact what he had to bear was the terrible accusation of the shame of the surrender at Sedan, and the loss of territory to Germany, both events that continued to be associated with the fallen dynasty. In this way the Empire was made guilty, as if the Empire had not been France itself. As for the Bonapartist party, what could a young man do even though he himself might wish to awaken it and to make it youthful? Princes in exile know less and less about the men and the things of their time, unlike the sovereigns who live in their capital in touch with the daily political life of the country they rule. Louis had informants, and he could read the newspapers, but as time passed he inevitably lost the *feel* of French political life, while being all too aware of the weakness and disarray among his supporters. Everything considered, it seems that the Prince Imperial would have probably grown old waiting, perhaps more and more sceptical and discouraged. He would have had the same destiny as all those other Pretenders to the French throne who were the result of the turmoil which had begun in 1789 and to which it had seemed only the Bonapartes and their regime could provide an answer.

In a sense the Bonaparte family had developed an almost symbiotic relationship with France, a relationship which had its origins in the growth of the French state as it emerged transformed by the Great Revolution, but which needed, during its most dangerous crisis, the action of a providential man who had appeared at a moment of social and political dissolution. Bonapartism claimed to be, and in fact was, the great reconciler, but because of the particular relationship between the family and the French people a great deal depended upon the maintenance of the almost mystical link between both parties. The dynasty had survived the shock of Waterloo, not just because of the legacy of greatness that had gone before, but also because the successor regimes had proved incapable of tapping into the *mystical* legacy of the Fourth Dynasty. Both the restored Bourbons and the monarchy of Louis-Philippe had tried in different ways to pick it up, but neither had been successful, while a Republican experiment had, by its introduction of universal suffrage, simply prepared the ground for a restored Empire by giving the people a voice.

After 1870, and the disasters caused by the war, Bonapartism had not disappeared, but it had taken a severe blow which had, certainly in the short term, knocked it out of the political arena. The long-term prospects were not good either: a sick man and a boy, both in exile, and a political class that was bemused and not sure what it wanted, but was fairly sure that it did not want an imperial restoration. Fortunately for them, the political elites were able to find a suitable compromise and establish a conservative Republic which, by a splendid irony, was held together by the administrative and legal structure bequeathed to it by Napoleon I. The most important legacy of Napoleon III and the Second Empire, apart from the economic growth of the country, was that it firmly established the principle, and the use, of universal male suffrage, making it an integral and irreversible part of France's political structure. It could be argued that the very success of the dynasty had made it surplus to requirements.

As the long nineteenth century drew to its close, for it really ended in 1914 with the outbreak of the First World War, the Bonaparte family had virtually disappeared from the political scene. At the same time its members had, by marriage, secured a place among the European royal establishment, being related to almost every major dynasty, an acceptance that would have pleased the founder.

In her residence at Farnborough Hill the Empress Eugénie maintained a 'court' because, as the last living representative of the Second Empire, she felt that this was her duty to her husband and son. It was a very unpretentious affair, though given her status it frequently had royal visitors, especially Queen Victoria with whom he maintained a close relationship until the Queen's death in 1901. Even this death did not end her links with the British royal family; she continued to be invited to stay at Windsor, and until her death, both King Edward VII and King George V visited Farnborough.

As far as the imperial dynasty was concerned, the Empress had always received Prince Victor formally as head of the Imperial House, making her curtsey to him, but it is doubtful if anyone believed that this represented anything other than the essential and traditional courtesies.

In 1904 Princess Mathilde died, the last *Princesse Française* of the Empire. The Empress made a point of going to France for her funeral, for, in spite of their far from easy relationship, Mathilde was the last representative of the generation that Eugénie had known when she had been on the throne. Times were changing, and as a further proof that old resentments and fears had disappeared, since the 1890s the Empress, with the consent of the French government, had been able to live in France during the winters, in a villa which she had built at Cap Martin.

Of Prince Napoleon's children Victor, as the head of the Imperial House, an undisputed title since the death of his father in 1891, married Princess Clementine of Belgium in 1910 and ensured the succession by producing two children, a daughter Marie-Clotilde, born in 1912, and a son, Louis born in 1914. Victor and his family frequently stayed at Farnborough Hill with the Empress, and in 1914 were to find refuge there when the Germans invaded Belgium. Of Prince Napoleon's other two children, Prince Louis spent his life in the Russian army, having a distinguished if not unremarkable career, and certainly displayed no great dynastic interest. The girl, Princess Letizia, had been born in 1866, and married in 1888 Prince Amadeo of Savoy, who had been for a short time King of Spain (1870–73). She was the only member of the family whose dynastic tendencies surfaced for a moment in 1911, when the newly created state of Albania was looking for a king and Letizia tried to persuade her brother Louis to take the throne. Fortunately, the Prince had more sense than his sister and refused to succumb to this dynastic temptation.

Prince Victor and his children lived with the Empress at Farnborough from 1914 until the end of the war, when they returned to Belgium. The Empress herself died in July 1920 while on a visit to her family in Spain, and was buried with her husband and her son in the Imperial Basilica which she had built at Farnborough. The three were finally united, and they remain there to the present day, in the care of the Benedictine community Eugénie established for that purpose.

On the death of Prince Victor in Brussels in 1926, his son, the young

Prince Louis became head of the Imperial House, and although Bonapartism had not totally disappeared from the political scene it was in a very weakened state. It maintained a media presence with two publications, *La Volonté Nationale* and, after 1930, *Brumaire*, but neither had a wide readership. The Third Republic, while virtually existing in a state of permanent political crisis, always survived, because the parties rallied to the system which guaranteed their political livelihood. Even the great crisis of 1932–33 did not produce a call for a Bonaparte, although during a serious riot outside the National Assembly a cry was heard 'Forward the grenadiers of Brumaire!', an appeal that found no response among the rioters.[12]

In any event, there was a familiar problem: Prince Louis was an exile in his teens. He continued to live in Belgium, where he attended the university of Louvain, and then in Switzerland, at the university of Lausanne. In 1939, on the outbreak of war, now of age, he closed down all Bonapartist political activity and offered to serve in the French army, but the offer was refused. Determined to be identified with France's struggle, he joined the Foreign Legion in which he served until 1940. In 1941, after the fall of France, the Prince returned to Switzerland, but at the end of 1942 he clandestinely entered Spain, determined to get back in the war. Together with three companions he attempted to cross the Pyrenees into France hoping to join the Resistance. Captured by the Germans, he was imprisoned by the Gestapo, who knew his identity (at over six feet in height the Prince was easily recognised). The Germans decided that they would try to use him and his name by having him publicly accept the occupation regime. The Prince's refusal was absolute, and so for the second time the Germans had failed to tap into the mystique of Napoleon and the Bonapartes, the first occasion being in December 1940 with the return of the body of the King of Rome from Vienna so that he could be buried in the Invalides beside his father. The gesture had been carefully calculated to appeal to French sentiment, since the chosen date of 15 December marked the centenary of the return of the body of Napoleon I from St Helena. It proved a failure. Prince Napoleon expressed outrage at the proposal that he should attend the ceremony, and even Marshal Pétain refused an invitation to attend, thereby thwarting a clumsy attempt to unite occupiers and occupied in a spurious legitimacy. The whole business turned into a public relations disaster and led to a rather cruel joke by the Parisians who said, 'we badly needed coal and the Germans sent us ashes!'

The Prince, released from prison, was put under house arrest, from which he managed to escape, and succeded in joining the Resistance. Severely wounded during an engagement with the enemy, in which Prince Murat was killed, Prince Louis was hospitalised, but on being discharged, he had the satisfaction of being admitted to serve in the French regular army, wearing the uniform of a French officer. It was the first time that a member of the dynasty had been able to serve since 1870. The Prince proved worthy of his inheritance, having at the end of the war, been awarded the Croix de Guerre and the Légion d'Honneur. Finally, in 1950, came the abrogation of the Law of Exile which had been in existence since 1886 and the family could return to France.

As head of the Imperial House, once again resident in France, the Prince made it plain that 'the only duty of someone who bore the name of Napoleon Bonaparte was to maintain this name in the service of France', and added, 'I serve, and I am not a Pretender' ('je sers et je ne prétends pas'). In a sense, the Prince's attitude and what he said, defined the position of the Bonapartes (who now use 'Napoleon' as their family name) in the modern world. Through choice, and an acceptance of change, as head of the Imperial House, Prince Louis officially ended the dynasty's link with Bonapartism as a political force. Until his death in 1997 he continued in his refusal to become involved in any political or partisan activity. His contribution to the maintenance of his family's links with France came though an unfailing interest in the history and importance of the dynasty's role in the development of the country. He was an enthusiastic patron of organisations he saw as fulfilling an educational function, enabling people to become fully aware of the nature and importance of the imperial epoch. As he said, 'I feel that in this I fulfil a pious obligation of the Emperors Napoleon I and Napoleon III towards France, by putting in the hands of the national museums the imposing patrimony which has been entrusted to me'. To this end, the imperial family gave large parts of their private possessions to enrich the collections of the various museums already linked in the public mind with the two empires.

The Prince fulfilled his dynastic duty by marrying in 1949 Alix de Foresta, a union which resulted in four children, the eldest of whom, Prince Charles Napoleon, was born in 1950. He too has a son, Prince Jean Christophe Napoleon born in 1986, so the dynasty, as a family, has assured continuity. It could be said of the Bonapartes that as a dynasty they no longer exist, having voluntarily given up the role of 'Pretenders', but they have been replaced by a family whose links with France, and with the French people, are impossible to ignore. Indeed the Fifth Republic, the present government of France, has a constitution which owes much to Bonapartist precedents. What is perhaps most extraordinary in this story is the very short space of time which this family, as a ruling dynasty, occupied in the long history of France, their two short periods in power, amounting to some forty years in all, seeming wholly disproportionate to the effect that they have had. But given that modern France is the product of the great upheaval of the Revolution, and that so much of what the Revolution hoped to achieve became identified with Napoleon, it is perhaps not so surprising.

Notes

Notes to Chapter 1: The Founder

1   For the relations between Bonapartists and Paolistas, see Charles Napoléon, *Bonaparte et Paoli* (Paris, 2000).
2   Emmanuel Las Cases, *Le Mémorial de Sainte Hélène*, Pléiade edition, ed. Walter (Paris, 1956), i, p. 80.
3   A critique of Bourrienne is in Jean Tulard, *Nouvelle bibliographie critique des mémoires sur l'époque Napoléonienne* (Geneva, 1991). This work is essential reading for anyone wishing to use the various memoirs of the period.
4   Jean Tulard, *Napoléon: ou le mythe du sauveur* (Paris, 1977), p. 44.
5   Napoléon, *Bonaparte and Paoli*, p. 189.
6   A good, balanced account of the Directory and its politics in Thierry Lentz, *Le 18 Brumaire* (Paris, 1997).
7   Las Cases, *Le Mémorial de Sainte Hélène*, i, p. 98.
8   Tulard, *Napoléon*, pp. 98–99, provides a sharp analysis of the reasons for the return to France.
9   The most recent account of this crucial event is in Lentz, *Le 18 Brumaire*, and in Steven Englund, *Napoleon: A Political Life* (New York, 2004), pp. 160–66.
10 In accord with Napoleon's view that a 'constitution should be short and obscure'.

Notes to Chapter 2: Towards a Dynasty

1   There was a great deal at stake. Thierry Lentz, *Le 18 Brumaire* (Paris, 1997), pp. 254–58, shows how well the family had done by 1799.
2   Napoleon confided to Las Cases, 'Without my wife I would never have been able to establish relations with this group', Emmanuel Las Cases, *Le Mémorial de Sainte Hélène*, Pléiade edition, ed. Walter (Paris, 1956), i, p. 582.
3   Isser Woloch, *Napoleon and his Collaborators* (New York and London, 2001), p. 55.
4   Felix Markham. *Napoleon* (London, 1963), p. 68, quotes this from the memoirs of Chaptal, the eminent scientist. See also, *Correspondance de Napoléon Ier, publiée par ordre de l'Empereur Napoléon III* (Paris, 1858–69), letter 4639.
5   Michael Ross, *The Reluctant King: Joseph Bonaparte, King of the Two Sicilies and Spain* (London, 1976), pp. 95–96.

6 Latreille and Rémond, *Histoire du Catholicisme en France* (Paris, 1962), iii, pp. 161–78 also Steven Englund, *Napoleon: A Political Life* (New York, 2004), for comments on the Concordat. For Napoleon's relations with Pius VII, see E.E.Y. Hales, *Napoleon and the Pope* (London, 1961).

7 Jean Tulard, *Napoléon: ou le mythe du sauveur* (Paris, 1977), p. 137.

8 Elizabeth Sparrow, *Secret Service: British Agents in France, 1792–1815* (1999), pp. 226–34, gives an account of the murder and English involvement.

9 Sparrow, *Secret Service*, pp. 286–91.

10 Jean-Pierre Babelon and Suzanne d'Huart, *Napoleon's Last Will and Testament* (facsimile), translated by Alex de Jonge (New York and London, 1977), p. 38.

11 Thierry Lentz, *Le Grand Consulat* (Paris, 1999), pp. 540–41 and 546.

12 Léon Duguit and Henry Monnier, *Les constitutions et les principales lois politiques de la France depuis 1789* (Paris, 1915), pp. 144–45.

13 Ibid., p. 165.

Notes to Chapter 3: The Revolution Crowned

1 Letter to the King of Spain, 25 Prairial, Year XII (14 June 1804), in Thierry Lentz, *Le Grand Consulat* (Paris, 1999), p. 581.

2 The bicentenary of the event in 2004 led to the appearance of several works of note. The most interesting is *Le Sacre de Napoléon*, general editor Thierry Lentz, Fondation Napoléon (Paris, 2004).

3 Thierry Lentz, *Nouvelle Histoire du Premier Empire*, i, *Napoléon a la conquête de l'Europe, 1804–1810* (Paris, 2002), p. 122.

4 Details in Owen Connelly, *Napoleon's Satellite Kingdoms* (New York, 1965). The Emperor's views on his family and its uses are in Emmanuel Las Cases, *Le Mémorial de Sainte Hélène*, Pléiade edition, ed. Walter (Paris, 1956), i, pp. 582–83.

5 The most recent account of the Continental System is in Steven Englund, *Napoleon: A Political Life* (New York, 2004), pp. 294–97 and 365–68.

6 For Joseph's attempts to 'rule wisely' see Connelly, *Napoleon's Satellite Kingdoms*, pp. 236ff.

7 Felix Markham, *Napoleon* (London, 1963), pp. 151–59.

8 Bernard Chevallier, *Douce et incomparable Joséphine* (Paris, 1999), thinks that as early as 1807 there was talk of a divorce, but the decisive factor was the pregnancy of Marie Walewska in 1809. Chevallier also points out how attached Napoleon remained to Josephine. In April 1814, he wrote from Fontainebleau, 'never forget the memory of one who never forgot you and never will'. Ibid., p. 228.

9 For Austrian policy, see C.A. Macartney, *The Habsburg Empire, 1790–1918* (London, 1968), pp. 192–93.

10 Lucien's tribulations dealt with in Frank McLynn, *Napoleon* (London, 1998), p. 472.

Notes to Chapter 4: An Heir without a Throne

1   For Marie-Louise, see Paul Ganière, 'Marie-Louise d'Autriche', article in *Dictionnaire Napoléon*, ed. Jean Tulard (Paris, 1987).

2   Philip Mansel, *The Eagle in Splendour* (London, 1987), gives an excellent account of the Napoleonic court. See also Jean Tulard, *Napoléon et la noblesse d'Empire* (Paris, 1979), pp. 55–66.

3   Mansel, *The Eagle in Splendour*, especially chapter 3, 'A Passion for Palaces'.

4   E.E.Y. Hales, *Napoleon and the Pope* (London, 1961), pp. 119–78. Napoleon's version of the issues is in Emmanuel Las Cases, *Le Mémorial de Sainte Hélène*, Pléiade edition, ed. Walter (Paris, 1956), pp. 1042–49.

5   André Ratchinski, *Napoléon et Alexandre Ier: la guerre des idées* (Paris, 2002), especially pp. 247–91.

6   Thierry Lentz, *Nouvelle Histoire*, ii, *L'éffondrement du système napoléonien* (Paris, 2004). Lentz challenges the accepted figure for the losses in Russia, ibid., pp. 319–23.

7   Ibid., pp. 334–39.

8   Léon Duguit and Henry Monnier, *Les constitutions et les principales lois politiques de la France depuis 1789* (Paris, 1915), pp. 169–77, senatus consultum, 5 February 1813.

9   Hales, *Napoleon and the Pope*, pp. 179–196. Napoleon's comment in *Le Mémorial de Sainte Hélène*, i, p. 1044.

10   The Pope's letter to the Allied sovereigns in Hales, *Napoleon and the Pope*, pp. 206–7.

11   Both quotes in Felix Markham. *Napoleon* (London, 1963), pp. 189 and 192.

12   Ibid., p. 198.

13   There seems little doubt that Clarke, as Minister for War, played a highly ambiguous role. Details are in René Reiss, *Clarke, maréchal et paire de France*, (Strasbourg, 1999), pp. 358–63.

14   Talleyrand's manoeuvres are well described in Lentz, *L'éffondrement*, pp. 561–64.

15   Emmanuel de Waresquiel and Benoit Yvert, *Histoire de la Restauration, 1814–1830* (Paris, 1996), pp. 93–97, show how fragile was the position of the restored monarchy.

16   The key work for the episode is Dominique de Villepin, *Les Cent-Jours: ou l'esprit de sacrifice* (Paris, 2001).

17   Waresquiel and Yvert, *Histoire de la Restauration, 1814–1830*, pp. 118–21.

18   Text in Jean Tulard *Napoléon II* (Paris, 1992), p. 121.

Notes to Chapter 5: No Justice for the Bonapartes in France

1   Lord Rosebery, *Napoleon: The Last Phase* (London, 1900), p. 57: '[An `Englishman] must regret that his government ever undertook the custody of Napoleon and he must regret still more that the duty should have been discharged in a spirit so ignoble and through agents so unfortunate.'

2   Joseph succeeded in recovering his, literally, buried treasure from his château at Prangins. The diamonds alone were estimated at five million francs.

3   Murat had decided to fight *with* rather than for Napoleon in the hope of becoming ruler of most of Italy. See Owen Connelly, *Napoleon's Satellite Kingdoms* (New York, 1965), pp. 320–24.

4   Ibid., pp. 185–93 and 221–22.

5   It was this vexatious treatment which provoked Rosebery's strictures.

6   Emmanuel Las Cases, *Le Mémorial de Sainte Hélène*, Pléiade edition, ed. Walter (Paris, 1956), i, p. 1051.

7   The circumstances of Napoleon's death have produced a considerable literature, a great deal of it polemical, mostly concerned with the possibility of poisoning. There is a choice of candidates for the role of assassin so the reader can play detective. Even biographers writing in English are involved: see Frank McLynn, *Napoleon* (London, 1998), pp. 655–62.

Notes to Chapter 6: Hope Deferred

1   'Created by default, dead through stupidity.' The verdict of Waresquiel and Yvert, *Histoire de la Restauration, 1814–1830* (Paris, 1996).

2   Blanchard Jerrold, *Life of Napoleon III* (London, 1874), i, pp. 155–57, reproduces a letter to him from Count Arèse, a close friend of Louis-Napoleon, stressing the Prince's sympathy with the Italian cause but denying any contact with the Carbonari.

3   Details in Georges Duval, *Napoléon III: enfance-jeunesse* (Paris, 1895), pp. 91–97. Also F.A. Simpson, *The Rise of Louis Napoleon* (London, 1968; reprint of 1909 edition), pp. 62–78.

4   Simpson, *The Rise of Louis Napoleon*, pp. 71–75.

5   *Madame Mère* died at Rome on 2 February, 1836.

6   The *coup* failed, but proved that there was now an active Bonapartist pretender. 'Bonapartism [as a political force] was born at Strasbourg', William Smith, *Napoléon III* (Paris, 1982), p. 56.

7   Jerrold, *Life of Napoleon III*, ii, p. 39.

8   Louis Napoleon to Joseph, letter of 12 July, 1837, in Smith, *Napoléon III*, p. 61.

9   Ibid., pp. 65–71, for an account of his life and activities in England. For the Prince's views, see Simpson, *The Rise of Louis Napoleon*, pp. 163–66.

10   Account of the Boulogne attempt in Simpson, *Rise*, pp. 171–184.

11   Complete text in Napoléon III, *Oeuvres* (Paris, 1869), i, pp. 435–37.

12   Marcel Emerit (ed.), *Lettres de Napoléon III à Madame Cornu* (2 vols, Paris, 1937).

13   This brochure, the first serious attempt to produce a simple analysis of the 'social question', and to propose remedies, had an enormous impact in the 1840s. It had no real rivals until Marx produced his *Communist Manifesto*.

14   There are several accounts, but probably the most reliable is in Jerrold, *Life of Napoleon III*, ii, pp. 343–59. Jerrold knew the Emperor well and visited him at Chislehurst.

Notes to Chapter 7: The Restoration

1   See H.A.C. Collingham, with R.S. Alexander, *The July Monarchy* (London, 1988). For the Bonapartist element, J. Lucas Dubreton, *Le culte de Napoléon* (Paris, 1960), pp. 388–420, and Frédéric Bluche, *Le Bonapartisme* (Paris, 1980), especially pp. 260ff.
2   Ivor Guest, *Napoleon III in England* (London, 1952), pp. 77–86.
3   Jasper Ridley, *Napoleon III and Eugénie* (London, 1979), p. 205, gives the text.
4   The best account of his life in the article by Fernand Beaucour, 'Persigny', in *Dictionnaire du Second Empire*, edited by Jean Tulard (Paris, 1995), pp. 995–97.
5   The Prince sold his lands in Italy, and various friends in London contributed – especially Miss Howard, who gave him £80,000. In all, it was not a great sum with which to fund an electoral campaign.
6   William Smith, *Napoléon III* (Paris, 1982), p. 116, quote the full text.
7   Roger Price, *The Second French Republic* (London, 1972), pp. 159–62, and 186–89. Ines Murat, *La deuxième République* (Paris, 1987), p. 270, thinks that there was a general feeling of disillusionment among the workers who had expected so much from the establishment of the Republic.
8   For the attitude of the deputies, see Smith, *Napoléon III*, p. 122, particularly the fatuous comment by Lamartine.
9   Quoted in Adrien Dansette, *Louis Napoléon à la conquête du pouvoir* (Paris, 1962), p. 252.
10 For Morny's role, see the most recent biography by Jean-Marie Rouart, *Morny: un volupteux au pouvoir* (Paris, 1995), pp. 132ff.
11 Article on 'Walewski' by Joseph Valynseele, in *Dictionnaire du Second Empire*.
12 Georges Duval, *Napoléon III: enfance-jeunesse* (Paris, 1895), pp. 239–42, for the insulting letters sent to Louis Napoleon.
13 Smith, *Napoléon III*, p. 135.
14 *Letters of Queen Victoria, 1837–1861* (London, 1908), ii, pp. 341 and 353. Also Louis Girard, *Napoléon III* (Paris, 1986), p. 142.
15 *The Secret of the Coup d'Etat: Correspondence Edited by the Earl of Kerry* (London, 1924).
16 Girard, *Napoléon III*, pp. 154–56.
17 Napoléon III, *Oeuvres*, iii, pp. 287–88.
18 Ibid., i, p. 342.
19 Ibid., iii, pp. 341–43, full text of the speech.
20 Léon Duguit and Henry Monnier, *Les constitutions et les principales lois politiques de la France depuis 1789* (Paris, 1915), p. 292.
21 Jules Ferry, *La lutte électorale à Paris en 1863* (Paris, 1863), p. 142.

Notes to Chapter 8: The Empire Restored

1   *Lettres de Guizot à sa Famille et a ses amis* (Paris, 1884), pp. 342–44.
2   William Smith, *Napoléon III* (Paris, 1982), pp. 167–68.

3   Letter to Prince Napoleon of 6 November 1852, in E. d'Hauterive, *Napoléon III et le Prince Napoléon: correspondance inédite* (Paris, 1925), p. 58.

4   Napoléon III, *Oeuvres*, pp. 357–60, the Emperor's speech to the Senate, Legislative body and the Council of State, 22 January 1853.

5   Harold Kurz, *The Empress Eugénie, 1826–1920* (London, 1964), pp. 57–58, for a description of the ceremony at Notre-Dame.

6   For the Empress, see Kurz, *The Empress Eugénie*; also William Smith, *Eugénie, Impératrice des Français* (Paris, 1998). The most recent work in English is Desmond Seward, *Eugénie: The Empress and her Empire* (Thrupp, 2004).

7   For this non-dynastic branch of the Bonapartes, see Olga Bonaparte-Wyse, *The Spurious Brood* (London, 1969).

8   The Court is described in William Smith, *Napoleon III and the Pursuit of Prestige* (London, 1991), chapter 3.

9   Queen Victoria, *Letters*, iii, pp. 135–37.

10 Prosper Mérimée, *Lettres à Madame de Montijo* (Paris, 1995), ii, pp. 59–60, gives an amusing account of the ceremony.

11 Latreille and Rémond, *Histoire du Catholicisme* (Paris, 1962), iii, pp. 312–14. See also Jacques-Olivier Boudon, *Paris: capitale religeuse sous le Second Empire* (Paris, 2001), pp. 346–50. See also S. Hazaree Singh, 'Religion and Politics in the Saint Napoleon Festivity, 1852–1870: Anticlericalism, Local Patriotism and Modernity', *English Historical Review*, 119 (2004).

12 Smith, *Napoleon III and the Pursuit of Prestige*, pp. 59–72.

13 Queen Victoria, *Letters* (London, 1908), iii, pp. 122–26, a memorandum by the Queen giving her assessment of Napoleon III and of the importance of the French alliance.

14 Ibid., pp. 135–140.

15 The most recent analysis of the social policy is in Pierre Milza, *Napoléon III* (Paris, 2004), pp. 406–15.

Notes to Chapter 9: Triumph and Catastrophe

1   Queen Victoria, *Letters* (London, 1908), iii, p. 138, indicates how successful the Emperor's contacts had been. For the war, William Smith, *Napoléon III* (Paris, 1982), pp. 208–15; also Clive Ponting, *The Crimean War: The Truth Behind the Myth* (London, 2004), pp. 1–12 and 337–41. The author possibly underestimates the importance for Britain of the Treaty of Paris. London's insistence on the Black Sea clauses effectively prevented a Franco-Russian entente.

2   The Emperor was seriously perturbed by the hostile public reaction to the Prince's departure, and adjured him 'to return to the army as soon as possible'. Letter of 23 November 1854. D'Hauterive, *Correspondance* (Paris, 1925), p. 75.

3   Napoleon III to the Austrian Ambassador, in S. Bobr-Tylingo, *Napoléon III: l'Europe et la Pologne* (Rome,1963), p. 14.

4   Denis Mack Smith, *Cavour* (London, 1985), for a neat summation.

5   The meeting and the Queen's comments in William Smith, *Eugénie, Impératrice des Français* (Paris, 1998), pp. 95–96.

6   Ibid., pp. 99–100, 'Killing Is No Crime'.

7   Lynn M. Case, *French Opinion on War and Diplomacy during the Second Empire* (New York, 1972).

8   Queen Victoria, *Letters*, iii, p. 234. There is also a personal letter to the Empress in the Alba Archives (Fonds Montijo), Madrid, caja 42.

9   William Smith, *Napoléon III* (Paris, 1982), chapter 14, for the Mexican imbroglio.

10 The Emperor blamed England for the collapse of the congress project and told the Prussian ambassador 'I shall have to change my alliances'. See W.E. Echard, *Napoleon III and the Concert of Europe* (Baton Rouge, Louisiana, and London, 1983), p. 202.

11 Emile Ollivier, *L'Empire libéral* (17 vols, Paris, 1895–1918), vii, p. 414, comments on the Prince's sense of dynastic loyalty.

12 William Smith, *Napoleon III and the Pursuit of Prestige* (London, 1991), pp. 88–89.

13 Lord Cowley, the British ambassador and a friend of the Emperor, thought there was nothing serious, letter to Lord Broomfield, 31 July 1866, in Cowley Papers, National Archive, London. But Napoleon was already adept at concealing his illness.

14 Jasper Ridley, *Napoleon III and Eugénie* (London, 1979), pp. 544–48.

15 Ibid., pp. 551–54. See also Smith, *Napoléon III*, pp. 318–19.

16 Details in Lynn M. Case, *French Opinion on War and Diplomacy during the Second Empire* (New York, 1972).

17 Bismarck's account, plus the two versions of the telegram, in *Bismarck: His Reflections and Reminiscences* (London, 1898), ii, pp. 94–100.

Notes to Chapter 10: The Débâcle

1   The Emperor's attitude is examined in William Smith, *Napoleon III and the Pursuit of Prestige* (London, 1991), pp. 98–99.

2   The situation of the Empress, and her activities, is examined in William Smith, *Eugénie, Impératrice des Français* (Paris, 1998), pp. 154–56.

3   Quoted in Henri Welschinger, *La Guerre de 1870: causes et responsabilités* (Paris, 1911), i, pp. 267–68.

4   Charles Chesnelong, *Les derniers jours de l'Empire* (Paris, 1930), p. 176.

5   Text in Smith *Eugénie*, p. 175.

6   Ibid., pp. 113–15, for an account of the flight.

7   Exchange of letters between the Emperor and Prince Napoleon, in d'Hauterive, *Correspondance* (Paris, 1925), pp. 315–19.

8   William Smith, *Napoléon III* (Paris, 1982), p. 328.

9   Christopher Hibbert, *Queen Victoria in her Letters and Journals* (London, 1984), p. 221.

10 Ibid., p. 224.

11 Comtesse des Garets, *L'Impératrice Eugénie en exil* (Paris, 1929), p. 47.

12   Augustin Filon, *Le Prince Impérial, 1856–1879* (Paris, 1935), pp. 121–24 and 129–34.

13   Emperor's note in ibid., p. 124.

14   Ivor Guest, *Napoleon III in England* (London, 1952), p. 194.

15   If one includes Napoleon II, then all three Emperors died in exile.

Notes to Chapter 11: 'The Prince is Down!'

1   Robert Gildea, *The Past in French History* (New Haven and London, 1994), especially pp. 73–78.

2   Hostility was not simply a reaction to his 'radicalism' but was based on his conduct during the Second Empire.

3   In 1874 a pamphlet, 'Il n'est pas trop jeune!' by 'Louis de Rozen' (the Bonapartist historian, Masson), argued, 'He is our child, he is of the people, like his dynasty'.

4   Augustin Filon, *Le Prince Impérial, 1856–1879* (Paris, 1935), p. 191, comments on the Prince's difficulties with Rouher and on how badly informed Louis was.

5   See Jean-Claude Lachnitt, *Le Prince Impérial: Napoléon IV* (Paris, 1997), pp. 269–70.

6   *Lettres familières de l'Impératrice Eugénie*, published by the Duke of Alba (Paris, 1935), ii, p. 83.

7   There is a good and straightforward account in William Peter Phillips, *The Death of the Prince Imperial in Zululand, 1879*, Hampshire Museum Publications (2nd edn, 1998).

8   Ibid.

9   At this point it was decided that the Empress must not view the body because of its condition.

10   The Empress to her mother, *Lettres familières*, 23 August, 1879.

11   Gildea, *The Past in French History*, pp. 74–75.

12   Gildea, *The Past in French History*, p. 77, makes the point that, while there was vestigial Bonapartism between the wars, 'support had dwindled to a hard core of professional nostalgics'.

Select Bibliography

Alexander, R. S, *Bonapartism and the Revolutionary Tradition in France* (Cambridge, 1991).

—, *Napoleon* (London, 2000).

Antonetti, Guy, *Louis-Philippe* (Paris, 1994).

Aronson, Theo, *The Golden Bees: The Story of the Bonapartes* (London, 1964).

Babelon, Jean-Pierre, and d'Huart, Suzanne, *Napoleon's Last Will and Testament (Facsimile)*, translated by Alex de Jonghe (New York and London, 1977).

Bertin, Célia, *La dernière Bonaparte* (Paris, 1982).

Bluche, Frédéric, *Le Bonapartisme* (Paris, 1980).

Bonaparte, Joseph, *Mémoires* (Paris, 1858–60).

Bonaparte, Lucien, *Memoirs* (London, 1836).

Bonaparte-Wyse, Olga, *The Spurious Brood* (London, 1969).

Boudon, Jacques-Olivier, *Napoléon et les cultes* (Paris, 2002).

Bourachot, Christophe, *Bibliographie critique des mémoires sur le Second Empire* (Paris, 1994).

Bourgoing de, Jean, *Le fils de Napoléon* (Paris, 1950).

Bourrienne de, Louis-Antoine, *Mémoires* (Paris, 1829).

Broglie de, Gabriel, *Guizot* (Paris, 1990).

—, *McMahon* (Paris, 2000).

Bruce, Evangeline, *Napoleon and Josephine: An Improbable Marriage* (London, 1995).

Bury, J. P. T. and Tombs, R. P, *Thiers, 1797–1877: A Political Life* (London, 1986).

Carmona, Michael, *Haussmann* (Paris, 2000).

Carrington, Dorothy, *Napoleon and his Parents: On the Threshold of History* (London, 1990).

Chevallier, Bernard and Pincemaille, Christophe, *L'Impératrice Joséphine* (Paris, 1996).

Chevallier, Bernard, *Douce et incomparable Joséphine* (Paris, 1999).

Collingham, H. A, *The July Monarchy* (London, 1988).

Connelly, Owen, *Napoleon's Satellite Kingdoms* (New York, 1965).

—, *The Gentle Bonaparte: Joseph* (New York and London, 1968).

Corley, T. A. B, *Democratic Despot: A Life of Napoleon III* (London, 1961).

Crook, Malcolm, *Napoleon Comes to Power: Democracy and Dictatorship in Revolutionary France* (University of Wales Press, 1998).

Dansette, Adrien, *Histoire du Second Empire*, 2 vols (Paris 1961–76).

Daudet, Lucien, *Dans l'ombre de l'Impératrice Eugénie* (Paris, 1935).

Des Cars, Jean, *Eugénie, la dernière impératrice* (Paris, 2000).

Des Garets, Comtesse (Marie de Larminat), *Auprés de l'Impératrice Eugénie* (Paris, 1928).

—, *L'Impératrice Eugénie en exil* (Paris, 1929).

Englund, Steven, *Napoleon: A Political Life* (New York, 2000).

Eugénie, Empress, *Lettres familières*, ed. the Duke of Alba, 2 vols (Paris, 1935).

Filon, Augustin, *Le Prince Impérial, 1856–1879* (Paris, 1935).

—, *Recollections of the Empress Eugénie* (London, 1920).

Fisher, H. A. L, *Bonapartism* (London, 1908).

Fournier, August, *Napoleon I*, 2 vols (London, 1911).

Gildea, Robert, *The Past in French History* (New Haven, 1994).

Godechot, Jacques, Hyslop, Beatrice F., and Dowd, David L., *The Napoleonic Era in Europe* (New York and London, 1971).

Guest, Ivor, *Napoleon III in England* (London, 1953).

Hales, E. E. Y., *Napoleon and the Pope: The Story of Napoleon and Pius VII* (London, 1962).

Jerrold, Blanchard, *The Life of Napoleon III*, 4 vols (London, 1874–82).

Jourdan, Annie, *L'empire de Napoléon* (Paris, 2000).

—, *Napoléon: héros, imperator, mécène* (Paris, 1998).

Kératry, Comte de, *Le dernier des Napoléon* (Paris, 1874).

Kurz, Harold, *The Empress Eugénie* (London, 1964).

Lachnitt, Jean-Claude, *Le Prince Impérial: Napoléon IV* (Paris, 1997).

Las Cases, Emmanuel, *Le mémorial de Sainte Hélène*, ed. Walter, i (Paris, 1956).

Legge, Edward, *The Empress Eugénie and her Son* (London, 1916).

Lentz, Thierry, *Le 18 Brumaire* (Paris, 1997).

—, *Le grand Consulat* (Paris, 1999).

—, *Nouvelle histoire du Premier Empire*, i, *Napoléon à la conquête du pouvoir* (Paris, 2002).

—, *Nouvelle histoire du Premier Empire*, ii, *L'éffondrement du système naploléonien* (Paris, 2004).

Lucas-Dubreton, J., *Le culte de Napoléon, 1815–1848* (Paris, 1960).

McLynn, Frank, *Napoleon* (London, 1998).

McMillan, James, F., *Napoleon III* (London, 1991).

Mansel, Philip, *The Eagle in Splendour* (London, 1987).

Markham, Felix, *Napoleon* (1963).

Melchior-Bonnet, Bernardine, *Le roi Jérôme* (Paris, 1979).

—, *Dictionnaire Napoléon*, ed. Jean Tulard (Paris, 1987), articles on Jérôme, Letizia, Caroline and Pauline Bonaparte.

Ménager, Bernard, *Le Napoléon du Peuple* (Paris, 1998).

Mérimée, Prosper, *Lettres à Madame de Montijo*, 2 vols (Paris, 1995).

Milza, Pierre, *Napoléon III* (Paris, 2004).

Napoléon III et le Prince Napoléon, correspondance inédite, ed. E. d'Hauterive (Paris, 1921).

Napoleon III, *Oeuvres*, 5 vols (Paris, 1869).

Napoléon, Prince Charles, *Bonaparte et Paoli* (Paris, 2000).

Oddie, E. M., *Marie-Louise, Empress of France* (London, 1931).

—, *Napoleon II, King of Rome* (London, n.d.).

Ollivier, Emile, *L'Empire libéral*, 18 vols (Paris, 1895–1918).

Paoli, Dominique, *Clémentine, Princesse Napoléon, 1872–1955* (Paris, 1992).

Pietromarchi, A., *Lucien Bonaparte, prince romain* (Paris, 1985).

Pilbeam, P., *Republicanism in Nineteenth-Century France, 1814–1871* (London, 1995).

Pimienta, Robert, *La propagande Bonapartiste en 1848* (Paris, 1911).

Pincemaille, Christophe, *L'Impératrice Eugénie: de Suez á Sedan* (Paris, 2000).

—, *The French Second Empire: An Anatomy of Political Power* (Cambridge, 2001).

Richardson, Joanna, *Portrait of a Bonaparte: The Life and Times of Joseph-Napoléon Primoli, 1851–1927* (London, 1987).

Ridley, Jasper, *Napoleon and Eugénie* (London, 1979).

Rosebery, Lord, *Napoleon: The Last Phase* (London, 1900).

Ross, Michael, *The Reluctant King: Joseph Bonaparte, King of the Two Sicilies and Spain* (London, 1976).

Rouart, Jean-Marie, *Morny: un voluptueu au pouvoir* (Paris, 1995).

Schom, Alan, *Napoleon Bonaparte* (New York, 1997).

Séguin, Philippe, *Louis Napoléon le Grand* (Paris, 1990).

Seward, Desmond, *Eugénie: The Empress and her Empire* (Thrupp, 2004).

Smith, William H. C., *Eugénie, Impératrice des Français* (Paris, 1998).

—, 'Grande Bretagne', in *Dictionnaire Napoléon*, ed. Jean Tulard (Paris, 1987).

—, *Napoléon III* (Paris, 1982).

—, *Napoleon III: The Pursuit of Prestige* (London, 1991).

Suissa, Jean-Luc, 'Lucien Bonaparte', in *Dictionnaire Napoléon*, ed. Jean Tulard (Paris, 1987).

Thompson, J. M, *Napoleon Bonaparte: His Rise and Fall* (Oxford, 1963).

Tulard, Jean, 'Joseph Bonaparte', 'Louis Bonaparte', in *Dictionnaire Napoléon* (Paris, 1987).

—, *Le Grand Empire* (Paris, 1982).

—, *Napoléon II* (Paris, 1992).

—, *Napoléon at la noblesse d'Empire* (Paris, 1980).

—, *Napoléon: ou le mythe du sauveur* (Paris, 1977).

Vidal, Florence, *Elisa Bonaparte, sœur de Napoleon 1er* (Paris, 2004).

Villepin de, Dominique, *Les Cent-Jours: ou l'ésprit de sacrifice* (Paris, 2001).

Wagener, Françoise, *La Reine Hortense* (Paris, 1992).

Waresquiel de, Emmanuel, and Yvert, Benoît, *Histoire de la Restauration, 1814–1830* (Paris, 1996).

Woloch, Isser, *Napoleon and his Collaborators* (New York and London, 2001).

Index